STUDY GUIDE

Jeannie D. DiClementi
Indiana University—Purdue University Fort Wayne

ABNORMAL

PSYCHOLOGY

Eleventh Edition

Irwin G. Sarason

Barbara R. Sarason

Upper Saddle River, New Jersey 07458

Printed in the United States of America
10 9 8 7 6 5 4

ISBN 0-13-118113-0

Table of Contents

INTRODUCTION: SUGGESTIONS FOR STUDYING ABNORMAL PSYCHOLOGY

This guide is for you to use as an aid to your studies only. You should not use it as a substitute for reading your textbook or going to class. Success in this course depends on your ability to learn a lot of new material, and the more organized your studying is, and the more you stick with it, the more successful you will be. Important components of a successful learning experience include: reading the textbook, taking notes in class, having the right study environment, and studying and preparing for the tests.

READING THE TEXTBOOK

Opening a substantial textbook for the first time can be a daunting task. Often people will look at the first few pages and think, 'I will never understand all of this.' But, with some determination and an organized effort, the reading will soon become less mysterious and more understandable.

Students who use an organized method for studying can significantly increase their comprehension of the material and their success in a course. A popular and effective system for studying and learning textbook material is the SQ3R system[1]. Detailed descriptions of this system can be found on a number of university websites. The steps of the SQ3R system are 1) Survey, 2) Question, 3) Read, 4) Recite, and 5) Review.

Survey. You make a fairly quick glance through the chapter, looking at the introductory and concluding paragraphs and the section headings. Pay attention to picture and graph captions, section headings, aids such as terms in bold or italic print, objectives, and questions at the end of the chapter. This will familiarize you with the material and what the author is trying to get across.

Question. As you read through the text again, look at all the boldface headings and subheadings in the chapter. Write down as many questions as you think will be answered by the information found in that section. Write these questions on your paper, leaving several blank lines between them. You are creating a structure for your learning, organizing your thoughts, and keeping yourself on track.

Read. You will now read each section for answers to the questions that you wrote earlier. Be sure that each question is answered in the reading. If not, then change the question. Also feel free to make up additional questions as you are reading. You are not only creating your own study guide, but you are also predicting questions that might be on the test. In fact, you may be surprised to discover that many of your questions are similar to or the same as questions your instructor puts on your test.

Recite. Say out loud to yourself or a study partner what you have just read and written. The more senses you use when studying, the more likely you are to understand and remember it.

Review. Look your notes over whenever you have a few minutes. Don't wait until the night before the test, but rather space this out over time throughout the term. Engage classmates in short conversations about the material.

The chapters in this study guide are organized to help you with the important points of each topic that are presented in your book. Use the outline at the beginning of each chapter in this guide to help you organize your study of the book. For example, copy each section of the outline in your notebook, leaving several spaces between the lines. Then, as you read your text, write the questions you develop from each section of reading into the outline you have copied on your paper.

The essay questions in this guide will also be valuable in helping you to study each chapter section. Use these as models for the questions you will be developing as you go through your book. But don't forget to answer the questions in the study guide, too.

Additionally, this guide has a list of important terms you will need to know in order to understand the material. Write out the definition of each term on a separate paper, then look it up in the text. After you have 'graded' yourself, repeat the process until you can write out the correct definition for each term. Another suggestion is to use index cards and write the term on one side and the definition on the other side and have your study partner quiz you with these flash cards.

NOTE TAKING STRATEGIES

A task as seemingly simple as taking notes during lectures is actually one of the more difficult tasks facing students. What to write, writing too little, writing too much all are concerns of students. Many of us have had the experience of having been busy writing down something the instructor has said, only to find that we have missed the next few sentences of the lecture. Note taking must be as organized and systematic as reading the text.

One system for note taking is the Cornell system[2], which can also be found in detail on the Web. Basically this system has three steps. First is preparation. Get a large notebook and use only one side of the paper. This is not the time to conserve paper. Draw a vertical line about 2 ½ inches from the left margin of your paper. You will write your notes on the right side of the page, leaving the column you created for key words and phrases you will add later.

Second, during the lecture, write your notes in paragraph form, recording general ideas, not illustrations or examples. Write legibly, using abbreviations, and skip lines to indicate separate thoughts or ideas.

Finally, after the lecture, read through your notes and add clarifications if necessary. Do this while it is still fresh. Write in the left column key words or phrases that will cue you to the instructor's ideas written on the right. Try covering up your notes and, using the key words in the left column, recite the ideas the instructor presented. This is your study guide.

Additional suggestions to enhance this system include listening before you write whenever possible. By automatically writing down everything you hear, you may miss important points the instructor is trying to convey. Listen for cues as to the important points. These may include repetition of points, change in voice inflection, or numbered lists. Most lectures present a few main points accompanied by explanatory material and numerous minor points. Learn to listen for the main points and discern what is explanatory or illustrative. This is a skill that can develop with practice and as you become familiar with the instructor's lecture style.

Ask questions if you miss something or for clarification. Assume that everything written on the board is important and copy it down. Instructors usually use the board for emphasizing important points and students should pay attention to this.

Additionally, always look over your notes soon after the lecture and frequently thereafter. This will enhance your recall and understanding of the material. And sit in the front of the class whenever possible. This will reduce distractions and it will be easier to see and hear.

YOUR STUDY ENVIRONMENT

OK, we're all certain that we know the best places and ways to study, whether it's in bed or stretched out on the carpet with the stereo on. But it's a good idea to periodically take stock of your study environment to see if it is really conducive to learning.

Things to consider when evaluating your study environment include lighting, temperature, seating, foot traffic, and distractions such as TV, stereo, telephones. Also consider the availability of snacks and if you will be able to stretch and walk around periodically. Libraries are fine, for example, but many do not allow food and if you need to take a walk, you may have to pack up all your belongings to take with you. Studying at home can work, too, unless you are too tempted to turn on the TV, or answer the phone, or nap. The dining room table would be a better location than bedroom or living room couch.

The ideal study environment would be one with good lighting and comfortable room temperature. Desk and chair should be comfortable with plenty of room to spread your study materials out. Distractions should be at a minimum, and if you use background music to block out distracting noises, make sure the music is not a distraction itself. Have energy snacks and water available.

STUDYING AND TAKING TESTS

Quality studying takes planning and consistency. Once you have found the right environment, there are several important tips to follow that can greatly improve your studying.

Schedule your study time consistently, and stick with the schedule. Decide how much material you will cover, making sure it's realistic, and give yourself a deadline.

Research has shown that "spaced" time intervals are more effective than "massed" intervals for learning material. In other words, read your book or study your notes for brief periods each day, followed by rest, rather than saving it for an all-day Saturday marathon.

When you get tired or bored, stop what you are doing and take a break. Make sure you are at a stopping place, though, so you can easily pick up where you left off.

Study buddies are helpful. You can compare notes, quiz each other, discuss the material, and keep each other on track.

To prepare for the test, find out what will be covered, what won't be covered, and what kind of test it will be (objective, essay, or a combination).

Get a good night's rest the night before the test and don't take the test hungry.

There are different types of test questions: factual, application, and synthesis. Each requires a slightly different strategy for preparation. Factual questions require memorization of facts and figures. Application questions usually require you to take some bit of knowledge and apply it to a hypothetical situation. Synthesis questions ask you to integrate several pieces of knowledge into some new conceptualization. For the most part, preparing for a multiple choice exam in the same way as you would prepare for an essay exam is a good strategy. Memorize key terms and lists of items, stress concepts, and elaborate.

In addition to the essay questions, this study guide has several other types of questions available for practice: multiple choice, true/false, and matching. When you are ready to practice, answer each question by writing your choice on a separate piece of paper. When you are done with the questions, grade yourself by checking your answers against the key at the end of the chapter. For each question you missed, look up the appropriate section in your textbook and read the information relevant to the question. Then take the test again. Repeat this process until you can answer all questions correctly.

When taking a multiple choice test, use a process of elimination: pick out the answers you know are correct, pick out the ones you know are not correct, rule out all answers with wrong options and those which have left out options you are sure of. Select the best remaining answer. Also remember that even though an answer may 'jump out' at you, it may be jumping out because it is familiar, not because it is correct.

Using these strategies to learn this material may seem like a tedious, time-consuming activity, but once you get into a routine and acquire some good study skills, you may find that it gets easier. And, you may even find the process becoming enjoyable, especially as you master it.

SAMPLE FLASH CARDS

These are only suggestions in order to give you an idea of how to write flash cards and to help get you started. The best flash cards are the ones you write yourself. The advantages to using flash cards are that they can easily be carried around in a pocket and they contain a lot of information that you can look over any time you have a few minutes.

Chapter 1

Side one	Side two
COPING SKILLS	Techniques people use to deal with stress
PHRENOLOGY	Mental faculties could be determined by feeling bumps on the head
VULNERABILITY	The likelihood of maladaptive response
RESILIENCE	Ability to function effectively and recover from stress
STRESS	People's reactions to demanding situations

Chapter 2

Side one	Side two
DENDRITES	The branches of the receiving end of the neuron
NEUROTRANSMITTERS	Chemical messengers that carry messages between neurons
MONOZYGOTIC TWINS	Identical twins; identical genetic material
ORAL STAGE	The first of Freud's stages; gratification through the mouth
SHAPING	Learning new behavior through reinforcement of successive approximations

Chapter 3

Side one	Side two
SYSTEMATIC DESENSITIZATION	Based on classical conditioning; involves gradual exposure to the feared object to acquire a conditioned relaxation response
RATIONAL-EMOTIVE THERAPY	Based on the idea that problems are caused by faulty thinking; replaces faulty thinking with rational thoughts
BEHAVIOR THERAPY	Uses principles of classical and operant conditioning to change behavior
ADHERENCE	The degree to which a patient follows treatment recommendations
META-ANALYSIS	Combining the data from several different studies to re-analyze; used in outcome research

Chapter 4

Side one	Side two
AXIS I	All diagnoses except personality disorders and mental retardation
RELIABILITY	The extent to which a classification decision is reproducible
MENTAL STATUS EXAMINATION	A structured interview technique for determining current level of function
MMPI	True-false personality inventory; objective test
RORSCHACH INKBLOTS	Personality test; projective test

Chapter 5

Side one	Side two
COGNITIVE MODIFICATION	Learning to think about anxiety-producing situations in a different way
DISSOCIATIVE IDENTITY DISORDER	Formerly called multiple personality disorder; different personalities that may or may not be aware of each other
DISSOCIATIVE FUGUE	Travel to a new location, adopting a new identity, inability to remember old identity
RELAXATION TRAINING	Structured approach to tension reduction
COPING PROCESS	Acquiring information, considering alternatives, deciding on a course of action, and behavior

Chapter 6

Side one	Side two
TYPE A PERSONALITY	Characterized by hostility, competitiveness, and time urgency; risk factor for heart attacks
HYPERTENSION	High blood pressure
HOMEOSTASIS	Balance in functioning
PSYCHOSOMATIC HYPOTHESIS	Links the development of physical symptoms to blocked emotional expression
BEHAVIORAL MEDICINE	Focused on improving diagnosis, treatment, and rehabilitation

Chapter 7

Side one	Side two
SOMATOFORM DISORDERS	Bodily complaints for which there are no actual physical impairments
HYPOCHONDRIASIS	Unrealistic fears of illness and excessive preoccupation with health
ACTIVE COPING	Actively seeking information and solutions to problems
FACTITIOUS DISORDER	Physical symptoms are deliberately induced in order to obtain medical care and attention
MALINGERING	Faking an illness for secondary gain such as financial gain

Chapter 8

Side one	Side two
ANXIETY	Diffuse, vague, unpleasant feelings of fear
SPECIFIC PHOBIAS	Irrational fears of specific objects, such as animals
BENZODIAZEPINES	A class of anti-anxiety medications
RESPONSE PREVENTION	Based on the principle of extinction, involves exposure to a feared object until the fear response extinguishes
AMYGDALA	Believed to be the emotion center of the brain

Chapter 9

Side one	Side two
FETISHISM	Uses a nonliving object as the primary source of sexual arousal and gratification
FROTTEURISM	Sexual gratification by rubbing up against an unsuspecting stranger while in a crowd of people
PEDOPHILIA	Targets children as the main source of sexual gratification
SADISM	Achieves orgasm through humiliating or inflicting pain on others
COVERT SENSITIZATION	Deviant sexual fantasies are paired with mental images of distressing consequences

Chapter 10

Side one	Side two
PERSONALITY	A person's characteristic ways of responding
PERSONALITY DISORDERS	Longstanding, inflexible, maladaptive patterns of behavior
SPLITTING	Failure to integrate the positive and negative aspects of experiences with other people; seeing people as either all good or all bad
PROTOTYPAL APPROACH	Diagnosing on the basis of number of characteristics present, not on any single characteristic
DIMENSIONAL MODEL	Focuses on patterns of personality characteristics

Chapter 11

Side one	Side two
DEPRESSED MOOD	Temporary feelings of sadness that fade when the situation changes
DYSTHYMIC DISORDER	Chronic and mild depressive symptoms
BIPOLAR DISORDER	Characterized by extreme moods ranging from depression to mania; formerly called manic depressive illness
SUICIDE CONTAGION	The copycat effect; after a publicized suicide by a well-known person, suicide rates temporarily increase
CYCLOTHYMIC DISORDER	Mood shifts similar to bipolar disorder, but without the extremes; dysthymia alternating with hypomania

Chapter 12

Side one	Side two
CATATONIA	Motor disturbance; either immobility or extreme agitation
DELUSION	False beliefs
NEGATIVE SYMPTOMS	The absence of behaviors that should be present
DOPAMINE HYPOTHESIS	Posits that dysfunctional dopamine systems are responsible for schizophrenic symptoms
TARDIVE DYSKINESIA	Permanent irreversible movement disorder stemming from long-term use of some antipsychotic medications

Chapter 13

Side one	Side two
DEMENTIA	Brain deterioration involving a gradual loss of intellectual abilities without clouding of consciousness
DELIRIUM	Global cognitive impairment, disorientation, confusion, and clouding of consciousness
KORSAKOFF'S SYNDROME	Brain deterioration resulting from combined alcoholism and vitamin B1 deficiency
APHASIA	Disturbance in speech and language function either receptive language or production of language or both
CONFABULATION	Creating information to fill in gaps in memory; the person is usually not aware that she or he is doing it

Chapter 14

Side one	Side two
SUBSTANCE DEPENDENCE	Characterized by development of tolerance and onset of withdrawal upon cessation of use
TOLERANCE	The need to use increasing amounts of a substance in order to achieve the same effects
SUBSTANCE ABUSE	Continued use in spite of negative consequences of use
BARBITURATES	Anti-anxiety or anti-convulsion drugs; central nervous system depressants
INTERACTIONAL ORIENTATION	The view that both the person and situation are important factors in the development of addiction

Chapter 15

Side one	Side two
EXTERNALIZING DISORDERS	Disorders in which children are undercontrolled; fights, temper tantrums, disobedience, destructive behavior
INTERNALIZING DISORDERS	Undercontrolled; depression, anxiety, shy, withdrawn
CONDUCT DISORDER	Violation of social norms and rules; often involves criminal behavior
SEPARATION ANXIETY DISORDER	Cannot tolerate separation from major attachment figures
COPROLALIA	Uttering of obscenities; common in Tourette's

Chapter 16

Side one	Side two
MICROCEPHALY	Head is much smaller than normal for the child's age; found in Rett's disorder
TRANSLOCATION	Occurs when material from the 21st chromosome pair breaks off and attaches to another pair
TRISOMY	Refers to the existence of three chromosomes instead of two
NONDISJUNCTION	In Down syndrome, an extra chromosome exists at the site of chromosome pair no. 21 so that there are three and not two
AMNIOCENTESIS	Amniotic fluid is tested to determine the presence of genetic disorders in the developing fetus

Chapter 17

Side one	Side two
PRIMARY PREVENTION	Administered to everyone in a target population to prevent or reduce new cases of disorders
INSANITY	Legal term referring to the person's state of mind at the time of committing a criminal act; can't tell right from wrong, or can't stop an impulse
COMPETENCY	Refers to the person's state of mind at the time of a judicial proceeding; understanding the legal proceeding
CRIMINAL COMMITMENT	Commitment of a person to a mental hospital when the criminal act is judged to be the result of insanity
DUTY TO WARN	Exception to confidentiality; therapist must warn potential victims of a patient's intent to harm them

Notes
[1] adapted from the University of Arizona website
[2] adapted from the Virginia Polytechnic Institute and State University website

Chapter 1
INTRODUCTION

CHAPTER OVERVIEW

This chapter introduces you to the field of abnormal psychology and the concept of abnormal behavior. Abnormal behaviors are maladaptive behaviors that are related to situational stress, vulnerability, deficits in coping and which cause concern for the individual, family or friends, or society. The epidemiology of maladaptive behavior is discussed and treatment facilities and professionals are described. Research techniques, methods of data analysis, and ethical concerns are reviewed.

LEARNING OBJECTIVES

After studying this chapter, you should be able to answer these questions:
1. What is abnormal behavior?
2. What is meant by the stigma of abnormal behavior?
3. What is the difference between adaptive and maladaptive behavior?
4. How did the ancient Greeks account for abnormal behavior?
5. What views of mental illness existed in the Middle Ages?
6. What advances in attitudes toward mental illness were put forth in the Renaissance?
7. How did attitudes toward mental illness change in the seventeenth and eighteenth centuries?
8. What was the Reform Movement, and how did it affect the treatment of the mentally ill?
9. What are the main approaches to understanding abnormal behavior today?
10. What are the differences between the psychological and organic approaches to abnormal behavior?
11. How do the concepts of vulnerability, resilience, and coping help explain mental illness?
12. What is the role of epidemiology in explaining maladaptive behavior?
13. How do the concepts of prevalence, incidence, and risk factors help us understand mental illness?
14. What are the reasons that people seek help for mental illness, and what are the sources of such help?
15. What roles do observation and self-observation play in abnormal psychology research?
16. What roles do theories play in abnormal psychology?
17. What are the vital steps in scientific research into abnormal behavior?
18. What are the main types of research in abnormal psychology and how do they differ?
19. What statistical procedures aid in understanding abnormal psychology research?
20. What ethical considerations guide abnormal psychology research?

CHAPTER OUTLINE

1. What Is Abnormal Behavior? (p.5)
    A. Triggers of Mental Health Problems
       Triggers can be either external (extreme stress, for example), or internal

    B. The Stigma of Abnormal Behavior
       Stigma refers to a label indicating a defect. Stigmatization increases the stress associated with mental illness, and can reduce access to services.

C. Adaptive and Maladaptive Behavior

Adaption refers to the balance between what the individual wants to do and the requirements of the environment. Maladaption refers to the existence of problems in living. Maladaptive behavior is always deviant, meaning it deviates from the norm. Deviant behavior is not always maladaptive, however.

2. Historical Background of Modern Abnormal Psychology (p.9)

Theories of maladaption, whether correct or not, have been repeated throughout history. Abnormal behavior was often explained by supernatural and magical forces. Treatment consisted of various means to remove spirits that were the cause of the abnormal behaviors.

A. The Ancient Western World

The rational approach of the philosophers set the historical foundation for modern science, with their emphasis on rationality, the organismic approach, and the quest for natural causes.

B. The Middle Ages

St. Augustine helped lay out the groundwork for modern psychodynamic theory. Other major changes in this era, particularly the rise of Christianity, affected the views of abnormal behavior. On one hand, people still believed in demonic possession as the cause of mental illness and advocated the institutionalization of the mentally ill, others made serious efforts to provide for the humane treatment of mentally ill individuals.

C. The Renaissance

Johann Weyer brought forth the notion that psychological conflict and disturbed relationships were at the root of mental disorders, rather than demons and spirits. He emphasized the need for medical rather than spiritual treatment for mental illness.

D. The Age of Reason and the Enlightenment

Reasoning and the scientific method came to replace religious faith and dogma as the prevailing approach to the conceptualization of abnormal behavior.

E. The Reform Movement

The growth of the scientific movement led to an increase in reform of treatment of the mentally ill, both in Europe and America. Wider acceptance of humanitarian ideas led to investigation of and improvement of institutions providing treatment of mental disorders.

3. Recent Concepts of Abnormal Behavior (p.19)

Twentieth-century focus was on the value of research in identifying the causes and treatment of maladaptive behavior.

A. The Psychological Approach

Emphasized the role of irrational thinking on both normal and abnormal behavior.

B. The Organic Approach

Emphasized disturbances in brain function as the basis of mental disorders. An implication of this viewpoint was the need to further understand the biological workings of the brain.

C. The Approaches Converge

The biopsychosocial approach considers maladaptive behavior in terms of biological, psychological, and social variables. The roles each of these takes differs between individuals and across the life span.

D. Vulnerability, Resilience, and Coping

Vulnerability refers to how likely we are to respond maladaptively to situations, while resilience refers to the ability to function effectively in the face of adversity.

4. The Epidemiology of Maladaptive Behavior (p.22)

Findings from epidemiological research help with our understanding patterns of maladaptive behaviors and a variety of environmental and behavioral factors.

A. Prevalence, Incidence, and Risk Factors

Prevalence describes the frequency of occurrence of a given condition among a certain population at a specific point in time. Incidence describes the number of new cases that arise during a particular period of time. Risk factors refers to those characteristics, variables, or hazards that make it more likely that an individual will develop a disorder.

5. Seeking Help for Abnormal Behavior (p.24)

A. Reasons for Clinical Contacts

Personal unhappiness, concerns of others, legal and community problems are all reasons that people seek treatment.

B. Sources of Help

Treatment facilities and a variety of individual mental health professionals all offer treatment services. Clinical or counseling psychologists, psychiatrists, psychiatric social workers, and psychiatric nurses all are qualified to offer specific types of services to the mentally ill.

C. Obstacles to Treatment

Poverty, mistrust of mental health services, lack of education all contribute to persons' inability or reluctance to seek mental health treatment, especially for members of ethnic minority groups.

6. Research in Abnormal Psychology

A. Observing Behavior

Observation and description are the first steps in the scientific process. Observational data include the stimuli that elicit responses, the subjective response to the stimuli, the behavioral response to the stimuli, and the consequences of the behavior.

B. The Role of Theory

Theories provide explanatory frameworks, and a foundation on which to build knowledge. Theories must be testable and must account for relationships that are not possible as well as those that are.

C. The Research Journey

Steps involved are identifying the problem, reviewing the literature, developing a specific hypothesis, selecting a research strategy, conducting the study, analyzing the results, and reporting the findings.

D. Types of Research

Case studies, correlational studies, assessment, followup, longitudinal, and experimental studies are all different types of research studies that psychologists conduct. Two primary types of experiments are hypothesis-testing experiments, and behavior-change experiments.

E. Research Design, Statistical Analyses, and Inference

A well-designed study has both internal validity and external validity. Descriptive statistics are used to summarize observations. Measures of central tendency provide descriptive summaries of a group's responses. These include the mean, median, and mode. Inferential statistics are used to determine whether or not between-group differences are attributable to chance or to some systematic difference.

F. Ethical Aspects of Research

Regardless of the merits of the research, the welfare of the subjects is the most important aspect of any study. All research subjects must be informed as to the risks and benefits of participating in the studies, must be allowed to withdraw at any time, must be fully debriefed if the study used deception. Strict guidelines have also been developed for research with vulnerable populations, including children, mentally retarded, seriously mentally ill, and prisoners.

TIPS FOR TESTING YOURSELF

Write each of the following key words and concepts on one side of an index card. Then, for each, look up the correct definition in your textbook. Write the definition on the opposite side of the corresponding index card. Now, you have flash cards to study. Keep the cards with you and whenever you have a few minutes, pull them out and test yourself. When you are studying with a study partner, you can test each other. You can also share the duties of looking up the definitions and writing them on the cards. Study them a little each day.

KEY TERMS AND CONCEPTS
abnormal psychology (p.5)
adaptation and maladaptive behavior (p.8)
exorcism (p.9)
shaman (p.10)
trephination (p.11)
organismic approach (p.12)
four humors (p.13)
physiognomy (p.15)
phrenology (p.15)
psychological approach (p.20)
organic approach (p.20)
interactional (biopsychosocial) approach (p.20)

stress (p.21)

vulnerability (p.21)

resilience (p.21)

coping (p.22)

epidemiological research (pp.22-24)

incidence (p.23)

prevalence p.23)

risk factor (p.24)

deinstitutionalization (p.26)

clinical psychologist (p.27)

counseling psychologist (p.27)

psychiatrist (p.27)

psychiatric social worker (p.27)

psychiatric nurse (p.27)

observational methods (p.29)

self-observations (p.29)

observational data (p.29)

independent variables (p.31)

dependent variables (p.31)

hypothesis (p.31)

descriptive statistics (p.31)

inferential statistics (p.31)

case studies (p.31)

correlational studies (p.32)

assessment studies (p.32)

longitudinal studies (p.33)

follow-up studies (p.33)

cross-sectional studies (p.33)

hypothesis testing experiments (p.34)

behavior-change experiment (p.34)

clinical trials (p.35)

placebo (p.37)

double-blind method (p.37)

internal validity (p.37)

external validity (p.37)

mean (p.38)

median (p.38)

mode (p.38)

range (p.38)

standard deviation (p.38)

null hypothesis (p.38)

correlation coefficient (p.38)

confounding (p.38)

reactivity (p.38)

demand characteristics (p.38)

expectancy effects (p.38)

sampling (p.39)

```
TIPS FOR TESTING YOURSELF

In developing answers for the following questions, turn to the section of your chapter that covers the
pertinent material. Read the section thoroughly and spend some time thinking about the information
before attempting to frame your answer. Write out each answer without referring to the book, and when
you have completed all of them, check their accuracy by returning to the corresponding section in the
book. For each question you missed, write out the correct answer. Then test yourself again. Repeat the
process until you can answer all the questions correctly.
```

SHORT ANSWER ESSAY QUESTIONS

1. Discuss internal and external stigmatization associated with mental illness. In what ways does stigmatization affect the individual—both directly and indirectly?

2. List seven problems that can arise when mental health deteriorates, and a specific example of each problem in practice.

3. What is the meaning of "adaptation" and how does it differ from "adjustment"?

4. Maladaptive behavior is always deviant, but deviant behavior is not always maladaptive. Explain.

5. What factors are implied in the label "maladaptive"?

6. Discuss the range of causes of maladaption.

7. Why is it important to understand the historical background of abnormal psychology?

8. Compare and contrast the supernatural, organic, and psychological perspectives of abnormal behavior from a historical perspective.

9. What was the practice of trephining and what therapeutic value was it supposed to have?

10. How did the ancient Greeks conceptualize the causes of abnormal behavior?

11. In what way did the treatment of abnormal behavior change during the Middle Ages? What were the two major causes of these changes? Describe the contribution of St. Augustine.

12. Explain the impact of "enlightened humanism" on changes in the conceptualization and treatment of mental illness during the Renaissance.

13. Science and rationalism replaced spiritual conceptualizations of abnormal behaviors gradually during the eighteenth and nineteenth centuries. Discuss the major contributions to this change.

14. What was the primary underlying mechanism of Anton Mesmer's treatment approach, and how is it still relevant?

15. Pinel, Rush, Dix, and Beers held views that directly impacted the treatment of institutionalized individuals. What were these views and how did they bring about reform?

16. Discuss the interaction between organic and psychological explanations of abnormal behavior. Give examples.

17. Characterize resilience in children and adults, and discuss the role of situational and individual factors in dealing with adversity.

18. How are stress, coping, and vulnerability related to maladaption? Name some common sources of vulnerability.

19. What is the function of epidemiological research? Include a discussion of prevalence, incidence, and risk factors.

20. People seek treatment for abnormal behavior for a variety of reasons. Discuss the reasons and the internal cognitive steps involved in seeking help.

21. What are some important cross-cultural issues in mental health treatment?

22. What has been the impact of deinstitutionalization on mentally ill individuals and on society as a whole?

23. List the various types of mental health professionals presented in this chapter and identify their differences in terms of training and function.

24. Discuss the process of moving from observation to theory, outlining the steps, and discussing the functions and usefulness of theory.

25. Now, describe the steps involved in developing and conducting a research study.

26. Describe the strengths and weaknesses of the following types of research strategies: case, correlational, longitudinal, and cross-sectional studies.

27. Experimental studies enable researchers to examine cause-and effect relationships. How is this accomplished? List the types of experiments presented.

28. Discuss the differences between inferential and descriptive statistics. Explain the roles of measures of central tendency, measures of variability, and the correlation coefficient in research.

29. Describe the four most important threats to the validity of research results.

30. What are the ethical standards for conducting research?

TIPS FOR TESTING YOURSELF

The following sections of self-test questions will test your understanding of the material presented in the chapter. On a separate piece of paper, write the correct answer for each item in the section, then compare your answers with those at the end of the chapter. After you have graded yourself, turn to the chapter and look up the questions you missed. Write out the correct answers. Then test yourself again. Continue doing so until you can answer all the questions correctly.

MULTIPLE CHOICE

1. The term _____ refers to survival of the species.
   a. adjustment
   b. coping
   c. adaptation
   d. vulnerability

2. Distress can be caused by
   a. an identifiable life event.
   b. environment.
   c. personality factors.
   d. all of the above.

3. Mental health includes the capacities
   a. to think on your feet, manage difficulties on a day-to-day basis, and mimic emotional maturity.
   b. to modulate your thoughts to make them acceptable, to stifle daily turmoil, and reflect normality.
   c. to think rationally and logically, cope effectively with stress and the challenges that arise in situations through the life course, and demonstrate emotional stability and growth.
   d. to imagine that you are healthy, balance the distress of everyday occurrences, and dramatize an adult demeanor in public situations.

4. Which of the following statements is (are) true?
   a. All maladaptive behavior is deviant behavior.
   b. Deviant behavior is always maladaptive.
   c. There are few causes of maladaptive behavior.
   d. both a and b.

5. How people react to situations that pose demands, constraints, or opportunities is called
   a. adaptation.
   b. coping.
   c. stress.
   d. vulnerability.

6. By examining the historical background of abnormal behavior, one can see how there are recurring theories of why people
   a. develop psychological problems.
   b. see that we have been able to discard the old, obsolete methods for treating psychological problems.
   c. become aware that much of what seems modern only developed after science proved how incorrect past views were.
   d. see how there was no attempt to treat troubled people in ancient times.

7. Trephination involves
   a. having the shaman remove a "demon possessed" stone from the victim's ear or mouth.
   b. making a small hole in the skull.
   c. a generally fatal procedure carried out in a nonsterile environment.
   d. casting out evil spirits through prayer.

8. _____ proposed the "organismic point of view," which sees behavior as a product of the totality of psychological processes.
   a. Hippocrates
   b. Plato
   c. Socrates
   d. Aristotle

9. According to Galen, _____ were believed to be related to the temperamental qualities of an individual.
   a. brain dysfunctions
   b. demons
   c. irrational thoughts
   d. humors

10. Saint Augustine helped lay the groundwork for modern
    a. humanistic psychology.
    b. behavioral theories.
    c. organic views of mental disorders.
    d. psychodynamic theory.

11. Spinosa believed that
    a. mind and body were separate entities.
    b. mind and body were inseparable.
    c. exorcism was the only effective way to eliminate demonic possession.
    d. St. Augustine was incorrect in his assumptions about human behavior.

12. A person during the nineteenth century might visit Franz Gall, who would attempt to identify personality characteristics by feeling the bumps on the person's skull. The technique Gall used was called
    a. phrenology.
    b. bacquet.
    c. mesmerism.
    d. animal magnetism

13. The Scottish physician, Cullen, treated his patients with
    a. bloodletting and physiotherapy.
    b. music and food.
    c. relaxation and baths.
    d. prayers and fasting.

14. Anton Mesmer believed that people developed psychological problems because
    a. they were possessed by demons.
    b. the bumps on the skull inaccurately reflected underlying personality structures.
    c. people had poor diets.
    d. their magnetic fluids were out of balance.

15. Mesmer's treatment appears to have been effective because of the patient's
    a. physical health.
    b. belief in the gods.
    c. age.
    d. suggestibility.

16. The term "bedlam" derived from
    a. Pinel's "Treatise on Insanity."
    b. the work of William Cullen.
    c. the atmosphere at St. Mary of Bethlehem hospital.
    d. comments regarding Virginia's hospital for "idiots and lunatics."

17. The movement of reform in Europe led directly to
    a. children being placed in halfway houses.
    b. the creation of institutions for psychologically disturbed kids.
    c. the popularity of the psychoanalytic movement.
    d. the foster care movement.

18. The people most responsible for the reform movement in America were
    a. Pinel and Mesmer.
    b. Hone, Cruikshank, and Facquier.
    c. Rush, Dix, and Beers.
    d. Freud, Heinroth, and Griesinger.

19. Clifford Beer's book that documented his experiences as a mental patient
    a. is directly responsible for the development of the insanity plea.
    b. argues in favor of the organic view of maladaptive behavior.
    c. was instrumental in gaining popular support for the mental health movement in America.
    d. was a bestseller in its time.

20. *Echoes From a Dungeon Cell* by Perry Baird was:
    a. an optimistic glimpse inside modern psychological hospitals.
    b. an expose of conditions in a 1940s era psychopathic hospital which likened hospitalization there to ancient jails such as Bedlam.
    c. a stirring story about one man's journey from insanity to health.
    d. an historical account of the surgical procedure known as a prefrontal lobotomy.

21. The organic approach assumes that
    a. irrational feelings lead to physical illnesses.
    b. animal magnetism eventually resulted in insanity.
    c. most mental disorders have a physical basis.
    d. most psychological problems are caused by deficiencies in rational thought processes.

22. Whether or not a behavior is considered deviant is based on
    a. scientific evaluation and careful observation.
    b. evidence that an organic problem is present.
    c. society's values and attitudes at the time the behavior occurs.
    d. whether there is evidence of hysteria in the behavior.

23. Vulnerability is best defined as
    a. the likelihood of maladaptive responses in certain situations.
    b. the likelihood of maladaptive responses in all situations.
    c. the likelihood of the person being resilient in certain situations.
    d. the likelihood of the person being resilient in all situations.

24. _____ refers to how people deal with difficulties and attempt to overcome them.
    a. Adaptation
    b. Adjustment
    c. Deviance
    d. Coping

25. Clinical interventions are ways of helping people cope with _____ more effectively.
    a. adaptation
    b. coping
    c. stress
    d. vulnerability

26. The rate of the number of new cases during a defined period of time is called _____, while the rate of both new and old cases for a specific period is termed _____.
    a. incidence; prevalence
    b. prevalence; incidence
    c. epidemiology; incidence
    d. deviance; prevalence

27. Which of the following has been identified as a risk factor for violent behavior?
    a. being raised in a single parent home
    b. prior history of psychiatric hospitalization
    c. habitual alcohol use and dependence
    d. low motivation or drive

28. Which of the following is not a risk factor associated with increased rates for mental disorders?
    a. marital happiness
    b. contact with friends
    c. low self-esteem
    d. education

29. Mary and John have been married for seven years. Recently, John confessed to an affair because guilt kept him from sleeping. If John seeks help from a clinician it is most probably because of
    a. his age.
    b. his unhappiness.
    c. the fact that adultery is a crime.
    d. the nature of his admission.

30. Select the following statement that is true.
    a. Since the 1960s, deinstitutionalization has been on the decrease.
    b. Community-based care is delivered in several forms including group homes.
    c. The failure of states to mandate community-based treatment has resulted in an increase in the number of inpatient treatment facilities.
    d. Community-based treatment is less effective overall than inpatient treatment.

31. A _____ has a medical degree and is allowed to prescribe medication.
    a. clinical psychologist
    b. psychiatrist
    c. psychiatric social worker
    d. psychotherapist

32. Because of different theoretical orientations, psychologists tend to emphasize _____, while psychiatrists focus on _____.
    a. diagnosis; medication regimens
    b. the importance between onset and course of a mental illness; factors related to onset of the illness
    c. the relationship between a person's psychological state of mind and relationships with friends and family; a biological approach to treatment
    d. somatic therapies; specific forms of talk therapy

33. Which of the following would likely be the first steps in the research process?
    a. observing and describing behaviors
    b. hypothesis formation and developing operational definitions
    c. interpretation of data and theory formation
    d. hospital and clinical situation application

34. A clinician observes that whenever a particular staff member comes in contact with patient X, the patient displays aggressive behavior. Which type of observation is the clinician using?
    a. consequences of behavior
    b. stimuli that elicit particular types of responses
    c. behavioral response to the stimuli
    d. subjective responses to the stimuli

35. A useful theory should be
    a. testable.
    b. correct.
    c. intuitive.
    d. controversial.

36. In a study testing the effects of listening to music on anxiety, the music would be the _____, while anxiety would be the _____.
    a. independent variable; dependent variable
    b. dependent variable; independent variable
    c. hypothesis; dependent variable
    d. correlational evidence; dependent variable

37. A(n) _____ involves the in-depth study of an individual's behavior.
    a. case study
    b. correlational study
    c. assessment study
    d. self-observation

38. Correlational studies allow the researcher
    a. to follow up with patients by retesting them.
    b. to study a single individual over a long period of time.
    c. to determine that variable A caused variable B.
    d. to establish relationships between variables.

39. Observing the same group of subjects for a long period of time is typical of
    a. a survey.
    b. a longitudinal study.
    c. a cross-sectional study.
    d. a self-observation.

40. Which of the following is not a problem when doing longitudinal studies?
    a. They tend to take a long time to complete.
    b. They are often expensive.
    c. Subjects used in the study may move or die.
    d. They are used much too often to be of real value.

41. In one study, subjects were given a self-report measure of anxiety. Six months later, these same individuals took the test again to see if their level of anxiety had changed. This study was probably designed to be a _____ study.
    a. hypothetical
    b. longitudinal
    c. cross-sectional
    d. follow-up

42. A researcher wants to find out the average height and weight of children between the ages of two and five years. The most efficient way of gathering this information would be to do a(n)
    a. longitudinal study.
    b. cross-sectional study.
    c. prevalence measure.
    d. inferential design.

43. Hypothesis-testing experiments
    a. tend to pose many ethical problems for researchers.
    b. involve making a prediction based on a theory.
    c. are always double-blind.
    d. involve the development of new therapeutic techniques.

44. A researcher wants to test the effectiveness of a new drug for depression. She obtains two comparable groups of depressed patients. To the one group, she administers the new drug; while the other group receives some form of control treatment. This methodology may be described as
    a. a double-blind.
    b. a clinical trial.
    c. an assessment procedure.
    d. a follow-up study.

45. In a double-blind study, neither the subjects nor the experimenter are aware
    a. that an experiment is being conducted.
    b. that a placebo will be used.
    c. what the independent variable will be.
    d. of what dependent variable might occur.

46. Internal validity refers to _____, while external validity refers to _____.
    a. experimental conditions; generalization of findings to the real world
    b. the soundness of the hypothesis; the ability of the hypothesis to predict behavior outside the laboratory
    c. manipulation of the dependent variable; manipulation of the independent variable
    d. none of the above

47. A study finds that the average age for first drink of an alcoholic beverage among teenagers is 13.4 years of age. This statistic is a
    a. median.
    b. mean.
    c. mode.
    d. correlation.

48. Which of the following refers to changes in behavior that occur when subjects are aware of the fact that they are being observed?
    a. confounding
    b. expectancy effects
    c. reactivity
    d. demand characteristics

49. If valid conclusions are to be drawn from a study, then
    a. the population should not be representative of the sample.
    b. the researcher should be blind to the sample under study.
    c. confounding must be maximized.
    d. the sampling must be representative of the population.

NEXT, TRY YOUR HAND AT TRUE/FALSE QUESTIONS.

TRUE/FALSE QUESTIONS

Indicate whether each statement is true or false. Check your answers at the end of this chapter.

T   F   1. Distress is almost always caused by an easily identifiable life event, for example, losing a job.

T   F   2. High self-regard, heightened competence, and lowered physiological reactivity are all signs of mental health deterioration.

T   F   3. Adaptation refers to individual mastery of the environment.

T   F   4. The idea that supernatural or magical forces like evil spirits can explain abnormal behavior can still be encountered today.

T   F   5. In ancient Greece, mental deviations came to be viewed as natural phenomena for which rational treatments might be developed.

T   F   6. During the Middle Ages, music and dance were thought to cure insanity by restoring the chemical balance within the body.

T   F   7. The term "non compos mentis" is Latin for mentally retarded from birth.

T   F   8. During the seventeenth and eighteenth centuries, people accepted the idea that demons and supernatural forces were the causes of abnormal behaviors.

T   F   9. Gall's theory that bumps on the skull reflect underlying brain structures is called physiognomy.

T   F   10. Moral treatment involved exorcism and an attempt to improve the morals of people in insane asylums.

T   F   11. Beer's book, *A Mind that Found Itself*, demonstrates that humane and humanistic treatment was widespread and popular during the early 1900s.

T   F   12. After enduring the pain of straitjackets and inhumane treatment at a 1940s mental hospital, Perry Baird concluded in *Echoes from a Dungeon Cell* that he had been treated quite humanely, considering his condition.

T   F   13. Theories of abnormality are almost never brand new.

T   F   14. Heredity can increase vulnerability.

T   F   15. Some areas of the U.S. have higher rates for schizophrenia than other areas.

T   F   16. The occurrence of a given condition at a particular point in time is called prevalence.

T F 17. Less educated people have higher rates of diagnosed mental disorders than people who have more education.

T F 18. In the past ten years there has been an increase in the number of beds in state mental hospitals.

T F 19. Psychologists prescribe medications for their clients.

T F 20. The last step in the research process is to analyze the results.

T F 21. For the most part, explanations of behavior occur after the fact in case studies.

T F 22. One limitation of the assessment study is that it provides little if any useful information.

T F 23. Experiments on animals have been conducted to investigate both biological and social factors in behavior.

T F 24. Placebos are inactive substances that never affect a person's behavior.

T F 25. Descriptive statistics allow the researcher to test comparisons between groups.

T F 26. Occasionally, prisoners or mental patients must be forced to participate in research for their own good.

KEEP GOING.....MATCHING IS NEXT.

MATCHING

Match the following terms with information provided below. The answers are at the end of this chapter.

a. confounding
b. demand characteristics
c. risk factor
d. deinstitutionalize
e. independent variable
f. inferential statistics
g. mode
h. social worker

i. hypothesis
j. placebo
k. natural fool
l. stress
m. shaman
n. physiognomony
o. St. Augustine

_____ 1. human reaction to a situation that poses demands, constraints, or opportunities

_____ 2. most frequently occurring score among subjects

_____ 3. an educated guess

_____ 4. focuses on link between disordered behavior and home environment

_____ 5. manipulated by researcher to assess impact on outcome measure

_____ 6. results from failure to control other influences on the dependent variable

_____ 7. an inactive substance

_____ 8. release from a psychiatric hospital

_____ 9. identified on basis of a relationship between two variables

_____ 10. subject's perception of what is expected of him/her

_____ 11. mentally retarded person with childlike intellectual qualities

_____ 12. used to judge personality characteristics on the basis of physical appearance

_____ 13. wrote "Confessions" using introspection

_____ 14. medicine man who is a spiritual medium

_____ 15. the correlation coefficient is an example

GOOD, NOW CHECK YOUR ANSWERS. WHEN YOU'RE DONE GRADING YOURSELF, COVER YOUR ANSWERS, AND START ALL OVER AGAIN. KEEP TESTING YOURSELF UNTIL YOU CAN ANSWER THEM ALL CORRECTLY.

CHAPTER 1 ANSWER KEY
Multiple Choice

1	c		26.	a
2.	d		27.	c
3.	c		28.	c
4.	a		29.	b
5.	c		30.	b
6.	a		31.	b
7.	b		32.	c
8.	b		33.	a
9.	d		34.	c
10.	d		35.	a
11.	b		36.	a
12.	a		37.	a
13.	a		38.	d
14.	d		39.	b
15.	d		40.	d
16.	c		41.	d
17.	b		42.	b
18.	c		43.	b
19.	c		44.	b
20.	b		45.	c
21.	c		46.	a
22.	c		47.	b
23.	a		48.	c
24.	d		49.	c
25.	d			

True/False

1.	F	14.	T
2.	F	15.	T
3.	T	16.	T
4.	T	17.	F
5.	T	18.	F
6.	T	19.	F
7.	F	20.	F
8.	F	21.	T
9.	F	22.	F
10.	F	23.	T
11.	F	24.	F
12.	F	25.	F
13.	T	26.	F

Matching

1. l
2. g
3. i
4. h
5. e
6. a
7. j
8. d
9. c
10. b
11. k
12. n
13. o
14. m
15. f

Chapter 2
THEORETICAL PERSPECTIVES ON MALADAPTIVE BEHAVIOR

CHAPTER OVERVIEW

The role of theory in the field of abnormal psychology is presented in this section. Theories provide frameworks for understanding the causes of maladaptive behavior. Theories representing the biological, psychodynamic, behavioral, cognitive, humanistic-existential, and community-cultural perspectives are featured and discussed. No one theory can fully explain all behavior; each theory deals with different aspects of reality. Some theories deal with causes of behavior, others with coping strategies, and still others explain human vulnerability. The chapter closes with a look at the integration of approaches to maladaptive behavior.

LEARNING OBJECTIVES

After studying this chapter, you should be able to answer these questions:
 1. What are the roles of theory in abnormal psychology?
 2. What is the biological perspective of abnormal psychology?
 3. What role do genetic factors play in abnormal behavior?
 4. What are DNA, genes, and chromosomes, and what do they have to do with abnormal behavior?
 5. What is meant by penetrance and heritability?
 6. What is behavior genetics?
 7. What are the main components of the nervous system?
 8. What are the main parts of the neuron?
 9. What is the brain's role in abnormal behavior?
10. What is meant by brain plasticity?
11. How do the brain and endocrine system interact?
12. What is the difference between neuroanatomy, neuropathology, neurochemistry, neuropharmacology, and neuropsychology?
13. How do computerized axial tomography (CT), magnetic resonance imaging (MRI), magnetic resonance spectroscopy (MRS), single photon emission computed tomography (SPECT), and positron emission tomography (PT) depict different aspects of brain structure and function?
14. What is the role of neuropharmacology in helping to understand and treat mental illness?
15. What is psychoneuroimmunology and how does it help us understand abnormal behavior?
16. How do the biological and psychological systems interact to produce maladaptive behavior?
17. What is the psychodynamic perspective of abnormal behavior?
18. What is Freud's theory of personality and personality development?
19. What did Freud think were the stages of psychosexual development, and what was the significance of each stage?
20. What is the difference between primary process and secondary process thinking?
21. What are defense mechanisms and what role do they play in adaptive and maladaptive behavior?
22. How does psychoanalysis work?
23. What are the more recent approaches to psychoanalysis and how are they different from each other?

24. What is the behavioral perspective of abnormal behavior?
25. What is classical conditioning?
26. How are the principles of operant conditioning used in a clinical setting?
27. What is social conditioning and which of its principles are used in a clinical setting?
28. How does the cognitive perspective explain abnormal behavior?
29. What have Aaron Beck and Albert Ellis contributed to the understanding of abnormal behavior and its treatment?
30. How do the humanistic and existential perspectives explain and treat abnormal behavior?
31. What has the community-cultural perspective contributed to understanding abnormal psychology?
32. What is meant by the integrative approach to abnormal behavior?

CHAPTER OUTLINE

1. The Role of Theory in Abnormal Psychology (p.45)

A. Thoughts, feelings, perceptions, and skills together influence mental states and behaviors. Scientific theory organizes what we know about these processes and help to explain their meanings.

B. The Orientation of This Book

Maladaptive behavior is presented in terms of individual vulnerabilities and resilience. Theories in this book will be presented in such a way as to profile assets and liabilities as well as discussing methods needed for reducing vulnerabilities and increasing resilience.

2. The Biological Perspective (p.47)

Medical research supports the role of biological factors in some, but not all, mental conditions. This perspective includes genetics, the brain and nervous system, and endocrine glands and their influence on behavior.

A. Genetic Factors

While genetic factors have a powerful role in human behavior, the emphasis of research is on the interaction between genetics and other factors, such as environment. The focus of scientific attention is on the interaction of nature and nurture.

B. The Nervous System and the Brain

The complexities of the structures of the brain and its neurochemistry have significant impact on human behavior. There is a preponderance of evidence showing that various behavioral deficits result from defects in the nervous system, but it often is not a one-to-one relationship. That is, it can be difficult to predict exactly the effects of damage to brain tissue on the individual's behavior.

C. Integration of Biological and Psychological Systems

Research is showing that most diseases, including mental illness, have multiple determinants that include physical, psychological, environmental, and heredity factors.

3. The Psychodynamic Perspective (p.59)

This perspective is based on the idea that behavior is the result of intrapsychic, unconscious processes.

A. Freud and Psychoanalysis

Freud's emphasis was on understanding one's deepest emotions and feelings in order to discern their effects on behavior. He believed that all behavior is determined by prior mental events, and that much of this mental material resides in the unconscious mind, out of awareness of the individual.

B. More Recent Approaches to Psychoanalysis

These approaches to psychoanalysis have broadened the theory to account for the influences of interpersonal relationships and other aspects of the social environments on maladaptive behavior.

C. Evaluating Psychoanalytic Theory

An evaluation of psychoanalytic theory is difficult at best because the events it hypothesizes are not directly observable and hence not subject to scientific investigation.

4. The Behavioral Perspective (p.66)

Behaviorism developed because many believed Freud's theory was vague, complicated, and untestable. Behaviorism is based on the idea that all behavior can be explained by environmental factors.

A. Classical Conditioning

The basic premise of classical conditioning is that a response that an organism automatically makes to a stimulus is transferred to other stimuli through an association between the stimuli. The most famous example of classical conditioning is the research conducted by Ivan Pavlov with laboratory dogs.

B. Operant Conditioning

In operant conditioning, otherwise known as instrumental conditioning, the organism must make a response before a reinforcement occurs. The organism 'operates' on the environment and produces an effect.

C. Social Learning Theories

Researchers believe that social processes play an important role in the influence that reinforcement and conditioning have on behavior. For example, modeling is one way to change behavior because people can learn by watching how others do things and by seeing the consequences of those behaviors.

5. The Cognitive Perspective (p.71)

This perspective places its emphasis on mental processes involved in the acquisition, interpretation, storage, and retrieval of information.

A. Maladaptive Behavior and Cognition

Maladaptive thought processes result in maladaptive behaviors.

B. Cognitive Therapies

Cognitive therapy is based on three assumptions: 1) cognitive activity affects behavior, 2) cognition can be monitored, analyzed, and changed, and 3) behavior change can be achieved through change in cognition.

6. The Humanistic-Existential Perspective (p.75)

Believes that science is missing its mark by only focusing on observable behaviors. Also posits the belief that inner experience and people's search for the meaning of their existence should be the focus of psychology.

A. The Humanistic View

Central assumption is that every person is striving toward 'self-actualization' and that maladaptive behavior is formed by environments that block the person's striving.

B. The Existential View

Existential perspective focuses in self-determination, choice, and individual responsibility.

7. The Community-Cultural Perspective (p.76)

Maladaptive behavior results from the inability to cope effectively with stress, and is also seen as partly the failure of the individual's social support system. Attempts to reduce maladaptive behavior before it begins through preventative measures.

A. Social Roles and Labeling

All persons belong to social and cultural groups, which shape behavior and influence every aspect of individuals' lives. Social roles are those functions that persons fill as members of groups.

B. Labeling refers to categorizing people on the basis of group membership.

C. Contributions of the Community-Cultural Perspective

Produced new approaches to maladaptive behavior that helps to reach groups that psychology has previously ignored, as well as help understand the ways in which the social environment can enhance lives.

8. An Interactional Approach (p.78)

Looks at the most valuable contribution of each theoretical perspective to our understanding of maladaptive behavior.

```
┌─────────────────────────────────────────────────────────────────────┐
│ TIPS FOR TESTING YOURSELF                                             │
│                                                                       │
│ Write each of the following key words and concepts on one side of an  │
│ index card.  Then, for each, look up the correct definition in your   │
│ textbook.  Write the definition on the opposite side of the           │
│ corresponding index card.  Now, you have flash cards to study.  Keep  │
│ the cards with you and whenever you have a few minutes, pull them out  │
│ and test yourself.  When you are studying with a study partner, you    │
│ can test each other.  You can also share the duties of looking up the  │
│ definitions and writing them on the cards.  Study them a little each   │
│ day.                                                                   │
└─────────────────────────────────────────────────────────────────────┘
```

KEY TERMS AND CONCEPTS
biological perspective (p.47)
psychodynamic perspective (p.59)
behavioral perspective (p.71)
cognitive perspective (p.75)
humanistic-existential perspective (p.76)
community-cultural perspective (p.78)
chromosomes (p.48)
chromosomal anomalies (p.48)
genes (p.48)
genome (p.48)
deoxyribonucleic acid (DNA) (p.49)
penetrance (p.49)
gene expression (p.51)
heritability (p.49)
behavior genetics (p.49)
population genetics (p.49)
pedigree studies (p.49)
monozygotic twins (p.49)
dizygotic twins (p.49)
concordance (p.50)
nonshared environment (p.51)
central nervous system (p.51)
peripheral nervous system (p.51)
somatic system (p.52)
autonomic system (p.52)
neuron (p.52)
axon (p.52)
dendrites (p.52)
neurotransmitter (p.52)
synapse (p.52)
cerebral cortex (p.54)
electroencephalogram (EEG) (p.54)
limbic system (p.54)
hypothalamus (p.55)
endorphins (p.55)

neural plasticity (p.55)
endocrine system (p.55)
stressor (p.56)
adrenal cortex (p.56)
neuroscience (p.56)
adrenal corticosteroids (p.56)
neuroscience revolution (p.56)
brain imaging (p.57)
neuropharmacology (p.58)
agonist (p.58)
antagonist (p.58)
psychoneuroimmunology (p.58)
antigens (p.58)
lymphocytes (p.58)
psychic determinism (p.60)
conscious (p.60)
preconscious (p.60)
unconscious (p.60)
libido (p.61)
psychosexual development (p.61)
oral stage (p.61)
anal stage (p.61)
phallic stage (p.61)
genital stage (p.62)
fixation (p.62)
regression (p.62)
psychic apparatus (p.62)
id (p.62)
ego (p.62)
superego (p.62)
primary process thinking (p.62)
pleasure principle (p.62)
secondary process thinking (p.62)
anxiety (p.62)
defense mechanisms (pp.63-64)
repression (p.63)
psychoanalysis (p.63)
free association (p.63)
ego psychology (p.66)
object relations psychology (p.66)
self-psychology (p.66)
determinism (p.67)
reinforcement (p.67)
classical conditioning (p.67)
conditioned stimulus (CS) (p.67)
unconditioned response (UCR or UR) (p.67)
unconditioned stimulus (UCS or US) (p.67)
conditioned response (CR) (p.67)

avoidance or escape responses (p.67)
extinction (p.67)
operant conditioning (p. 67)
positive reinforcer (p.68)
negative reinforcer (p.68)
punishment (p.68)
shaping (p.68)
schedule of reinforcement (p.69)
modeling (p.70)
role playing (p.70)
implicit learning (p.71)
self-efficacy (p.72)
cognitive therapy (p.73)
rational-emotive therapy (p.74)
social learning (p.74)
self-actualization (p.75)
community psychology (p.76)
social causation theory (p.76)
social selection theory (p.76)
social roles (p.78)
labeling (p.78)
interactional approach (p.78)
mediators (p.79)

SHORT ANSWER ESSAY QUESTIONS

1. In what ways are theories of maladaptive behavior useful?

2. From the biological perspective, what are the physiological causes of abnormal behavior? Advances in which scientific fields made the biological perspective so popular in the eighteenth and nineteenth centuries?

3. Define the following terms: genetic penetrance, behavior genetics, and genetic concordance.

4. Explain the nature versus nurture controversy. What is the position held by most psychologists?

5. Describe the new field of neuroscience and its contribution to the understanding of maladaptive behavior.

6. What are the underlying assumptions regarding the causes of human behavior from the psychodynamic perspective?

7. What is the function of defense mechanisms, according to Freud? Name and discuss the most important of the defense mechanisms.

8. In what ways do the more recent psychodynamic theories differ from the traditional Freudian views?

9. Discuss how learning theorists view behavior. What does the behavioral approach have in common with the psychoanalytic approach?

10. Compare and contrast classical and operant conditioning.

11. Enumerate six schedules of reinforcements and briefly define each.

12. Explain the role of modeling and covert mediators in the social learning explanations of abnormal behavior.

13. How do cognitive psychologists differ from those of the psychodynamic perspective in their study of the psychological processes involved in abnormal behavior?

14. What are the underlying assumptions of cognitive theory?

15. How have learning theorists like Albert Bandura incorporated cognitions into their understanding of abnormal behavior?

16. How do cognitive therapists attempt to alter maladaptive cognitions during therapy?

17. In what ways to the humanistic-existential theories from the behaviorist and psychodynamic perspective?

18. Briefly summarize the community-cultural perspective on abnormal behavior. What are the underlying assumptions? In what ways is this perspective different from other theories of maladaptive behavior?

19. What are social roles and how are they involved in shaping people's behavior?

20. Describe the interactive approach to the study of abnormal behavior.

TIPS FOR TESTING YOURSELF

The following sections of self-test questions will test your understanding of the material presented in the chapter. On a separate piece of paper, write the correct answer for each item in the section, then compare your answers with those at the end of the chapter. After you have graded yourself, turn to the chapter and look up the questions you missed. Write out the correct answers. Then test yourself again. Continue doing so until you can answer all the questions correctly.

MULTIPLE CHOICE

1. The biological perspective
   a. became popular during the seventeenth century.
   b. gained popularity with the discovery of the link between bodily infections/defects and disordered behavior.
   c. suggests that high levels of psychological stress are responsible for psychological disorders.
   d. has established that there is a physiological cause for all psychological disorders.

2. The Phineas Gage story of 1848 is important because it reveals:
   a. man's ability to survive catastrophic injury, as well as the hazards of manual labor in the industrial age.
   b. that the control of emotional responses could be affected without affecting other mental capacities.
   c. that to some extent mental functions are encapsulated in specific brain pathways.
   d. both b and c.

3. A major factor in some genetic abnormalities appears to be
   a. irregularities in the structure or number of an individual's chromosomes.
   b. the absence of DNA.
   c. the high rate of penetrance.
   d. none of the above.

4. Which of the following represents a correct association?
   a. monozygotic–chromosomal anomaly
   b. monozygotic–fraternal twins
   c. dizygotic–fraternal twins
   d. dizygotic–identical twins

5. _____ in twin studies refers to the relationship between twins or other family members with respect to a given characteristic or trait.
   a. Penetrance
   b. Anomalies
   c. Psychoimmunology
   d. Concordance

6. The fact that there is not a 100 percent concordance rate for schizophrenia between identical twins suggests
   a. error measurement in those studies.
   b. a genetic mutation.
   c. the environment influences behavior.
   d. that the twins are actually dizygotic.

7. Today, most psychologists view behavior to be a function of
   a. nature only.
   b. nurture only.
   c. nature and nurture.
   d. nurture if siblings, but nature if identical twins.

8. The central nervous system includes
   a. the brain and spinal cord.
   b. the glands and hormones that regulate behaviors.
   c. the thymus and adrenal glands.
   d. 100 percent of the nerve cells in the body.

9. A _____ is a messenger chemical sent to dendrite receptor sites.
   a. synapse
   b. axon
   c. neuron
   d. neurotransmitter

10. In the brain, the _____ controls our distinctive human behaviors.
    a. hypothalamus
    b. midbrain
    c. cerebral cortex
    d. medulla

11. Endorphins are associated with
    a. chromosomal anomalies.
    b. opiate receptors in the brain reward system.
    c. endocrine hormones.
    d. EEG spikes characteristic of petit mal epilepsy.

12. Which of the following is (are) true?
    a. The development of the brain is not influenced by environmental factors.
    b. The brain uses the outside world to shape itself.
    c. The brain goes through critical periods in which its cells require stimulation to develop certain functions.
    d. both b and c

13. Under stress, the hypothalamus releases a substance called
    a. corticotrophin-releasing factor.
    b. corticosteriod.
    c. adrenocorticotrophic-releasing factor.
    d. endorphin.

14. A _____ would be a neuroscience specialist who might conduct an investigation on the relationship between Alzheimer's disease and abnormalities in the brain structure.
    a. neurochemist
    b. neuropsychologist
    c. neuroendocrinologist
    d. neuropathologist

15. Select the following statement that is true.
    a. It appears that many factors may cause mental illness.
    b. Recent research confirms the fact that most mental illness is primarily due to brain abnormalities.
    c. Deficiencies in the command center of the brain have not been found to be responsible for mental illness.
    d. The stress of daily living, although worrisome, does not contribute to mental illness.

16. _____ is a form of brain imaging used to study subjects while they perform various kinds of cognitive tasks.
    a. Computed tomography
    b. Single photon emission computed tomography
    c. Magnetic resonance imaging
    d. Positron emission tomography

17. Psychoneuroimmunology involves the study of
    a. antigens and lymphocytes.
    b. psychoactive drug actions on psychotic behavior.
    c. psychological, neural, and immunological processes.
    d. the pain-relieving properties of endorphins.

18. The two major tasks of the immune system are
    a. reproduction and distribution of antigens.
    b. producing and dispersing endorphins.
    c. producing ACTH and deactivation of the hypothalamus.
    d. recognition and removal/inactivation of foreign materials.

19. Research on the relationship between bereavement and the immune system
    a. has shown little promise in light of new discoveries in the neurosciences.
    b. indicates that there appears to be a relationship between these variables.
    c. demonstrates that the absence of a social support network for the bereaved exacerbates suppression of the immune system.
    d. both b and c.

20. The psychodynamic perspective is based on the idea that
    a. stress can trigger psychological problems.
    b. stress can trigger physical disorders.
    c. thoughts and emotions are important causes of behaviors.
    d. psychological disorders are caused by hormonal imbalances.

21. Which of the following is the correct order for Freud's psychosexual stages of development?
    a. oral, anal, phallic, latency, genital
    b. oral, anal, latency, phallic, genital
    c. anal, oral, phallic, latency, genital
    d. latency, oral, anal, phallic, genital

22. Which of the following statements is accurate regarding the functioning of the psychic apparatus according to Freud?
    a. The ego uses guilt to keep the id in line.
    b. Primary process thinking is found in children but not in adults.
    c. The ego is the only structure present in the infant.
    d. The id is concerned with the maximization of pleasure.

23. The most basic defense mechanism is
    a. displacement.
    b. denial.
    c. repression.
    d. sublimation.

24. Rationalization involves
    a. a shift of feeling and attitudes from one object to another more acceptable substitute.
    b. externalizing characteristics or impulses that arouse anxiety by attributing them to others.
    c. a self-serving explanation and justification of behavior, serving as an excuse for doing something the person believes to be socially unacceptable.
    d. engaging in behavior designed to symbolically make amends for or negate previous thoughts, feelings or actions; expressing a wish and then denying it.

25. _____ involves expressing an unacceptable impulse by transforming it into its opposite.
    a. Projection
    b. Reaction formation
    c. Regression
    d. Sublimation

26. Freud would view a ten-year-old child who begins bed wetting after a new sibling is born as utilizing the defense mechanism of
    a. sublimation
    b. regression
    c. reaction formation
    d. projection

27. _____ viewed development as a life-long process proceeding in stages.
   a. Klein
   b. Erikson
   c. Alder
   d. Freud

28. _____ believed that psychological disorders were the direct result of deficits in the structure of the self.
   a. Freud
   b. Adler
   c. Bandura
   d. none of the above

29. You have a headache and take an aspirin. The headache goes away. Your behavior of aspirin-taking has been
   a. extinguished.
   b. negatively reinforced.
   c. punished.
   d. positively reinforced.

30. Which of the following mechanisms of behavior change results in a decrease in the frequency of the behavior?
   a. positive reinforcement
   b. negative reinforcement
   c. shaping
   d. extinction

31. In a continuous reinforcement schedule
   a. reinforcement is given after a fixed number of responses.
   b. reinforcement varies around an average number of responses.
   c. reinforcement occurs after a variable interval of time.
   d. reinforcement occurs after every response of a particular type.

32. Systematic desensitization procedures rely most heavily upon
   a. classical conditioning principles.
   b. operant conditioning principles.
   c. punishment.
   d. negative reinforcement principles.

33. Answering a telephone has been
   a. operantly conditioned.
   b. classically conditioned.
   c. extinguished through shaping.
   d. both b and c

34. Bandura proposed that
    a. all behaviors were learned through reinforcement.
    b. modeling is ineffective as a learning tool.
    c. no individual learns vicariously.
    d. a behavior can be learned without reinforcement.

35. Self-efficacy refers to
    a. irrational beliefs.
    b. hypothetical constructs.
    c. convictions about personal effectiveness.
    d. the mental life of the individual and personal schemata.

36. Rational-emotive therapy is based on the idea that
    a. disturbed emotions result in abnormal behaviors.
    b. anxiety and guilt decrease feelings of self-efficacy.
    c. people are motivated to strive toward self-actualization.
    d. irrational thoughts cause emotional overreactions.

37. Beck's concept of schema refers to
    a. a person's plan for achieving self-actualization.
    b. experiences in later life that affect our ability to deal with trauma.
    c. a cognitive structure in a particular domain.
    d. an individual's cognitive structure that serves as a conscience.

38. Humanistic-existential theorists believe that
    a. psychology should focus on observable behaviors.
    b. psychological problems are a product of illogical thoughts.
    c. inner experiences and a search for the meaning of existence should be the focus of psychology.
    d. the job of the therapist is to help clients restructure their thinking and replace maladaptive thoughts.

39. Which of the following represents a similarity between the ideas of Freud and the perspective of Rogers?
    a. Both believed the roots of anxiety lie in unconscious impulses.
    b. Both developed their theories by observing clients in psychotherapy.
    c. Neither believed that psychotherapists should provide interpretations during therapy.
    d. Neither believed that people are rational or socialized.

40. Which of the following viewpoints argues that lower socioeconomic groups show a greater incidence of maladaptive behavior because people who do not function well tend to experience downward mobility?
    a. existential
    b. community
    c. social-causation
    d. social-selection

41. _____ occurs whenever people are categorized on some basis, whether that basis is relevant and fair or not.
    a. Labeling
    b. Social role development
    c. Diagnostic classification
    d. Mediation

42. By an integrative approach, the authors of your text mean
    a. that behavior is a function of several factors.
    b. that the brain has primary influence on behavior.
    c. that each system of psychotherapy has importance depending on the disorder under consideration.
    d. that the best approach to treating mental illness is through a combination of drugs and psychotherapy.

NEXT, TRY YOUR HAND AT TRUE/FALSE QUESTIONS.

TRUE/FALSE QUESTIONS

Indicate whether each statement is true or false. Check your answers at the end of this chapter.

T F 1. At the extreme, the biological perspective assumes all disordered behaviors are due to bodily dysfunctions or defects.

T F 2. Monozygotic twins develop from the same fertilized egg.

T F 3. The somatic nervous system transmits information from sense organs to the muscles.

T F 4. The limbic system is not responsible for motivational or emotional functions.

T F 5. Neuroscientists have shown that behavior, perception, and cognition are the results of integrated actions of networks of nerve cells.

T F 6. Psychoneuroimmunology is the study of the effects of drugs on behavior.

T F 7. Freud changed behavior by attempting to identify and eliminate psychic determinants.

T F 8. Saving money for a goal would reflect primary process thinking.

T F 9. One of the goals of psychoanalytic therapy is the elimination of the use of defense mechanisms.

T F 10. Reaction formation involves the expresses of an anxiety-arousing aspect of the environment, as defined by Freud.

T F 11. Punishment is one of the most common forms of negative reinforcement.

T F 12. Operant conditioning deals with responses that occur relatively infrequently prior to being reinforced.

T F 13. The cognitive view seeks to account for behavior by studying the ways in which the person uses available information.

T F 14. Albert Ellis regards intense emotions and maladaptive behavior as the consequence of irrational thoughts.

T F 15. The community perspective suggests that psychological problems are closely related to problems existing only within the individual.

T F 16. The interactional approach suggests that the way a situation influences behavior depends on the particular capabilities of an individual experiencing a particular set of conditions.

KEEP GOING…..MATCHING IS NEXT.

MATCHING

Match the following terms with the information provided below. The answers are at the end of this chapter.

a. antigens
b. genome
c. preconscious
d. escape response
e. secondary process thinking
f. object relations
g. phallic psychosexual stage
h. classical conditioning
i. schedule
j. intervening variable
k. stressor
l. karyotypes
m. conditioned response
n. substantia nigra
o. population genetics
p. undoing
q. intermittent reinforcement schedule
r. seventh theory of maladaptive behavior

_____ 1. site in brain associated with Parkinson's disease

_____ 2. condition that makes it difficult to maintain biological and psychological adaptation

_____ 3. engaging in behavior designed to symbolically make amends or negate previous thoughts, feelings, or actions.

_____ 4. maps of chromosomes

_____ 5. basis for reinforcement

_____ 6. allows for the delay of gratification

_____ 7. only some responses are reinforced

_____ 8. model used by Pavlov with his dogs

_____ 9. contains information that may readily become conscious

_____ 10. a behavior that is learned to be associated with a particular stimulus

_____ 11. involves the use of an aversive US

_____ 12. foreign materials

_____ 13. the mind is composed of internal representations of significant others

_____ 14. complete set of a person's genes

_____ 15. pleasure is associated with the genitals

_____ 16. inferred variable

_____ 17. the integration of biological, psychodynamic, behavioral, cognitive, humanistic, and community-culture perspectives

_____ 18. study of gene distributions in groups of individuals

GOOD, NOW CHECK YOUR ANSWERS. WHEN YOU'RE DONE GRADING YOURSELF, COVER YOUR ANSWERS, AND START ALL OVER AGAIN. KEEP TESTING YOURSELF UNTIL YOU CAN ANSWER THEM ALL CORRECTLY.

CHAPTER 2 ANSWER KEY

Multiple Choice

1.	b		22.	d
2.	d		23.	c
3.	a		24.	c
4.	c		25.	b
5.	d		26.	b
6.	c		27.	b
7.	c		28.	d
8.	a		29.	b
9.	d		30.	d
10.	c		31.	d
11.	b		32.	a
12.	d		33.	a
13.	a		34.	d
14.	d		35.	c
15.	a		36.	d
16.	b		37.	b
17.	c		38.	c
18.	d		39.	b
19.	d		40.	d
20.	c		41.	a
21.	a		42.	a

True/False

1.	T		9.	F
2.	T		10.	F
3.	T		11.	F
4.	F		12.	T
5.	T		13.	T
6.	F		14.	T
7.	T		15.	F
8.	F		16.	T

Matching

1.	n		10.	m
2.	k		11.	d
3.	p		12.	a
4.	l		13.	f
5.	i		14.	b
6.	e		15.	g
7.	q		16.	j
8.	h		17.	r
9.	c		18.	o

Chapter 3
THE THERAPEUTIC ENTERPRISE: CHOICES, TECHNIQUES, EVALUATION

CHAPTER OVERVIEW
The major approaches to treating maladaptive behavior are reviewed in the present chapter. The approaches considered are: psychodynamic, cognitive, behavioral, cognitive-behavioral, interpersonal therapy, and humanistic-existential. Prominent group therapies are also highlighted. The effectiveness of the various therapeutic styles is evaluated and methodological research issues considered. Finally, the scope and effectiveness of biological approaches are reviewed, and the changing role of the psychiatric hospital considered.

LEARNING OBJECTIVES
After studying this chapter, you should be able to address these questions:
1. Regardless of theoretical orientation, what three tasks do psychotherapists perform?
2. What are the features of psychodynamic therapy and what techniques does it involve?
3. In what ways does psychoanalysis differ from psychodynamic therapy?
4. What is the focus of humanistic therapies and what type of atmosphere does a therapist try to provide?
5. What are the underlying questions of existential therapies?
6. Describe the perspective of Gestalt therapy.
7. Discuss the assumptions of cognitive psychotherapy and the techniques used to address them.
8. What is the essence of Aaron Beck's cognitive therapy?
9. Compare and contrast the focus of Albert Ellis's rational-emotive therapy with that of Aaron Beck's approach.
10. What does brief psychotherapy share with interpersonal therapy?
11. How is the effectiveness of psychotherapy researched? Discuss meta-analysis and its use in outcome research. What are the problems encountered by researchers studying therapeutic effectiveness?
12. What technique and interpersonal factors influence therapeutic effectiveness?
13. What is process research?
14. Name and describe the most common forms of behavior therapy.
15. What are the main techniques of cognitive-behavior therapy? What different kinds of modeling are used?
16. For what types of problems are cognitive-behavioral interventions particularly effective?
17. What is the growing interest in integrating diverse therapeutic approaches? What are the advantages of such integration?
18. What features do all types of group therapy share?
19. What is the focus of cognitive-behavioral group therapy?

20. What is the primary underlying idea guiding family therapy? How is this unique to family therapy? With which type of problems is family systems therapy particularly effective?
21. What takes place during psychodrama?
22. Discuss the effectiveness of group therapy.
23. What are the major tasks for researchers studying the various types of psychological therapies?
24. What are the various measures of therapeutic outcomes and why is it important for researchers to compare therapeutic approaches?
25. The growing cultural and ethnic diversity within the U.S. population present a number of challenges to psychotherapists and researchers. What are the treatment and research challenges?
26. What is behind the trend for greater integration of therapeutic approaches?
27. Discuss the primary classes of medications used to treat mental disorders and the effectiveness of each. What is a major reason that patients discontinue their use?
28. When is ECT appropriate to use and what is its effectiveness? What has been done in recent years to render ECT safer?
29. When are people with mental health problems hospitalized? What is the primary result of the move toward deinstitutionalize the mentally ill?

CHAPTER OUTLINE
1. Psychotherapy (p.95)

All forms of psychotherapy involve interchanges, both verbal and nonverbal, between the therapist and patient that are aimed at understanding what is on the patient's mind and which can be used to effect change. All therapists, regardless of theoretical orientation, performs three tasks: 1) listening, 2) understanding, and 3) responding.

A. Psychodynamic Therapy and Psychoanalysis

Insight is the goal of both psychodynamic therapy and psychoanalysis. Transference is an important feature of both, in which the patient displaces feelings for other important persons (e.g., mother, father) to the therapist. In this manner, the patient can gain insight into the unconscious conflicts that are driving her/his behavior.

B. Humanistic and Existential Therapies

Humanistic therapy emphasizes people's desire to achieve self-respect, while existential therapy emphasize the individual's need to confront basic questions of existence. Common to both is the importance of the client's experience in therapy and the view that each individual is the expert concerning her or his own experiences.

C. Cognitive Psychotherapy

The aim of cognitive therapy is to discover errors in thinking. By correcting these errors, behavior change is effected. Clients are encouraged to think about their beliefs and to develop alternative beliefs that are more rational.

D. How Effective is Psychotherapy?

Obtaining information about the effectiveness of psychotherapy is difficult, at best. Some therapies may be more effective than others with specific types of patients or problems than others. Meta-analysis is a technique used to summarize the results of many studies. Results of meta-analyses of the effects of psychotherapy generally support the benefits of psychotherapy when compared with no psychotherapy.

2. Cognitive-Behavioral Approaches (p.103)

These differ from the more traditional, interchange approaches in that they are more action-oriented and follow specific plans for strengthening or weakening target behaviors or responses.

A. Behavior Therapy

Behavior therapy uses techniques based on principles of operant and classical conditioning. Examples include behavior modification, biofeedback, and token economy methods.

B. Cognitive-Behavior Therapy

This approach is an integration of cognitive techniques with those of behavior therapy. Multiple components are frequently used to achieve behavior change. For example, while helping the patient change ideas about problem areas, the therapist might also reinforce adaptive behaviors, and use modeling and rehearsal to help the patient develop other adaptive behaviors.

C. How effective are cognitive and behavioral approaches?

They are particularly effective in treating anxiety and depression.

3. Integration and Extension of Psychological Therapies (p.106)

Two issues related to therapy concern 1) integration of different approaches to provide the most effective treatment, and 2) extension of such approaches for use with groups.

A. Integrative approaches to treatment

Combining techniques might be more common that expected. For example, while a psychodynamic approach emphasizing the transference in the clinical relationship is used, the therapist is also modeling appropriate and adaptive relationship behaviors.

B. Group approaches

Group therapy gives the patient the opportunity to observe others' adaptive and maladaptive behaviors. Groups are particularly effective in giving participants opportunities to learn new social skills through modeling. Common group approaches include psychodynamic, cognitive-behavioral, client-centered, and family therapy.

4. How Effective Are Group Approaches? (p.111)

Researchers believe that group approaches are effective and efficient, although research on the effectiveness of group therapy is difficult to conduct.

A. Research on the Psychological Therapies

Four issues are prominent: 1) features unique to particular treatments or common to all treatments, 2) criteria by which effectiveness is judged, 3) how to compare different therapeutic approaches, and 4) the ways in which cultural and ethnic diversity relates to therapy.

B. Common and Unique Features of Therapies

A common feature is the therapist's ability to instill hope in the patient. Research on the effectiveness of therapies has failed to include the therapist as an independent variable as well as account for the use of combinations of treatment approaches.

C. Therapeutic Outcomes

One of the most important questions is what the criteria for improvement should be, that is, what are the most important changes, and who is the best determinant of improvement, the patient or the therapist.

D. Comparing Therapies

Meta-analyses of comparative studies between two or more therapeutic approaches have revealed mixed results.

E. Recognizing Cultural and Ethnic Diversity

Consideration of the cultural and ethnic background of clients is relevant to successful treatment in terms of understanding the values different groups place on professional therapeutic services. For example, some groups place a greater value on talking with family members than someone outside the family group. Others do not perceive insight as important to their daily problems and situations.

5. Integration of Psychologically Based Therapeutic Approaches (p.114)

Integration of therapeutic approaches depends on the therapists' ability to recognize the roles of and relationships between the individual's cognition, emotion, and behavior.

Biological Therapies

These are treatment approaches that have developed directly from the biological orientation to maladaptive behavior.

A. Electroconvulsive Therapy (ECT)

In its current form, with many safeguards, ECT can be an effective treatment for severe depression that has not responded to medications or other therapies.

B. Drug Therapies

Medications have been effective with disorders in which schizophrenia, mania, depression, or anxiety are prominent features. The classeS of drugs are antipsychotics, antimanics, antidepressants, and antianxiety agents. Although effective, these drugs also carry a certain number of risks as well as adverse or uncomfortable side effects.

C. How Effective Are Biological Therapies?

For the most part, medications are effective in treating many disorders; however, the unpleasant side effects often induce people to discontinue the drugs.

6. Hospitalization (p.119)

Hospitalization is less frequent than it used to be, and an unfortunate side effect of deinstitutionalization is the isolation of patients, and limited or no access to professional services beyond brief contacts with physicians who prescribe medications.

```
TIPS FOR TESTING YOURSELF

Write each of the following key words and concepts on one side of an index card.  Then, for each, look
up the correct definition in your textbook.  Write the definition on the opposite side of the corresponding
index card.  Now, you have flash cards to study.  Keep the cards with you and whenever you have a few
minutes, pull them out and test yourself.  When you are studying with a study partner, you can test each
other.  You can also share the duties of looking up the definitions and writing them on the cards.  Study
them a little each day.
```

KEY TERMS AND CONCEPTS

psychotherapy (p.95)
psychodynamic therapy (p.96)
transference (p.96)
positive transference (p.96)
negative transference (p.96)
countertransference (p.96)
recovered memories (pp.96-97)
hypnosis (p.97)
humanistic-existential therapies (p.97)
client-centered therapy (p.97)
unconditional positive regard (p.98)
Gestalt therapy (p.98)
cognitive psychotherapy (p.98)
rational-emotive therapy (p.98)
interpersonal therapy (p.99)
meta-analysis (p.101)
process research (p.102)
behavior therapy (p.103)
behavior modification (p.103)
fading (p.103)
biofeedback (p.103)
cognitive-behavior therapy (pp.103-104)
relaxation therapy (p.104)
exposure therapy (p.104)
flooding (p.104)
implosive therapy (p.105)
systematic desensitization (p.105)
modeling (p.105)
assertiveness training (p.106)
multimodal therapy (p.107)
group therapy (p.107)
family therapy (p.109)
marital therapy (p.110)
psychodrama (p.111)
electroconvulsive therapy (ECT) (p.115)
drug therapies (p.116)
deinstitutionalization (p.121)

TIPS FOR TESTING YOURSELF

In developing answers for the following questions, turn to the section of your chapter that covers the pertinent material. Read the section thoroughly and spend some time thinking about the information before attempting to frame your answer. Write out each answer without referring to the book, and when you have completed all of them, check their accuracy by returning to the corresponding section in the book. For each question you missed, write out the correct answer. Then test yourself again. Repeat the process until you can answer all the questions correctly.

SHORT ANSWER ESSAY QUESTIONS

1. What are the characteristics common to all the various types of psychotherapy?

2. Describe the goals and procedures associated with traditional psychoanalysis. How does it differ from psychodynamic therapy?

3. What is the emphasis of humanistic therapy? Explain the client-centered approach of Carl Rogers.

4. Differentiate Gestalt therapy from existential therapy.

5. What is interpersonal psychotherapy and what does it share with brief therapy?

6. What are the assumptions and techniques associated with the cognitive psychotherapies?

7. Name and discuss the most common techniques used in behavior therapy.

8. Explain the nature of cognitive-behavioral approaches. List and describe techniques used by this therapeutic model.

9. Explain the concept of group therapy. What are some common features found among group therapies?

10. What is the primary idea underlying family therapy? What types of problems does it attempt to address?

11. How is marital therapy used?

12. What are some of the methodological issues that must be considered in studies of psychotherapy effectiveness?

13. How is therapy outcome measured? What are the problems inherent in such research?

14. What does the research comparing effectiveness of therapeutic interventions tell us?

15. What is meta-analysis and how is it used in outcome research?

16. Distinguish technique factors from interpersonal factors as components of effective therapy? How may therapy research be improved?

17. Describe the techniques used in biological therapies.

18. When is ECT appropriate to use and what is its effectiveness/

19. What are the classes of medications used in the treatment of mental disorders? Discuss the side effects of these medications.

20. List the major reasons for hospitalization. What ten steps does Paul (1969) recommend that hospitals take to increase effectiveness of the inpatient intervention?

21. Discuss the ways in which the role of the psychiatric hospital in treating disordered behavior is changing. What has been the result of deinstitutionalization?

TIPS FOR TESTING YOURSELF

The following sections of self-test questions will test your understanding of the material presented in the chapter. On a separate piece of paper, write the correct answer for each item in the section, then compare your answers with those at the end of the chapter. After you have graded yourself, turn to the chapter and look up the questions you missed. Write out the correct answers. Then test yourself again. Continue doing so until you can answer all the questions correctly.

MULTIPLE CHOICE

1. Regardless of theoretical orientation, psychotherapists must perform three tasks. They must
   a. listen, understand, and advise.
   b. listen, understand, and respond.
   c. listen, advise, and evaluate.
   d. listen, interpret, and explore.

2. Psychoanalysis
   a. requires multiple weekly sessions.
   b. does not require that the patient develop insight into problems.
   c. has the client and therapist sitting face to face.
   d. is not suited to the use of free-association.

3. During a session of psychoanalysis a client begins to react emotionally toward the psychoanalyst as though the analyst were a parent. Treating the psychoanalyst as though he or she were an important figure from one's past is part of psychoanalysis called
   a. free association.
   b. developing insight.
   c. transference.
   d. countertransference.

4. Through interpretations, psychodynamically oriented therapists
   a. attempt to expose areas of conflict.
   b. aid the client in gaining an understanding of past events.
   c. help the client put their motivation in perspective.
   d. all of the above

5. Which of the following statements is true regarding hypnosis?
   a. It is an acceptable treatment for severe mental disorders.
   b. It heightens a person's suggestibility.
   c. There are no harmful side effects.
   d. Dissociation and role-play do not appear to be associated with hypnosis.

6. Humanistic therapies emphasize the client's need
   a. to achieve insight.
   b. for achievement.
   c. for self-respect.
   d. to find the meaning of their existence.

7. Client-centered therapy is most associated with
   a. Kline.
   b. Rogers.
   c. Kelly.
   d. Frankel.

8. Fritz Perls, developer of Gestalt therapy, believed that the therapist's main task was to
   a. frustrate the client.
   b. provide unconditional positive regard.
   c. help the client understand the meaning of his/her own life.
   d. teach the client better methods of coping with problems.

9. According to cognitive therapists, unpleasant emotions such as depression and anger are caused by
   a. irrational beliefs.
   b. an inability to outwardly express emotions.
   c. early childhood traumas.
   d. a lack of unconditional positive regard.

10. During rational-emotive therapy (RET) the client must
    a. develop insight into personal problems.
    b. identify, dispute, and replace irrational beliefs with rational ones.
    c. explore the therapeutic relationship and examine any transference.
    d. achieve self-respect.

11. "Automatic thoughts" are a concept employed by
    a. RET.
    b. fixed-role therapy.
    c. Beck's cognitive model.
    d. brief psychotherapies.

12. Interpersonal therapy
    a. focuses on interpersonal relationships.
    b. was originally designed to be used in the treatment of depression.
    c. assists the client in examining suppressed thoughts.
    d. all of the above

13. Which of the factors below is a problem associated with evaluating the effectiveness of psychotherapy?
    a. therapists charge different patients different prices
    b. individual differences in therapists
    c. the personal biases of the researcher
    d. length of treatment

14. In a study by Najavits and Weiss (1994), therapeutic effectiveness was related to
    a. therapeutic orientation.
    b. the client's age.
    c. the length of treatment.
    d. the interpersonal skills of the therapist.

15. Which of the following is not a topic for process research?
    a. therapist/client perception of sessions
    b. therapist/client relationship
    c. treatment length
    d. content of therapeutic sessions

16. Select the therapist variable below that is not related to therapeutic change and outcome.
    a. warmth
    b. directness
    c. beliefs
    d. values

17. _____ is a method of quantifying therapeutic outcome measures so that they can be combined over several studies.
    a. Meta-analysis
    b. Factor analysis
    c. Systematic analysis
    d. Functional analysis

18. Which of the following is not a core characteristic of behavior therapy?
    a. Clients must thoroughly explore early childhood experiences.
    b. Most inappropriate behaviors can be modified through the application of social-learning principles.
    c. Treatment methods are objectively evaluated.
    d. Methods used during treatment are individually tailored to the differing needs of each client.

19. Which of the following is associated with behavior therapy?
    a. insight
    b. fading
    c. positive reinforcement
    d. both b and c

20. During therapy a phobic client learns to relax. Then while the client is relaxed, he or she imagines scenes that are related to the specific fear. The individual begins with imagining mildly upsetting scenes and gradually progresses to imagining highly upsetting scenes. This technique is known as
    a. meditation.
    b. autogenic training.
    c. systematic desensitization.
    d. in vivo exposure.

21. Sue's therapist asks her to hold a live snake because she reports having "snake phobia." The therapist is using
    a. fading.
    b. systematic desensitization.
    c. in vivo exposure.
    d. fantasy exposure.

22. Dylan tells his therapist that he is experiencing difficulty going to sleep at night. His therapist instructs him to remain awake at night as long as possible. The therapist is probably using a technique called
    a. modeling.
    b. paradoxical intention.
    c. implosion.
    d. aversion.

23. Select the factor below that influences the success of a modeling program.
    a. sex of the model
    b. observer's ability to copy model's behavior
    c. weight of the model
    d. observer's use of denial

24. Select the feature below that is not associated with group therapy.
    a. norm clarification
    b. self-containment
    c. social learning
    d. self-disclosure

25. Cognitive-behavioral group therapy would probably not emphasize
    a. graded task assignments.
    b. increasing social skills.
    c. analysis of transference.
    d. role playing.

26. A family therapist is likely to encourage the family to
    a. become more highly interdependent.
    b. work as a group to solve problems.
    c. become more closely knit and enmeshed.
    d. deal with problems in a more individual manner.

27. In _____, a group of individuals assembles under the leadership of a therapist and enacts events of emotional significance in order to resolve conflicts.
    a. family therapy
    b. marital therapy
    c. the systems approach
    d. psychodrama

28. Studies of improvement in psychotherapy should include which of the following?
    a. the client's evaluation
    b. the therapist's evaluation
    c. the evaluation of family and friends
    d. all of the above

29. Discussions that center on the effectiveness of a particular type of therapy are expected to continue into the future because
    a. not all persons who need treatment receive it.
    b. therapists resist evaluation of therapeutic interventions.
    c. all people benefit from some form of therapy.
    d. there are no uniform criteria for assessing therapeutic effectiveness.

30. Which of the following statements is false about ECT?
    a. Its use has increased in the past 20 years.
    b. A major risk is memory loss.
    c. Doctors don't know how ECT works.
    d. There is a risk of spontaneous seizures.

NEXT, TRY YOUR HAND AT TRUE/FALSE QUESTIONS.

TRUE/FALSE QUESTIONS

Indicate whether each statement is true or false. Check your answers at the end of this chapter.

T F 1. All forms of therapy are directed at finding out what is on the client's mind.

T F 2. Presently, there are a great number of psychodynamic approaches.

T F 3. Few psychologists today question the validity of repressed memories.

T F 4. The existential approach views the client as a "partner in treatment."

T F 5. Gestalt therapists do not believe that dreams are important sources of information about the client.

T F 6. Most cases of psychotherapy last fewer than twelve sessions.

T F 7. One useful approach in evaluating therapeutic effectiveness is to ask the patient.

T F 8. Psychoanalysis is clearly more effective than other therapies.

T F 9. Cognitive therapy appears to be the treatment of choice for panic attacks.

T F 10. Relaxation therapy is not effective for psychosomatic disorders.

T F 11. Cognitive-behavioral treatments are effective for anxiety disorders.

T F 12. Families often have certain "myths."

T F 13. Less than one hundred therapies are in use for adults according to Kazdin (1995).

T F 14. The average effectiveness rate for drugs used in treatment of maladaptive behavior is about forty percent.

KEEP GOING.....MATCHING IS NEXT.

MATCHING

Match the following terms with the information provided below. The answers are at the end of the chapter.

a. unconditional positive regard
b. spontaneous remission
c. covert modeling
d. free association
e. flooding
f. psychodrama
g. hypnosis

h. marital therapy
i. token economy
j. fixed role therapy
k. managed care
l. mantra
m. exposure
n. assertiveness training

_____ 1. altered state of consciousness induced by suggestion

_____ 2. a specially selected word on which an individual concentrates

_____ 3. a subtype of family therapy

_____ 4. client practices new roles and relationships

_____ 5. characterized by a natural flow of ideas

_____ 6. health insurance programs that pay for psychotherapy but place a limit on the number of therapy sessions for which payments will be made

_____ 7. uses operant principles to change behavior

_____ 8. form of exposure therapy

_____ 9. nonjudgmental stance of therapist

_____ 10. client asked to imagine observing a model

_____ 11. enhances the interpersonal skills one needs to stand up for one's self

_____ 12. getting better without treatment

_____ 13. a gradual approach to an anxiety-provoking situation

_____ 14. acting out conflicts

GOOD, NOW CHECK YOUR ANSWERS. WHEN YOU'RE DONE GRADING YOURSELF, COVER YOUR ANSWERS, AND START ALL OVER AGAIN. KEEP TESTING YOURSELF UNTIL YOU CAN ANSWER THEM ALL CORRECTLY.

CHAPTER 3 ANSWER KEY

Multiple Choice

1.	b		16.	b
2.	a		17.	a
3.	c		18.	a
4.	d		19.	d
5.	b		20.	c
6.	c		21.	c
7.	b		22.	b
8.	a		23.	b
9.	a		24.	b
10.	b		25.	c
11.	c		26.	b
12.	d		27.	d
13.	b		28.	d
14.	d		29.	d
15.	c		30.	d

True/False

1.	T		8.	T
2.	T		9.	T
3.	F		10.	F
4.	T		11.	T
5.	F		12.	T
6.	T		13.	F
7.	T		14.	F

Matching

1.	g		8.	e
2.	l		9.	a
3.	h		10.	c
4.	j		11.	n
5.	d		12.	b
6.	k		13.	m
7.	i		14.	f

Chapter 4
CLASSIFICATION
AND ASSESSMENT

CHAPTER OVERVIEW

This chapter presents various methods for classifying and assessing abnormal behaviors. The currently used diagnostic system, The Diagnostic and Statistical Manual, 4th Edition Text Revision (DSM-IV-TR) is described. This system is a multiaxial diagnostic system, meaning that individuals are diagnosed along five clinically important dimensions or factors. This helps to create a complete picture of the person and an understanding of problems in their contexts. Context includes recent experiences, the patient's vulnerabilities, and the patient's strengths. The five axes of the DSM are discussed, including the type of diagnosis or information included on each axis, and examples are presented. Various methods for assessing individuals are highlighted including: interviews, psychological tests, behavioral assessment, cognitive assessment, relational assessment, and bodily assessment.

LEARNING OBJECTIVES

After studying this chapter, you should be able to answer these questions:
1. Why is diagnosis an important step in the process of identifying and classifying a clinical condition?
2. What are the advantages and disadvantages of classifying abnormal behavior?
3. What is the purpose of having a multiaxial classification system in the DSM, and what are the five axes of the system?
4. What are the major diagnostic categories of the DSM-IV and on which axis are they found?
5. How has the DSM multiaxial approach helped in the classification and treatment of mental disorders?
6. What is meant by reliability and validity?
7. How does clinical judgment influence a diagnosis?
8. How does the cultural context affect judgments about abnormal behavior?
9. What is the difference between a diagnostic and therapeutic interview, and what types of information
   is sought in each?
10. What interviewer characteristics influence the course of an interview and its content?
11. What are the elements of a mental status examination, and what behaviors is the clinician attending to?
12. Why are standardized interviews useful?
13. Why is the Diagnostic Interview Schedule (DIS) such a valuable assessment tool?
14. What role do intelligence tests play in the assessment process?
15. How do the Stanford-Binet and Wechsler tests differ?
16. What are the major intelligence assessment instruments used with children?
17. What is the function of neuropsychological tests?
18. What are the main features of the Minnesota Multiphasic Personality Inventory-2 (MMPI-2) and the Million Clinical Multiaxial Inventory (MCMI) and how do they differ?

19. How are rating scales used in personality assessments, and what are some of their methodological problems?
20. What are the more common projective techniques and how do their goals and procedures differ?
21. What is the goal of behavioral assessments?
22. What is cognitive assessment and how is it carried out?
23. What is the rationale underlying relational assessment and how is it conducted?
24. What are the major bodily assessments and the advantages and limitations of each?

CHAPTER OUTLINE

1. Classification: Categories of Maladaptive Behavior (p.128)
A classification system groups disorders on the basis of similar symptoms. Classification is a way of understanding and learning from experience.

A. Advantages and Disadvantages of Classification
Usefulness of classification systems include communication between clinicians, tracking progress, maintaining statistics on incidence and prevalence, and in the planning of treatment programs and facilities. Disadvantages include lack of reliability, e.g., diagnoses can differ depending on each clinician's theoretical orientation or training.

B. Vulnerability, Resilience, and Coping
Maladaptive behavior must be understood in the context of the person's level of stress, vulnerabilities, resilience, coping strategies. The multiaxial system takes these factors into account.

C. The Multiaxial Approach
Summarizes diverse information about the person, rather than just offers a label. Also, provides information about the context in which maladaptive behavior occurs as well as describes the behavior.

D. DSM-IV-TR
The axes provide information about the psychological, biological, and social aspects of a person's condition. The first multiaxial system was presented in the third revision of the DSM, known as the DSM-III, published in 1980. This most recent revision, the DSM-IV-TR, was published in 2000. the current system, allows for identification of the etiology where possible as well as the subjective experiences of the patients.

E. The Major Diagnostic Categories
Axis I includes all of the disorders in the system except personality disorders and mental retardation. Axis II includes the personality disorders and mental retardation. Axis III describes medical conditions that seem relevant. Axis IV describes psychosocial and environmental problems. Axis V is a global assessment of functioning, i.e., a rating of the person's psychological, social, and occupational functioning,

F. Evaluation of the DSM Multiaxial Approach
It is concerned primarily with descriptions of disorders and continues to rely on clinical judgment. It is best viewed as a set of guidelines for characterizing clinical problems. More recent revisions of the classification system has reduced the amount of inference needed to make a diagnosis, and hence, increased its reliability.

G. Research on Classification

Several factors affect the clinical utility of a classification. Reliability refers to the reproducibility of a classification decision, that is, whether different clinicians using the system would arrive at the same diagnoses. Validity refers to the appropriateness of the system, in other words, whether or not the system groups together people with similar symptoms. The current classification system takes some cultural differences into account, but further research is needed to determine the influences of ethnic identity and cultural variation on the classification of maladaptive behavior.

2. Assessment: The Basis of Classification (p.137)

No single assessment tool is considered foolproof. In order to yield the most complete and accurate picture of the individual, assessment commonly uses more than one approach.

A. The Interview

The diagnostic interview gathers information and assesses behavior. The therapeutic interview occurs after a preliminary assessment and is aimed at modifying behavior and attitudes. Assessment, or diagnostic, interviews attempt to answer several questions: who is the client? how does the client think and feel? what is the history of the problem and the client's background? what is the client's present state? and how vulnerable and how resilient is the client? Structured interviews are often used, particularly when the information needs to be obtained in a standardized way. Mental status examinations are also often a part of the diagnostic interview.

B. Intelligence Tests

First developed to identify mentally retarded children, intelligence tests are widely used today as part of clinical assessment. They generally yield measures of global characteristics as well as scores for specific ability areas.

C. Neuropsychological Tests

These tests are given in batteries of several tests that assess cognitive function in a variety of areas. These areas include memory, attention, thinking, planning, verbal fluency, and motor functioning. They are employed to assess deficits believed to be related to brain abnormalities.

D. Personality Assessment

Personality inventories, rating scales, visual analogue scales, and projective techniques are all used to assess an individual's strengths and weaknesses, help decide if treatment is required, and in planning the treatment to be used.

E. Behavioral Assessment

Behavioral assessment is used to identify response deficits, which are then treated through behavioral techniques. Clinicians often use behavioral observations to get information that otherwise might not be obtained.

F. Cognitive Assessment

Cognitive assessment provides information about thoughts that precede, accompany, and follow maladaptive behavior. Questionnaires can be used. Electronic beepers have also been used to signal patients to record their thoughts at certain times of the day.

G. Relational Assessment

Relationships are important contextual variables and how a person functions in relationships is important information. The results of relational assessments can also provide information about the person's social network.

H. Bodily Assessment

Brain imaging and EEG recordings, as well as measures of pupil dilation, blood pressure, and electrical skin responses can al provide important data regarding a person's physiological responses to stress, for example. Biofeedback has been used therapeutically, as the patient is able to monitor her/his own bodily functions.

```
TIPS FOR TESTING YOURSELF

Write each of the following key words and concepts on one side of an index card.  Then, for each, look
up the correct definition in your textbook.  Write the definition on the opposite side of the corresponding
index card.  Now, you have flash cards to study.  Keep the cards with you and whenever you have a few
minutes, pull them out and test yourself.  When you are studying with a study partner, you can test each
other.  You can also share the duties of looking up the definitions and writing them on the cards.  Study
them a little each day.
```

KEY TERMS AND CONCEPTS

diagnosis (p.127-128)
Diagnostic and Statistical Manual of Mental Disorders (p.130)
DSM-IV-TR (p.130)
vulnerability (p.129)
resilience (p.129)
coping (p.129)
multiaxial classification system (p.130)
Axis I (p.130, 132)
Axis II (p.130, 133)
Axis III (p.130)
Axis IV (p.130)
Axis V (p.130)
global assessment of functioning (p.130)
reliability (p.134)
kappa statistic (p.135)
validity (p.135)
ethnic identity (p.136)
assessment (p.137)
diagnostic interview (p.137)
therapeutic interview (p.137)
mental status examination (p.140)
structured interview (p.141)
Diagnostic Interview Schedule (DIS) (p.141)
Structured Clinical Interview for DSM (SCID) (p.142)
mental age (p.142)
iIntelligence quotient (IQ) (p.142)
Binet tests (p.142)
Wechsler tests (p.142-143)
verbal IQ (p.142)
performance IQ (p.143)
full Scale IQ (p.143)
WISC-IV (p.143)
WPPSI--III (p.143)
neuropsychological tests (p.143)
Bender Visual-Motor Gestalt Test (p.143)

> **TIPS FOR TESTING YOURSELF**
>
> In developing answers for the following questions, turn to the section of your chapter that covers the pertinent material. Read the section thoroughly and spend some time thinking about the information before attempting to frame your answer. Write out each answer without referring to the book, and when you have completed all of them, check their accuracy by returning to the corresponding section in the book. For each question you missed, write out the correct answer. Then test yourself again. Repeat the process until you can answer all the questions correctly.

SHORT ANSWER ESSAY QUESTIONS

1. How is classification used? In what ways is classification useful? In what ways can classification cause problems for patients? Give examples.

2. What are the major sources of diagnostic unreliability?

3. What is the DSM? Describe the five axes.

4. What is the relationship between Axis I and Axis II diagnostic categories?

5. List the major differences between earlier and later versions of the DSM. What first appeared in the DSM-III?

6. Explain why reliability and validity are important concepts in classification. List the factors that influence clinical judgment.

7. Describe the major assessment methods used in gathering information about clients.

8. Describe the two types of clinical interviews. What are the general types of information sought during an interview? List the four components of the clinical interview.

9. What are the Binet and Wechsler tests? Explain the concept of intelligence/IQ as measured by these tests.

10. Briefly describe the dimensions that are assessed using the MMPI-2. How are the L, F, and K scales used?

11. What impact does the "halo effect" have on rating scales?

12. What is the rationale underlying the use of projective tests?

13. What are the goals of behavioral assessment? What questions are of interest to the clinician?

14. Know and understand the four components of the clinical interview.

15. Explain cognitive assessment.

16. Why would a clinician be interested in making a relational assessment? What relationships are likely to have the most influence on the patient's functioning?

17. Briefly describe the measures used in bodily assessment. What therapeutic technique has been developed directly out of bodily measurements?

18. Explain how the mental status examination is important in evaluating the current mental status of patients.

19. The concept of "IQ" and its measurement has been a topic of debate for many years. Proponents of IQ assessment believe it is a useful device, while those against it argue that it is a form of "labeling" and derived from tests that are culturally biased. What is your position on this topic? Support it.

TIPS FOR TESTING YOURSELF
The following sections of self-test questions will test your understanding of the material presented in the chapter. On a separate piece of paper, write the correct answer for each item in the section, then compare your answers with those at the end of the chapter. After you have graded yourself, turn to the chapter and look up the questions you missed. Write out the correct answers. Then test yourself again. Continue doing so until you can answer all the questions correctly.

MULTIPLE CHOICE

1. A classification statement that places a disorder within a system of conventional groupings is called a/an
   a. axis.
   b. diagnosis.
   c. interview.
   d. clinical judgment.

2. For Robert Bjorkland and Pete Harnisch, diagnosis played a critical role in resolving mental health issues because
   a. a correct diagnosis can lead to the correct classification of a condition, and a misdiagnosis can lead to stigmatization and inappropriate therapy.
   b. both men were incorrectly labeled by mental health professionals and thus discriminated against in their work environment.
   c. because each individual was a very sick man who needed a classification for the condition that was ailing them.
   d. none of the above

3. Two major sources of diagnostic unreliability are
   a. differences in training of therapists and the stigma associated with labeling an individual.
   b. the stigma associated with labeling and the lack of training of many professionals who do diagnostic interviews.
   c. differences in the training of therapists and the uniqueness of every individual.
   d. the uniqueness of every individual and the stigma associated with placing labels on individuals.

4. A good clinical classification system provides for causes of a condition, a common language for communication, a short- and long-term outlook, and
   a. considers the contribution of genetics.
   b. gives a low kappa statistic.
   c. shows low validity but high reliability.
   d. provides clues for treatment and prevention.

5. A multiaxial classification system gives the clinician an opportunity to
   a. provide a single label for the various dimensions of a person's psychological problems.
   b. describe an individual along several dimensions.
   c. decrease reliability while maximizing validity.
   d. select the single best description of maladaptive behavior and explain the behavior's etiology.

6. The first three axes of the DSM classification system contain
   a. case history information.
   b. a description of the symptoms and estimation about how long it will take for the person to improve with therapy.
   c. the probable cause of the disorder and suggestions for the best type of therapy and medications to use.
   d. diagnostic categories and general medical information.

7. Which of the following is not included in the Axis I categories?
   a. disorders of infancy and childhood
   b. sleep disorders
   c. sexual disorders
   d. mental retardation

8. Both DSM-III and DSM-IV have increased the reliability of diagnosis by
   a. providing a theoretical orientation for each disorder.
   b. reducing the sheer volume of information contained in the manuals.
   c. emphasizing descriptions of behavior.
   d. decreasing coverage of the range of disorders.

9. A major criticism of earlier versions of DSM lies in their
   a. reliance on statistical data.
   b. inability to accurately diagnose problems of childhood.
   c. unreliability of categories due to hypothesizing about underlying causes.
   d. use of multiple axes.

10. Which of the following is not a criticism of recent DSMs?
    a. Insufficient attention is paid to prior history.
    b. Too few field trials have been conducted on the categories to convince clinicians that these categories are stable.
    c. It has not been coordinated with the ICD.
    d. Consistency of diagnosis decreases when clinicians attempt to make distinctions in classification within the finer subdivisions of the general categories.

11. _____ refers to the diagnostic agreement among clinicians as to a particular individual.
    a. Reliability
    b. Stability
    c. Validity
    d. Cohesion

12. Which of the following is not implicated in the error of clinical research?
    a. clinician factors
    b. criteria factors
    c. age factors
    d. method factors

13. The purpose of the assessment interview is to
    a. modify maladaptive behaviors.
    b. identify problems and determine the nature of maladaptive behaviors.
    c. explain to the client the origins of his/her problems.
    d. identify the traumatic childhood events that form the roots of present problems.

14. Appearance, psychomotor behavior, concentration, perception, and insight are all important factors
    in
    a. the Diagnostic Interview Schedule.
    b. the Guide to Mental Health Status, Revision IV.
    c. the Mental Status Examination.
    d. the International Classification of Diseases, Revision IX (ICD9).

15. Select the statement that is true of cross-cultural research on maladaptive behavior.
    a. Regardless of the cultural setting, the expression of depression is the same.
    b. The experience of depression as an intrapsychic experience is universal.
    c. Rates of depression are higher in European countries than in the U.S.
    d. Asian Americans somaticize depression.

16. The concept of behavioral observations refers to
    a. the notion that a behavior must be observable in order to be significant.
    b. how a client perceives the therapist's behavior.
    c. observing the manner in which a client behaves.
    d. the use of physiological recording devices to measure a behavior.

17. Of the following, which characteristic of an interviewer might readily influence the course and
    content of an interview?
    a. gender
    b. hair color
    c. height
    d. manner of dress

18. A psychologist would use the Diagnostic Interview Schedule (DIS) during
    a. an unstructured interview.
    b. psychoanalysis.
    c. a standardized interview.
    d. personality assessment.

19. _____ were the first widely recognized psychological assessment tool.
    a. Intelligence Tests
    b. Personality inventories
    c. Rating scales
    d. The Diagnostic Interview Schedules

20. The Wechsler tests differ from the Binet tests in that the Wechsler tests provide
    a. a score for mental age.
    b. a verbal and performance IQ score.
    c. an IQ score for chronological ability.
    d. information about personality disorders.

21. The K-ABC's reported strength over other intelligence tests for children lies in its
    a. length.
    b. attempt to reduce cultural bias.
    c. reliance on verbal responses.
    d. ease of administration.

22. The most widely used personality inventory is the
    a. Thematic Apperception Test.
    b. WAIS-R.
    c. Rorschach inkblot test.
    d. MMPI.

23. The L, F, and K scales of the MMPI were designed to evaluate
    a. lethargy, fantasy, and kleptomaniac tendencies.
    b. impulses toward antisocial behaviors.
    c. bizarre thinking, delusions, and hallucinations.
    d. honesty, carelessness, and defensiveness.

24. The major contribution of the MMPI-2 over the MMPI lies in
    a. the former's deletion of culturally sensitive items.
    b. the addition of the K-scale.
    c. three new scales to measure reliability.
    d. none of the above.

25. Johnny is a seven-year-old who experiences problems of impulsivity in class. Which of the following tests would most likely be selected by a school psychologist to evaluate Johnny's problem?
    a. Behavior Rating Scale for Children
    b. Children's Visual Analogue Scale
    c. TAT
    d. Rorschach

26. An individual comes to a clinic complaining of chronic backache. In order to evaluate this condition, a clinician would most probably administer the
    a. Visual Analogue Scale.
    b. Thematic Apperception Test.
    c. Rorschach.
    d. sentence completion technique.

27. Defense mechanisms, latent impulses, and anxieties have all been inferred from data gathered in
    a. projective situations.
    b. rating scale interviews.
    c. neuropsychological tests.
    d. behavioral assessment.

28. A patient reports, "It looks like an apple tree in the middle of a huge forest...and   there's my mother lying on the ground under it. She was hit in the head by an apple while picking them. Hey, this is fun, it's like looking at clouds and seeing figures." Which of the following tests was the patient most probably taking?
    a. MMPI-2
    b. Rorschach
    c. Thematic Apperception Test
    d. none of the above

29. A word association test is an example of
    a. an unstructured interview.
    b. a projective intelligence test.
    c. a projective technique.
    d. a cognitive assessment.

30. Counting the number of times a young child hits other playmates is characteristic of
    a. cognitive assessment.
    b. behavioral assessment.
    c. bodily assessment.
    d. aggression assessment.

31. Cognitive assessment provides information about
    a. anxieties and insecurities.
    b. distortions in thinking that play a role in psychological problems.
    c. repressed wishes and conflicts stemming from early childhood traumas.
    d. latent impulses.

32. The Quality of Relationships Inventory is an example of a _____ instrument.
    a. projective
    b. baseline assessment
    c. behavioral assessment
    d. relational assessment

33. Which of the following is true regarding the polygraph?
    a. It measures feelings of guilt.
    b. It measures truthfulness.
    c. It measures level of interest in a subject.
    d. It measures physiological reactions.

NEXT, TRY YOUR HAND AT TRUE/FALSE QUESTIONS.

TRUE/FALSE QUESTIONS

Indicate whether each statement is true or false. Check your answers at the end of this chapter.

T   F   1. Diagnosis is a relatively unimportant step in the process of identifying and classifying a clinical condition, as it is irrelevant to effective treatment and appropriate therapy.

T   F   2. The most widely accepted classification system for abnormal behavior is the DSM.

T   F   3. Axis I refers to any physiological disorder that is relevant to the condition of a client.

T   F   4. DSM-I and DSM-II are criticized for focusing too heavily on psychoanalytic theory.

T   F   5. Since the advent of DSM-III, schizophrenia has been diagnosed less frequently.

T   F   6. A diagnosis is a product of present knowledge and opinion about abnormal behavior.

T   F   7. Although the validity of DSM-IV has been established, the reliability of its categories remains questionable.

T   F   8. Typically, the clinician relies on a single assessment tool in gathering information about a client.

T   F   9. The ability to quickly size up a situation and plan a treatment strategy based on the assessment is not particularly important as a clinical skill.

T   F 10. Cultural factors are significant not only with regard to exotic disturbances, but in relation to variations in emotional expression, body language, religious beliefs, and rituals.

T   F 11. An advantage of the Binet intelligence test is that it provides both verbal IQ and performance IQ scores.

T   F 12. Baseline observations are records of response frequencies taken in order to evaluate the effectiveness of a therapeutic technique.

T   F 13. Cognitive assessment attempts to identify thoughts and ideas.

KEEP GOING.....MATCHING IS NEXT.

MATCHING

Match the following with information presented below. The answers are at the end of the chapter.

a. verbal IQ
b. Axis III
c. cognitive assessment
d. WPPSI
e. biofeedback
f. TAT
g. Axis V
h. Behavior Rating Scale for Children

i. operant observations
j. kappa statistic
k. mental age
l. mental status examination
m. Millon Clinical Multiaxial Inventory
n. diagnosis
o. culture-bound syndromes

_____ 1. consists of 24 clinical scales, and 3 designed to assess tendencies to distort responses

_____ 2. refers to physical disorders

_____ 3. measure of reliability

_____ 4. usually takes place in an interview setting, and without a structured format

_____ 5. provides information about thoughts

_____ 6. global assessment of functioning

_____ 7. intelligence test for children

_____ 8. recording of response frequencies

_____ 9. provides a continuous recording of physiological measures

_____ 10. requires client to make up a story

_____ 11. measure provided by a Wechsler test

_____ 12. measures a child's degree of self-control

_____ 13. early explorers first noted the existence of these

_____ 14. construct developed by Binet

_____ 15. how the clinician seeks to answer the question, "What is the patient's problem?"

GOOD, NOW CHECK YOUR ANSWERS. WHEN YOU'RE DONE GRADING YOURSELF, COVER YOUR ANSWERS, AND START ALL OVER AGAIN. KEEP TESTING YOURSELF UNTIL YOU CAN ANSWER THEM ALL CORRECTLY.

CHAPTER 4 ANSWER KEY
Multiple Choice

1.	b	18.	c
2.	a	19.	a
3.	c	20.	b
4.	b	21.	b
5.	b	22.	d
6.	d	23.	d
7.	d	24.	d
8.	c	25.	a
9.	c	26.	a
10.	c	27.	a
11.	a	28.	b
12.	c	29.	c
13.	b	30.	b
14.	c	31.	b
15.	d	32.	d
16.	c	33.	d
17.	a		

True/False

1.	F	8.	F
2.	T	9.	F
3.	F	10.	T
4.	T	11.	F
5.	T	12.	T
6.	T	13.	T
7.	F		

Matching

1.	m		9.	e
2.	b		10.	f
3.	j		11.	a
4.	l		12.	h
5.	c		13.	o
6.	g		14.	k
7.	d		15.	n
8.	i			

Chapter 5
STRESS, COPING,
AND MALADAPTIVE BEHAVIOR

CHAPTER OVERVIEW
This chapter reviews the role of stress in contributing to maladaptive behavior. The chapter discusses responses to two types of situations, those that arise suddenly such as traumas, and those that develop more gradually, such as difficult life situations. We will also look at types of stress that have not received much attention in the literature, such as caregiver stress and lifelong racial stigmatization. The entire range of responses, from calm to collapse, along with coping techniques are evaluated. Failures of coping with stress that lead to adjustment disorders, acute stress disorder, and the dissociative disorders are presented. Students also need to keep in mind that stress plays a major role in other groups of disorders. The difference is that the disorders in this chapter are those in which the source of stress is most apparent. Therapeutic techniques for dealing with stressful situations are explored.

LEARNING OBJECTIVES
After studying this chapter, you should be able to answer these questions:
1. What are the factors that influence a person's vulnerability to stress?
2. What coping skills are effective in dealing with stressors?
3. What is the role of social support in coping with stress?
4. What are the psychological, bodily, and behavioral reactions to stress?
5. What are the characteristics of stress-arousing situations?
6. What are some examples of life transitions that lead to high stress levels?
7. What are the nature and characteristics of adjustment disorders?
8. What are the characteristics and diagnostic criteria for acute stress disorder?
9. What are the characteristics and diagnostic criteria for the various dissociative disorders?
10. What are the major therapies for treating stress-related problems?
11. What are some of the challenges clinicians face when trying to treat stress-related problems?

CHAPTER OUTLINE
1. Stress and Coping (p.158)
Stress refers to negative emotional experiences with associated changes that are related to perceived acute or chronic challenges. Coping skills are characteristic ways of dealing with difficulties.

A. Coping Skills
Successful coping reduces vulnerability. Task-oriented, matter-of-fact responses to situations are more effective than becoming anxious or angry. Denial, however, often gets in the way, as people underestimate or negate the significance of an event.

B. The Coping Process
People use their personal resources to master a problem, overcome an obstacle, or resolve a dilemma. Some of these resources include the ability to seek pertinent information, the ability to share

concerns, the ability to make a situation solvable, the ability to consider alternatives, and the use of humor to defuse a situation.

C. Social Support
Vulnerability increases as social support decreases. That is, social support serves as a buffer against the stresses of daily living, as well as during periods of acute stress.

D. Stressful Situations and Life Transitions
Stress causes uncomfortable psychological feelings as well as changes in physical functions, e.g., blood pressure, hormone levels, brain waves. Persons who experience multiple stressors are more vulnerable to the cumulative effects of those stressors.

E. Stress-Arousing Situations
Stress-arousing situations are those that require adjustment to certain situations. These situations have varying characteristics, and such situations as natural disasters, accidents, and combat evoke particularly high levels of stress that may interfere with normal functioning.

F. Personal Crises
The death of a loved one, the loss of a job, or the need to care for a terminally ill relative are all examples of personal crises. Rape is another type of personal crisis that is receiving increased attention. College women are particularly at risk for rape. Women who have been the victims of sudden and violent assaults are likely to remain fearful and depressed for an extended period of time. Bereavement and grief are also associated with stress responses.

F. Life Transitions
Some of these include: birth of a child, changes associated with adolescence, educational transitions, getting a job, marriage, moving, children's milestones, retirement.

2. Clinical Reactions to Stress (p.169)
Stress plays a role in most mental disorders. Stress disorders that go beyond what would be expected for the given situation require clinical attention. Difficulties in diagnosing abnormal behavior are caused by the blurring of lines between normal and abnormal stress reactions.

A. Adjustment Disorder
This disorder is characterized by the failure to adapt to one or more stressors that have occurred in the previous three months. Depression, anxiety, conduct disturbances, disturbances in sleep, poor performance in school or work, and social withdrawal are typical of adjustment disorders.

B. Acute Stress Disorder
Resulting from an extremely traumatic stressor, this disorder is characterized by major changes in behavior, thought, and emotions. These changes are marked by symptoms of dissociation that include a sense of numbness. Recovery is expected in a relatively short period of time.

C. Dissociative Disorders
These are characterized by a detachment from the reality of an overwhelming traumatic experience. Dissociation can be viewed as a severing of connection between ideas and emotions. Most persons dissociate to a certain extent under certain conditions. When the detachment becomes extreme,

they are classified as dissociative disorders. There are four disorders: dissociative amnesia, dissociative fugue, dissociative identity disorder, and depersonalization.

3. Treating Stress-Related Problems (p.177)

The clinician has two functions; to provide support, and to strengthen the patient's coping skills.

A. Supportive Therapy

The therapist listens sympathetically and provides encouragement. The client-therapist relationship is important in terms of facilitating adaptive coping.

B. Medications

These are often used in conjunction with supportive psychotherapy and can be effective in overcoming panic states and other maladaptive reactions to intense stress.

C. Relaxation Training

Involves the voluntary control of the autonomic nervous system. The steps involved are focusing attention on a series of muscle groups, tensing each group, maintain muscle tension for several seconds, telling oneself to relax followed by release of tension, and focusing attention on the muscle group as it relaxes.

D. Systematic Desensitization

This involves a combination of relaxation training and exposure to fear-producing stimuli until the fear response is extinguished.

E. Cognitive Modification

Cognitive modification involves learning new internal dialogue and ways of thinking about the situations and about oneself.

F. Social Intervention

This approach involves attempts to modify the client's work or home environment. Family therapy is one technique designed to modify the home environment as well as the family's interactions.

G. Challenges in Treating Stress-Related Problems

Stress-related disorders cannot be explained simply on the basis of the trauma of the events. The effects of the events on the individual also depend on the individual's perceptions of the event, how the person experiences the event, and the person's individual characteristics, such as vulnerability and resilience.

TIPS FOR TESTING YOURSELF

Write each of the following key words and concepts on one side of an index card. Then, for each, look up the correct definition in your textbook. Write the definition on the opposite side of the corresponding index card. Now, you have flash cards to study. Keep the cards with you and whenever you have a few minutes, pull them out and test yourself. When you are studying with a study partner, you can test each other. You can also share the duties of looking up the definitions and writing them on the cards. Study them a little each day.

KEY TERMS AND CONCEPTS

racism (p.157)
stressors (p.158)
coping skills (p.159)
coping process (p.159)
social support (p.162)
personal crises (p.166)
bereavement (p.167)
grief (p.167)
life transitions (p.168)
adjustment disorder (p.170)
acute stress disorder (p.171)
dissociative disorders (p.172)
dissociative amnesia (p.173)
dissociative fugue (p.174)
localized amnesia (p.174)
select amnesia (p.174)
generalized amnesia (p.174)
continuous amnesia (p.174)
systemized amnesia (p.174)
dissociative identity disorder (p.174)
depersonalization (p.175)
supportive therapy (p.177)
relaxation training (p.177)
systematic desensitization (p.178)
cognitive modification (p.178)
social intervention (p.178)
EMDR (p.178)

```
TIPS FOR TESTING YOURSELF

In developing answers for the following questions, turn to the section of your chapter that covers the
pertinent material. Read the section thoroughly and spend some time thinking about the information
before attempting to frame your answer.  Write out each answer without referring to the book, and when
you have completed all of them, check their accuracy by returning to the corresponding section in the
book.  For each question you missed, write out the correct answer.  Then test yourself again.  Repeat the
process until you can answer all the questions correctly.
```

SHORT ANSWER ESSAY QUESTIONS

1. How is a person's vulnerability to stress influenced by coping skills and social support?

2. Describe how two individuals, one highly resilient, the other very vulnerable, might deal with stressors.

3. Stress-arousing conditions fall into two broad categories: traumatic events/personal crises and developmental transitions. List typical stressors for each category. What psychological, bodily, and behavioral responses might a person experience as a result of these stressors?

4. Adjustment disorders, acute stress disorders, and dissociative disorders are all maladaptive attempts to cope with stress. Compare and contrast these disorders.

5. Date rape is a very serious concern on college campuses today. Briefly discuss its dimensions and the results of research efforts in this area.

6. What is the difference between bereavement and grief, and how can these processes lead to stress?

7. What positive life transitions lead to stress? What do you think accounts for this?

8. What are the therapeutic techniques used in treating stress-related disorders? How does each intervention attempt to aid the person in coping?

9. Why is adolescence such a period of high stress? Do you recall it as a particularly stressful time for you?

10. What three DSM-IV-TR clinical conditions are associated with high levels of stress?

11. How does adjustment disorder arise in the contest of developmental transitions and situational stressors?

12. List and explain the diagnostic criteria for acute stress disorders.

13. Compare and contrast the dissociative disorders that exist along the dissociative continuum.

14. The diagnosis of dissociative identity disorder is a controversial one. Many people believe that this disorder is simply faked by the individual. What is your position on this matter? Defend it.

15. What therapies are most useful for treating stress-related disorders. Which do you think would most appeal to you if you needed such treatment? Why?

TIPS FOR TESTING YOURSELF

The following sections of self-test questions will test your understanding of the material presented in the chapter. On a separate piece of paper, write the correct answer for each item in the section, then compare your answers with those at the end of the chapter. After you have graded yourself, turn to the chapter and look up the questions you missed. Write out the correct answers. Then test yourself again. Continue doing so until you can answer all the questions correctly.

MULTIPLE CHOICE

The following multiple choice questions will test your comprehension of the material presented in the chapter. Circle the correct choice for each question in the section, then compare your answers with those at the end of the chapter.

1. A person's _____ is influenced by his or her coping skills, and the social support available.
   a. primary appraisal
   b. secondary appraisal
   c. vulnerability to stress
   d. task orientation

2. Stressors are
   a. those chronic challenges that cause a reduction in a person's overall anxiety level.
   b. the most important factor in dealing with violence-prone individuals.
   c. negative emotional experiences which have little or no impact on a person's behavior.
   d. the negative emotional events that can stimulate behavioral, biochemical, and physiological changes in an individual.

3. Which of the following is false about using coping techniques when dealing with a stressful situation?
   a. Different coping strategies are effective in different types of situations.
   b. What you don't know can't hurt you.
   c. Successful copers have a varied array of personal resources for coping with situations.
   d. Successful copers have the ability to use humor to defuse a situation.

4. Which of the following is not considered to be a personal resource for coping?
   a. considering alternatives
   b. keeping your concern to yourself
   c. using humor
   d. redefining a situation

5. Which of the following is an example of a reinforcing self-statement used when dealing with a stressful situation?
   a. "I'm not going to worry about what happens."
   b. "I'll take things one step at a time."
   c. "I didn't handle that very well—just like usual."
   d. "I really did a good job handling that one."

6. Which of the following statements is false regarding the effects of social support on one's ability to deal with stressful situations?
   a. People should learn to be independent and not count on family or friends to help them.
   b. People who have high levels of social support are less vulnerable to illness than those with few social supports.
   c. There appears to be no minimum number of social supports that ensures satisfaction for everyone.
   d. People who are low in social support tend to be perceived by others as less interesting than people who are high in social support.

7. Select a characteristic below that is not a typical bodily response to stress.
   a. rapid pulse
   b. pounding heart
   c. increased or decreased sleeping
   d. increased perspiration

8. Research has shown that
   a. recent stressors exert less influence than past stressors on our lives.
   b. the experience of multiple stressors in the recent past is related to increased risk for depression and anxiety.
   c. at the present, there are no measures to assess the severity and perceptions of stressors.
   d. both a and c

9. Stress-arousing situations vary along several dimensions. These include: severity, degree of loss of control, the individual's level of self-confidence, suddenness, and
   a. predictability; generality.
   b. susceptibility; generality.
   c. predictability; duration.
   d. duration; sensitivity.

10. Witnessing a traumatic event such as an airplane crash may cause the observer
    a. to suffer immediate effects but no long-term effects.
    b. to suffer long-range problems as well as immediate effects.
    c. to suffer a psychological stress reaction but not a bodily one.
    d. to suffer emotional stress only.

11. Which of the following is false of date rape?
    a. The most prevalent fears for victims include being alone, going out, darkness, and encountering strangers.
    b. College women are a high risk group for date rape.
    c. Alcohol and drug use are not major contributing factors to nonconsensual sex.
    d. Typically, physical force is not used.

12. Which of the following are not diagnostic criteria for Acute Stress Disorder
    a. marked anxiety and arousal
    b. marked avoidance of stimuli associated with the traumatic event
    c. exposure to an extreme event that evokes fear, helplessness, and horror
    d. a sudden and brief upsurge in appetite, and a corresponding weight gain in less than 2 days

13. According to Sanders (1993), which of the following is a high risk factor for poor outcome of bereavement?
    a. emotional dependence on the deceased
    b. death of a child
    c. chronic illness
    d. being a widower

14. Select the aspect below that is not typically seen in bereavement.
    a. crying
    b. social withdrawal
    c. suicidal ideation
    d. anxiety

15. An adjustment disorder
    a. is often part of a lifelong pattern of maladaptive behavior.
    b. usually involves extremely bizarre behavior.
    c. is generally in direct proportion to the severity of the stressor; more severe stressors produce more severe adjustment disorders.
    d. involves poor adaptation to one or more stressors that have occurred in the previous three months.

16. Select the following statement(s) that is (are) true of adjustment disorders.
    a. Typical behaviors seen include truancy and reckless driving.
    b. The individual is expected to return to pre-stressor functioning within 6 months.
    c. War veterans are not likely to suffer this disorder.
    d. both a and b

17. The difference between PTSD and acute stress disorder lies in the
    a. time of onset of the symptoms.
    b. age of the client.
    c. nature of the stressor.
    d. all of the above

18. Choose the following statement that is true.
    a. Dissociative disorders tend to have gradual onsets.
    b. Dissociative disorders tend to last only a brief period.
    c. People suffering from dissociative disorders have a difficult time getting rid of the memories of the traumatic event.
    d. Dissociative disorders usually begin in childhood.

19. Which of the following associations is correct?
    a. Selective amnesia—entire life is forgotten
    b. Continuous amnesia—events during a particular period of time
    c. Localized amnesia—events during a particular period of time
    d. Generalized amnesia—memory for specific categories of information

20. A week after being fired from his job of 25 years, a husband does not recognize his wife or children. This man is most probably suffering from
    a. systematized amnesia.
    b. dissociative fugue.
    c. dissociative identity disorder.
    d. selective amnesia.

21. As dissociative disorders, fugue and amnesia have the following in common.
    a. Physical flight.
    b. Both involve behaviors similar to PTSD.
    c. The stressor remains conscious.
    d. The onset may be sudden or gradual.

22. As a process, dissociation may be viewed as
    a. a severing of the connections between various emotions and ideas.
    b. part of the psychotic process.
    c. inherently pathological.
    d. a phenomenon that is restricted to the U.S.

23. A twenty-five-year-old woman was found wandering the local interstate highway. Upon being taken to the local police station, the woman was not able to provide details as to her identity, address, etc. It was later revealed that the woman lived in a town 100 miles away and was last seen at the funeral of her only child. This woman was most probably suffering from
    a. dissociative identity disorder.
    b. dissociative fugue.
    c. dissociative amnesia.
    d. depersonalization.

24. Dissociative identity disorder
    a. is seldom psychogenic.
    b. tends to occur more frequently in males than in females.
    c. is seldom tied to early childhood trauma.
    d. occurs very rarely.

25. Identify the statement below that is incorrect.
    a. DID is a rare disorder.
    b. Males experience DID four times more frequently than females.
    c. In DID, the person may have alternate personalities that are different genders.
    d. Alternates often have different value systems and handwritings.

26. _____ may be leading to the underdiagnosing of dissociative identity disorder.
    a. The patient's attempts to hide alternate personalities
    b. The clinician's unfamiliarity with alternate personalities
    c. The concurrent diagnosis of schizophrenia
    d. The failure of DSM-IV to be explicit regarding the symptoms of DID

27. A person says to a therapist, "I feel as though I'm in a dream, like I'm doing this mechanically." This statement would be most characteristic of someone experiencing
    a. generalized amnesia.
    b. dissociative amnesia.
    c. depersonalization.
    d. dissociative fugue.

28. Which of the following would not be part of systematic desensitization training?
    a. focusing attention on specific muscle groups
    b. telling oneself to relax and releasing tension
    c. constructing a hierarchy of anxiety-producing stimuli
    d. attempting to contact alternate personalities

29. Which of the following therapies involves learning new internal dialogues?
    a. relaxation training
    b. systematic desensitization
    c. social intervention
    d. cognitive modification

30. _____ might typically involve the social worker going into the home to observe familial interactions.
    a. Reality therapy
    b. Cognitive family therapy
    c. Social intervention
    d. Familial intervention

```
NEXT, TRY YOUR HAND AT TRUE/FALSE QUESTIONS.
```

TRUE/FALSE QUESTIONS

Indicate whether each statement is true or false. Check your answers at the end of this chapter.

T   F   1. Past experiences influence the level of stress we experience in a situation and how we cope with it.

T   F   2. People sometimes fail to cope effectively with stress because of their high level of arousal.

T   F   3. The most stressful aspect of hospitalization for people is the pain often associated with illness and treatment.

T   F   4. Research with the Social Support Questionnaire has failed to demonstrate a relationship between social support and physical illness.

T   F   5. People who have experienced multiple stressors in the recent past are especially susceptible to depression.

T   F   6. College women are a high risk group for sexual assault.

T   F   7. A nineteen-year-old college student is attacked and robbed at gunpoint one night while walking across campus. Because of this event, the student will likely begin to sympathize with her attacker, and even long to encounter her assailant again.

T   F   8. Clinically significant symptoms lasting for a minimum of 2 days and a maximum of 4 weeks, emerging with 4 weeks of a traumatic event (not due to medication or substance abuse) could be seen as a criterion for Acute Stress Disorder.

T   F   9. Dissociative identity disorder was formerly called multiple personality disorder.

T   F   10. PTSD is the same thing as an acute stress disorder.

T   F   11. Therapists find it easy to be supportive of clients with dissociative identity disorder.

T   F   12. Cognitive modification involves learning new internal dialogues and new ways of thinking about situations.

KEEP GOING.....MATCHING IS NEXT.

MATCHING

Match the following terms with information provided below. The answers are at the end of the chapter.

a. supportive therapy	f. social intervention
b. denial	g. bereavement
c. dissociative disorder	h. grief
d. vulnerability	i. dissociative identity disorder
e. social support	

_____ 1. defense mechanism used to cope with bodily symptoms

_____ 2. involves disparate self-concepts

_____ 3. usually occurs after childhood with a history of serious family turmoil

_____ 4. may be accompanied by a sense of numbness and disbelief

_____ 5. treatment involving family members

_____ 6. the feeling of being cared about and loved by others

_____ 7. increases the likelihood of a maladaptive response to stress

_____ 8. loss of a loved one

_____ 9. therapist is noncritical

GOOD, NOW CHECK YOUR ANSWERS. WHEN YOU'RE DONE GRADING YOURSELF, COVER YOUR ANSWERS, AND START ALL OVER AGAIN. KEEP TESTING YOURSELF UNTIL YOU CAN ANSWER THEM ALL CORRECTLY.

CHAPTER 5 ANSWER KEY

Multiple Choice

1.	a		16.	d
2.	d		17.	a
3.	b		18.	d
4.	b		19.	c
5.	a		20.	d
6.	a		21.	d
7.	c		22.	a
8.	b		23.	b
9.	c		24.	d
10.	b		25.	b
11.	c		26.	a
12.	d		27.	c
13.	d		28.	d
14.	c		29.	d
15.	d		30.	c

True/False

1.	T		7.	F
2.	T		8.	T
3.	F		9.	T
4.	F		10.	F
5.	T		11.	F
6.	T		12.	T

Matching

1.	b		6.	e
2.	i		7.	d
3.	c		8.	g
4.	h		9.	a
5.	f			

Chapter 6
BODY MALADAPTIONS: EATING, SLEEPING, AND PSYCHOPHYSIOLOGICAL DISORDERS

CHAPTER OVERVIEW

The present chapter investigates the role of psychological, social, and bodily systems in the development of physical illness. A biopsychosocial model of illness that accounts for the interaction among biological, psychological, and social factors is presented and the impact of stress on physical functioning is highlighted. The relationships are not always linear, that is, physical symptoms are not always the result of stress. Conversely, stress does not always cause physical illness. For example, asthma is an allergic condition that leads to respiratory difficulties, but it can be exacerbated by stress. The text discusses the complexity of the relationships. The text reviews eating disorders, sleep disorders, cardiovascular disorders, cancer, and the diagnostic dilemmas represented by chronic fatigue syndrome, headaches, and irritable bowel syndrome.

LEARNING OBJECTIVES

After studying this chapter, you should be able to answer these questions:
1. What is the psychosomatic hypothesis?
2. What is the biopsychosocial model of abnormal behavior?
3. What do behavioral medicine and health psychology contribute to the understanding and treatment of abnormal behavior?
4. How does stress influence mental and physical health?
5. What are the characteristics of anorexia nervosa, and how do they differ from that of bulimia nervosa?
6. What is binge eating?
7. What factors influence the development of eating disorders?
8. What are the effective treatments for eating disorders?
9. What are the parasomnias and what are their main features?
10. What are the dyssomnias and what are their distinguishing characteristics?
11. What are the main cardiovascular disorders and how do they differ from each other?
12. What is the relationship between stress and cancer?
13. What is chronic fatigue syndrome?
14. What are the different types of headaches?
15. What bodily and psychological factors contribute to headache pain?
16. What are the causes of irritable bowel syndrome and how is it treated?

CHAPTER OUTLINE
1. Psychological, Social, and Bodily Interactions (p.184)

Early clinicians adopted the psychosomatic hypothesis, a Freudian view that bodily symptoms were caused by blocking emotional expression. Since then, research has focused on the bodily changes that occur in response to emotion-arousing stimuli. Illness has been shown to be correlated with conflict and aggression in interpersonal relationships, for example.

A. The Biopsychosocial Model
A person is regarded as a system, with interacting biological, psychological, and social subsystems. Sources of vulnerability and resilience can be found throughout this system.

B. Behavioral Medicine and Health Psychology
Behavioral medicine is concerned with improving diagnosis, treatment, and rehabilitation by using psychological techniques. Behavioral medicine research is concerned with direct patient evaluation and treatment. Health psychology is more concerned with research on the acquisition and modification of behavior that influences health.

C. Stress and Illness
All bodily systems work overtime when the individual is experiencing stress. The particular factors that increase the risk of illness include inability to adapt to change in environmental demands, inability to handle strong emotions and to express them realistically, inability to interpret demands and opportunities correctly, and the inability to form rewarding, lasting intimate relationships.

2. Eating Disorders (p.190)
People with eating disorders often have a preoccupation with thinness, are depressed much of the time, have low self esteem, poor social skills, and tend to be obsessive and perfectionistic.

A. Anorexia Nervosa
The hallmark of anorexia is that individuals see themselves as overweight even when dangerously thin. They often refuse to eat and develop unusual eating behaviors.

B. Bulimia Nervosa
Characterized by eating excessive amounts of food, followed by purging using laxatives, exercising, vomiting, or enemas.

C. Binge Eating
This involves frequent episodes of out-of-control eating without purging.

D. Can Eating Disorders be Prevented?
Educational interventions aimed at children and their parents that address the dangers of eating disorders and the risks of behaviors related to eating disorders.

3. Sleep Disorders (p.198)
Sleep is biologically determined and individuals need different amounts of sleep per night. Chronic sleep deficits can affect mood, behavior, schoolwork, and health.

A. Sleep Processes
Normal sleep occurs in a series of stages, and sleep-related problems play a role in a number of health problems and mental health problems.

B. Dyssomnias
These involve disturbances in the amount, quality, or timing of sleep. They include insomnia, narcolepsy, and sleep apnea.

C. Parasomnias

These are marked by unusual behavioral or psychological events that occur during sleep. They include nightmare disorder, sleep terror disorder, and sleepwalking disorder.

4. Psychophysiological Disorders (P.203)

These refer to physical conditions in which psychologically meaningful events are closely related to bodily disorders. Another way of thinking about this is that they are the end result of biopsychosocial processes.

A. Cardiovascular Disorders

Coronary heart disease and hypertension are particularly affected by psychological and social factors. Stress plays an important role in coronary disease, especially when it results in depression. The Type A personality, characterized as hurried, competitive, and hostile has long been associated with coronary disease; recent research points to hostility as having the greatest effect.

B. Cancer

Psychosocial factors are hypothesized to affect the initiation of a new cancer and the progression of an established cancer, in addition to detecting and taking action when symptoms are detected.

5. Diagnostic Dilemmas (P.212)

Some physical conditions that people experience are difficult to classify medically. One reason for this is the traditional assumption that mind and body are separate and, therefore, what can't be categorized medically, must be psychological.

A. Chronic Fatigue Syndrome

This disorder is characterized by extreme fatigue resulting in a reduction of activities by at least 50 percent, poor concentration, irritability, and pain. It is diagnosed by not only inclusion criteria (symptoms that are present) but also by exclusion criteria (the absence of other symptoms).

B. Headaches

Headaches are very common and are not always associated with organic disease. Headaches have three components: physiological changes, subjective experience of pain, and pain behavior. Although psychological treatments play an increasing role in the treatment of headaches, more research is needed on these approaches.

C. Irritable Bowel Syndrome

Characterized by gastrointestinal symptoms including abdominal pain, gas, bloating, altered bowel movements, this disorder is often accompanied by stress, strong emotions, and maladaptive behavior. The relationship is not clear, however, and more research is needed.

Write each of the following key words and concepts on one side of an index card. Then, for each, look up the correct definition in your textbook. Write the definition on the opposite side of the corresponding index card. Now, you have flash cards to study. Keep the cards with you and whenever you have a few minutes, pull them out and test yourself. When you are studying with a study partner, you can test each other. You can also share the duties of looking up the definitions and writing them on the cards. Study them a little each day.

KEY TERMS AND CONCEPTS
biopsychosocial model (p.185)
behavioral medicine (p.185)
health psychology (p.185)
eating disorders (p.190)
anorexia nervosa (p.190)
bulimia nervosa (p.194)
binge eating (p.194)
sleep disorders (p.198)
sleep processes (p.199)
REM sleep (p.199)
polysomnography (p.201)
dyssomnias (p.201)
parasomnias (p.201)
hypersomnia (p.201)
insomnia (p.201)
hypnogogic hallucinations (p.202)
sleep paralysis (p.202)
nightmare disorder (p.203)
sleep terror disorder (p.203)
sleepwalking disorder (p.203)
psychophysiological disorders (p.203)
cardiovascular disorders (p.204)
coronary heart disease (p.204)
Type A personality (p.205)
hypertension (p.208)
cancer (p.210)
diagnostic dilemmas (p.212)
Chronic Fatigue Syndrome (p.212)
tension headaches (p.213)
migraine headaches (p.213)
cluster headaches (p.214)
irritable bowel syndrome (p.215)

TIPS FOR TESTING YOURSELF

In developing answers for the following questions, turn to the section of your chapter that covers the pertinent material. Read the section thoroughly and spend some time thinking about the information before attempting to frame your answer. Write out each answer without referring to the book, and when you have completed all of them, check their accuracy by returning to the corresponding section in the book. For each question you missed, write out the correct answer. Then test yourself again. Repeat the process until you can answer all the questions correctly.

SHORT ANSWER ESSAY QUESTIONS

1. What is the psychosomatic hypothesis?

2. Describe the interactive nature of the effects of biological and psychosocial factors on health. Explain the Biopsychosocial Model of Health.

3. What psychological skills appear to decrease a person's risk for illness?

4. What are the similarities and differences between behavioral medicine and health psychology?

5. How does stress influence physical and mental health?

6. What are the causes, characteristics, and consequences of anorexia nervosa? How is it treated?

7. What are the causes, characteristics, and consequences of bulimia nervosa? How is it treated?

8. What are the main dyssomnias?

9. What are parasomnias and how are they treated?

10. What are the biological and psychological variables relating to coronary heart disease?

11. What are the sociocultural factors associated with coronary heart disease?

12. What are the characteristics of the Type A coronary-prone person? Discuss the findings of the Framingham study.

13. Describe the factors associated with hypertension.

14. What are some psychological factors that might be associated with cancer?

15. How may psychological factors influence the severity of asthma?

16. List and describe all inclusion and exclusion criteria for Chronic Fatigue Syndrome .

17. Why are Chronic Fatigue Syndrome (CFS), headaches, and Irritable Bowel Syndrome (IBS) referred to as diagnostic dilemmas?

TIPS FOR TESTING YOURSELF

The following sections of self-test questions will test your understanding of the material presented in the chapter. On a separate piece of paper, write the correct answer for each item in the section, then compare your answers with those at the end of the chapter. After you have graded yourself, turn to the chapter and look up the questions you missed. Write out the correct answers. Then test yourself again. Continue doing so until you can answer all the questions correctly.

MULTIPLE CHOICE

The following multiple choice questions will test your comprehension of the material presented in the chapter. Circle the correct choice for each question in the section, then compare your answers with those at the end of the chapter.

1. Bodily symptoms may be caused by blocking of emotional expression according to the
   a. psychosomatic hypothesis.
   b. general adaptation syndrome.
   c. biopsychosocial model.
   d. organ susceptibility hypothesis.

2. The _____ releases hormones under "flight or fight" conditions.
   a. adrenal medulla
   b. adrenal cortex
   c. pituitary system
   d. brain

3. Research has established that there are hormonal and blood pressure changes under conflict conditions in
   a. married couples.
   b. separated couples.
   c. divorced couples.
   d. both a and c

4. Which of the following is false regarding the biopsychosocial model?
   a. A person can be regarded as a system with interacting subsystems.
   b. Biopsychosocial problems occur when a person's life is disrupted.
   c. Illness is due mostly to the influence of external agents.
   d. The biopsychosocial model is relevant to the prevention and treatment of illness.

5. Health psychology is concerned with
   a. rehabilitation.
   b. diagnosis and treatment.
   c. promoting mental health.
   d. disease prevention.

6. Which of the following skills appears to be directly related to a decreased risk of illness?
   a. ability to remain inflexible in the face of change
   b. ability to be "stoic" and suppress feelings
   c. ability to deny circumstances
   d. ability to form loving relationships

7. Stress
   a. stimulates hormonal secretions.
   b. induces biochemical changes.
   c. alters the brain's electrical level.
   d. all of the above

8. The term _____ has been applied to physical conditions in which psychologically meaningful events are closely related to bodily symptoms.
   a. biofeedback
   b. longevity
   c. hardiness
   d. psychophysiological

9. Anorexia may lead to
   a. dry skin.
   b. death.
   c. cardiac arrhythmia.
   d. all of the above.

10. Bulimia nervosa
    a. is more common in men than in women.
    b. begins earlier than anorexia.
    c. occurs only in the Caucasian population.
    d. begins later than anorexia.

11. Adults spend ___ percent of total sleep time in REM sleep.
    a. 50
    b. 30
    c. 20
    d. 25

12. Which sleep disorder has been related to a cluster of genes on chromosome number 6?
    a. insomnia
    b. REM sleep disorder
    c. sleep apnea
    d. narcolepsy

13. Sleep terror disorder
    a. occurs during REM sleep.
    b. only occurs during childhood.
    c. occurs early in the sleep cycle.
    d. causes people to get out of bed and act out their dreams.

14. Psychophysiological disorders include disorders of the
    a. cardiovascular system.
    b. brain.
    c. skin.
    d. both a and c

15. The three components of headache pain are physiological changes, subjective experience of pain, and
    a. duration of pain.
    b. behavior motivated by the pain.
    c. intensity of pain.
    d. both a and c

16. A significant number of migraine sufferers experience
    a. depression.
    b. isolation.
    c. anxiety.
    d. both a and c

17. Cluster headaches
    a. are more frequent in women.
    b. are often confined to one side of the head.
    c. rarely occur at night.
    d. tend not to be severely painful.

18. The number one cause of death and disability in the United States is
    a. asthma.
    b. coronary heart disease.
    c. cancer.
    d. none of the above.

19. Myocardial infarction
    a. is rare in the elderly.
    b. is the least lethal of CHD types.
    c. is the same as a "heart attack."
    d. is directly associated with overexercise.

20. Factors known to increase the risk of CHD include age, cigarette smoking, high blood pressure, and
    a. diabetes.
    b. liver disease.
    c. work habits.
    d. migraines.

21. A study evaluating the effects of lifestyle on coronary heart disease risk in identical twins (Liljefors and Rahe, 1970) found that
    a. genetics proved to be the best predictor of the disease.
    b. diet was directly related to coronary heart disease.
    c. lifestyle was an important factor in the disease.
    d. both b and c

22. Friedman and Rosenman (1974) found that
    a. there is little difference in risk for CHD between type A and type B personalities.
    b. Type B had twice the risk for CHD than type A.
    c. Type B personalities tended to be competitive and hostile.
    d. none of the above

23. A study using husbands' and wives' ratings of hostility (Kneip et al., 1993) found
    a. the higher the spouse-rated hostility, the higher the likelihood of CHD.
    b. the higher the spouse-rated hostility, the lower the likelihood of CHD.
    c. no relationship between hostility and risk of CHD.
    d. that wives were not accurate in assessing their husbands' latent hostility.

24. Choose the following statement that is true.
    a. There are no cultural differences in rates of CHD.
    b. Japan and the U.S. have the highest rates of CHD.
    c. Japan has the highest rate for CHD of all countries studied.
    d. none of the above

25. _____ and _____ have been identified as important factors in the development of hypertension.
    a. Chronic anger; anger suppression
    b. Hostility; passivity
    c. Chronic anger; explosive behavior
    d. Passivity; denial

26. Research suggests that _____ may help people cope with cancer.
    a. biofeedback
    b. individual counseling
    c. group psychotherapy
    d. a belief in God

27. Chronic Fatigue Syndrome (CFS) is currently characterized by the following inclusion criteria and exclusion criteria:
    a. inclusion criteria: sore throat, unexplained fatigue, acute onset of symptoms not resulting from ongoing exertion. Exclusion criteria: psychotic disorders, dementia, eating disorder, severe obesity.
    b. inclusion criteria: psychotic disorders, dementia, eating disorder, and severe obesity. Exclusion criteria: sore throat, unexplained fatigue, acute onset of symptoms not resulting from ongoing exertion.
    c. both a & b
    d. none of the above

28. Studies have shown a high prevalence of _____ in Irritable Bowel Syndrome (IBS) patients.
    a. depression
    b. anxiety
    c. hypochondriasis
    d. both a and b

NEXT, TRY YOUR HAND AT TRUE/FALSE QUESTIONS.

TRUE/FALSE QUESTIONS

Indicate whether each statement is true or false. Check your answers at the end of this chapter.

T   F   1. The quality of close relationships can influence the functioning of the immune system.

T   F   2. Evidence exists that stress plays an important role in health and illness.

T   F   3. Prolonged stress has only a short-term impact on physical health.

T   F   4. Homeostasis refers to a state of balance in the body.

T   F   5. Hostility is related to high risk for coronary heart disease.

T   F   6. Deficits in social support are not associated with CHD.

T   F   7. Environmental factors may influence the functioning of the immune system in humans.

T   F   8. The blood pressures of African-American adults tend to exceed those of white adults.

T   F   9. Belief that one's state of mind influences the body is a relatively new theory.

T   F   10. Medications have been successful in reliably changing eating behavior.

T   F   11. Males are equally prone to be diagnosed with bulimia nervosa and anorexia nervosa.

T   F   12. During REM sleep, the body is in a heightened physiological state.

T   F   13. The leading cause of death and disability in the United States is cancer.

T   F   14. There are no age, sex, and racial or ethnic differences in mortality rates from coronary heart disease.

T   F   15. Ethnicity plays no role in cancer survival and recovery rates.

KEEP GOING.....MATCHING IS NEXT.

MATCHING
Match the following terms with information provided below. The answers are at the end of the chapter.
    a. psychosomatic hypothesis
    b. binge eating
    c. sleep apnea
    d. hypersomnia
    e. sleepwalking disorder
    f. narcolepsy
    g. catecholamines
    h. Chronic Fatigue Syndrome (CFS)
    i. psychophysiological disorders
    j. stress reduction techniques

_____ 1. a disorder in which people fall easily into a deep sleep

_____ 2. may improve immune system functioning

_____ 3. links bodily symptoms to lack of emotional expression

_____ 4. physical conditions in which psychological experiences play a part

_____ 5. disruption in breathing

_____ 6. hormones secreted in times of stress

_____ 7. marked by fatigue in the absence of physical exertion

_____ 8. complex motor behaviors may begin in sleep but continue upon awakening

_____ 9. too much sleep

_____ 10. large quantities of food are eaten without purging

CHAPTER 6 ANSWER KEY

Multiple Choice

1.	a	15.	b
2.	a	16.	d
3.	a	17.	b
4.	c	18.	b
5.	d	19.	c
6.	d	20.	c
7.	d	21.	c
8.	d	22.	d
9.	d	23.	a
10.	d	24.	d
11.	c	25.	a
12.	d	26.	c
13.	c	27.	a
14.	d	28.	d

True False

1.	T	9.	F
2.	T	10.	F
3.	F	11.	F
4.	T	12.	T
5.	T	13.	F
6.	F	14.	F
7.	T	15.	F
8.	T		

Matching

1.	f	6.	g
2.	j	7.	h
3.	a	8.	e
4.	i	9.	d
5.	c	10.	b

Chapter 7
DISORDERS OF BODILY PREOCCUPATION

CHAPTER OVERVIEW

The present chapter investigates the disorders of bodily preoccupation, also known as somatoform disorders. They consist of bodily complaints for which no actual physical disease or underlying dysfunction can be found. Many persons suffering from a somatoform disorder are unwilling to consider that their symptoms may have a psychological basis rather than being purely biological. Diagnosis is often difficult because there often are no clear cut distinctions between what is medical and what is psychological. We discussed some of these diagnostic dilemmas in the last chapter. In those disorders, however, physical symptoms were affected by psychological factors. In the present group of disorders, the psychological is the primary underlying factor. Somatization, conversion, body dysmorphic, and pain disorders, as well as hypochondriasis, are explored. Epidemiology and treatment options are also examined.

LEARNING OBJECTIVES

After studying this chapter, you should be able to answer these questions:
1. What are somatoform disorders?
2. What are the characteristics and causes of somatization?
3. What are conversion disorders and where do they come from?
4. What do people with body dysmorphic disorder feel about their bodies?
5. What is difficult about treating pain disorders?
6. What are the most helpful interventions for people suffering from pain disorders?
7. What is hypochondriasis?
8. What is the defining feature of factitious disorders?
9. What is factitious disorder by proxy?
10. How does malingering differ from factitious disorder?

CHAPTER OUTLINE

1. Somatoform Disorders (p.219)

These disorders are characterized by physical symptoms in the absence of physical disease.

A. Pain Disorders

Severe, prolonged pain without organic symptoms or in excess of what would be expected to accompany organic symptoms characterize pain disorders. A difficulty in assessing pain disorders is that pain affects different individuals differently, depending on different psychological and social factors.

B. Somatization Disorder

This is marked by multiple physical complaints that are chronic or recurrent. The most common include heart palpitations, fatigue, nausea, vomiting, fainting spells, allergies, menstrual and sexual problems.

C. Conversion Disorders

Persons with conversion disorders report the loss of part of all of a basic bodily function. They usually involve a single disturbance at a time, but can affect different sites in subsequent episodes.

D. Hypochondriasis

This diagnosis is appropriate for a person who has a persistent belief lasting at least six months that she or he has a serious disease despite medical evidence to the contrary. This person has an obsessive preoccupation with her or his bodily function and continuously worries about her or his health.

E. Body Dysmorphic Disorder

This disorder is characterized by a morbidly excessive preoccupation with imagined defects in appearance.

2. Factitious Disorders and Malingering (p.231)

Factitious disorder involves the deliberate self-inducement of symptoms by the patient for the single goal of assuming the role of patient. Malingering is motivated by some gain such as evading police, or disability pension.

TIPS FOR TESTING YOURSELF

Write each of the following key words and concepts on one side of an index card. Then, for each, look up the correct definition in your textbook. Write the definition on the opposite side of the corresponding index card. Now, you have flash cards to study. Keep the cards with you and whenever you have a few minutes, pull them out and test yourself. When you are studying with a study partner, you can test each other. You can also share the duties of looking up the definitions and writing them on the cards. Study them a little each day.

KEY TERMS AND CONCEPTS
bodily preoccupation (p.219)
somatoform disorders (p.220)
pain disorders (p.220)
active coping (p.222)
passive coping (p.222)
acute pain disorder (p.220)
chronic pain disorder (p.220)
biofeedback (p.224)
somatization disorders (p.225)
conversion disorders (p.227)
hypochondriasis (p.228)
body dysmorphic disorders (p.229)
body image (p.230)
muscle dysmorphia (p.231)
factitious disorders (p.231)
malingering (p.232)
Munchausen syndrome (p.232)

SHORT ANSWER ESSAY QUESTIONS

1. What are six questions asked in clinical interviews to assess the presence and intensity of a pain disorder?

2. Compare and contract passive and active coping skills for dealing with pain.

3. Discuss four self-management strategies for coping with pain.

4. What is biofeedback and how is it used to treat pain disorders?

5. What are the six guidelines used by clinicians in the treatment of somatization disorders?

6. Give five reasons why people somatize.

7. Describe the somatoform disorders and list the key characteristics of each.

8. Compare factitious disorders and malingering, noting the similarities and differences.

┌───┐
TIPS FOR TESTING YOURSELF

The following sections of self-test questions will test your understanding of the material presented in the chapter. On a separate piece of paper, write the correct answer for each item in the section, then compare your answers with those at the end of the chapter. After you have graded yourself, turn to the chapter and look up the questions you missed. Write out the correct answers. Then test yourself again. Continue doing so until you can answer all the questions correctly.
└───┘

MULTIPLE CHOICE

1. Which of these individuals exhibits symptoms that would meet the criteria for factitious disorders?
   a. Amanda, whose physical symptoms are stress induced
   b. Darryl, whose symptoms are associated with a bad ankle sprain
   c. Zoë, whose symptoms are psychosomatic in origin
   d. Carmelita, who is feigning symptoms.

2. How does biofeedback work?
   a. progressive relaxation
   b. systematic desensitization
   c. neurotransmitter balance
   d. amplification of bodily signals

3. What have studies of the Yogi practitioner Swami Rama revealed concerning the claimed abilities to control bodily functions?
   a. His claims were false.
   b. There are limits to biofeedback.
   c. Physical processes thought to be involuntary can be consciously controlled.
   d. Yoga is just another form of exercise.

4. A major limitation of biofeedback is
   a. the high cost of treatment.
   b. it alters brain electrical activity.
   c. it is not very effective in reducing symptoms after training stops.
   d. it takes years of training to be good at it.

5. Somatization, conversion disorders, pain disorders, and hypochondriasis are classified by the DSM-IV as
   a. anxiety disorder.
   b. factitious disorders.
   c. somatoform disorders.
   d. psychophysiological disorders.

6. A person with hypochondriasis is
   a. convinced that he is very sick.
   b. pretends to be sick to avoid responsibility.
   c. always complains about vague aches and pains.
   d. has symptoms that make no anatomical sense.

7. Another name for Briquet's syndrome is
   a. hypochondriasis.
   b. conversion disorder.
   c. somatization disorder.
   d. depersonalization disorder.

8. Which disorder is often associated with unnecessary surgeries?
   a. malingering
   b. dissociative fugue
   c. conversion disorder
   d. somatization disorder

9. Robert is unable to hear, but a physical examination finds no medical cause for this. Robert may be diagnosed with
   a. hypochondriasis.
   b. depersonalization disorder.
   c. conversion disorder.
   d. malingering.

10. Glove anesthesia is an example of
    a. factitious disorder.
    b. conversion disorder.
    c. somatization disorder.
    d. histrionic personality disorder.

11. Someone with body dysmorphic disorder is likely to be concerned about
    a. having AIDS.
    b. having cancer.
    c. having too much facial hair.
    d. being overweight.

12. Which is most likely to contribute to more rapid recovery from pain?
    a. regular work
    b. regular exercise
    c. taking time off of work
    d. obtaining the sympathy of others

13. During the "B" phase of the A-B-A-B research design
    a. a baseline measure of behavior is recorded.
    b. reinforcement is given for changing behaviors.
    c. the person is interviewed about his experiences.
    d. reinforcements for changing behavior are removed.

14. Repeated, conscious simulation of illness for the purpose of obtaining medical attention would likely be diagnosed as
    a. malingering.
    b. hypertension.
    c. hypochondriasis.
    d. Munchausen syndrome.

15. A mother caught putting some of her own blood into her son's urine sample after bringing in her son for examination would most likely be diagnosed with
    a. Munchausen syndrome.
    b. schizophrenia.
    c. factitious disorder by proxy.
    d. malingering.

16. Research suggests that _____ may help people with pain cope better.
    a. biofeedback
    b. individual counseling
    c. group psychotherapy
    d. a belief in God

17. Which of the following is not a statement that a somatizer might make?
    a. "I really can't take it much longer."
    b. "I feel as weak as a cat."
    c. "I throw up every evening."
    d. "I often feel I'm in the wrong body."

18. Susan appears to be obsessed by her bodily condition and fears developing a disease. Her behavior is most typical of someone experiencing
    a. hypochondriasis.
    b. a conversion disorder.
    c. a factitious disorder.
    d. a conversion disorder.

19. Linda goes to a plastic surgeon complaining of her "ugly and lopsided chin." Upon examination, the surgeon remarked that her chin looked normal and symmetric. If Linda experiences a heightened self-consciousness due to her chin, she would probably be diagnosed as having a(n)
    a. conversion disorder.
    b. identity disorder.
    c. body dysmorphic disorder.
    d. factitious disorder.

20. Pain disorders are frequently accompanied by
    a. an inability to attend work.
    b. substantial use of medications.
    c. interpersonal problems.
    d. all of the above

NEXT, TRY YOUR HAND AT TRUE/FALSE QUESTIONS.

TRUE/FALSE QUESTIONS

Indicate whether each statement is true or false. Check your answers at the end of this chapter.

T   F   1. It appears that biofeedback training skills are lost soon after training ends.

T   F   2. Exercise has been used to facilitate pain management.

T   F   3. Conjuring up pleasant, pain-free visions and thinking about topics not related to pain is a pain self-management strategy known as cognitive restructuring.

T   F   4. Malingering is another term for factitious disorder.

T   F   5. The head and face are most often the focus of preoccupation in body dysmorphic disorder.

T   F   6. *La belle indifference* is a characteristic of Munchausen syndrome.

T   F   7. Biofeedback was a discovery of the German medical profession.

T   F   8. Hysteria was formerly thought to be only a woman's disorder.

KEEP GOING.....MATCHING IS NEXT.

MATCHING

Match the following terms with information provided below. The answers are at the end of the chapter.

    a. muscle dysmorphia
    b. glove anesthesia
    c. A-B-A-B research design
    d. malingering
    e. hysteria
    f. somatization disorder
    g. perception of one's own bodily features
    h. *la belle différence*

_____ 1. an anatomical impossibility

_____ 2. seeking medical attention to achieve some specific goal

_____ 3. physical symptoms result from blocked emotional expression

_____ 4. a repeated measures design that allows for a subject to act as his own control group

_____ 5. Briquet's syndrome

_____ 6. though not yet part of the official diagnostic nomenclature this is gaining considerable attention

_____ 7. associated with conversion disorders

_____ 8. body perception

CHAPTER 7 ANSWER KEY

Multiple Choice

1.	d		11.	c
2.	d		12.	a
3.	c		13.	b
4.	c		14.	d
5.	c		15.	c
6.	c		16.	a
7.	c		17.	c
8.	d		18.	a
9.	c		19.	c
10.	b		20.	d

True/False

1.	T		5.	T
2.	T		6.	F
3.	F		7.	F
4.	F		8.	T

Matching

1.	b
2.	d
3.	e
4.	c
5.	f
6.	a
7.	h
8.	g

Chapter 8
ANXIETY DISORDERS

CHAPTER OVERVIEW

The focus of this chapter is on describing five different types of anxiety disorders that have intense feelings of tension, panic, and anxiety at their core. The types presented are: generalized anxiety disorder, panic disorder, phobic, obsessive-compulsive disorder and posttraumatic stress disorder. These disorders are then discussed from the psychodynamic, learning, cognitive, and biological perspectives.

LEARNING OBJECTIVES

After studying this chapter, you should be able to answer these questions:
1. What are the components of anxiety?
2. What are the causes, course, and consequences of generalized anxiety disorder?
3. What are panic attacks?
4. What is panic disorder and how does it differ from panic attacks?
5. What are phobias and where do they come from?
6. What are the most common types of specific phobias?
7. What are the two types of agoraphobia?
8. What treatments are helpful for phobias?
9. What are the defining features of obsessive-compulsive disorder?
10. What are the most common obsessions and compulsions?
11. What causes posttraumatic stress disorder?
12. Why is posttraumatic stress disorder a controversial diagnosis?
13. What is the most effective treatment for posttraumatic stress disorder?
14. How do the psychodynamic, behavioral, cognitive, and biological perspectives differ in explaining and treating anxiety disorders?
15. What are three main concepts underlying behavior therapy?
16. What are the three types of therapy that utilize the exposure principle?
17. What are the principles that underlie cognitive-behavioral therapy?
18. What are the main medications used to treat anxiety disorders?
19. What is the evidence for a genetic basis for anxiety disorders?
20. Why are antidepressant drugs sometimes useful in treating anxiety disorders?

CHAPTER OUTLINE

1. The Experience of Anxiety (p.238)

Anxiety is defined as a diffuse, vague, very unpleasant feeling of fear and apprehension. The anxious person worries a lot, especially about unknown dangers. Persons often have intrusive thoughts in the form of worries about possible future events and outcomes or catastrophic thinking about past events.

2. Generalized Anxiety Disorder (p.240)

GAD is characterized by prolonged vague and unexplained intense fears that are not attached to any object or event. These feelings resembling normal fears occur in the absence of any actual danger. Individuals suffering from GAD worry about minor things that have not happened, but they often feel worried and tense when nothing at all has occurred. Typical symptoms include: worry and apprehensive feelings about the future, hypervigilance, motor tension, and autonomic reactivity.

3. Panic Disorder (p.241)

Panic attacks are episodes of sudden and intense anxiety rising to a peak that is either cuedby the presence of or thoughts about particular cues, or that occurs spontaneously and unpredictably. Worry over the consequences of the panic attacks is a key aspect of this disorder. One worry in particular, the worry of having a panic attack in public, often results in the development of agoraphobia, which is discussed later in this chapter.

4. Phobias (p.245)

These are characterized by intense fear, panic, dread, or fright in response to specific objects, people, or situations. Stimuli that provoke phobias are not random, and the most common fear-arousing stimuli tend to be objects, animals, or events that present real dangers at some point early in human evolution. Phobic individuals do not need the actual presence of the feared object or situation to evoke feelings of panic; imagining about the source of their fear can be enough to provoke panic.

A. Specific Phobias

This is a miscellaneous category of marked, persistent, and irrational fears to specific stimuli. Some examples of specific phobias include intense and irrational fears of particular animals, heights, closed-in spaces. Specific phobia is the most common type of phobia.

B. Social Phobias

Social phobias are characterized by intense fear and embarrassment in dealings with others. Fear of public speaking and eating in public are frequently experienced by social phobics. Shyness is different from social phobia in that shyness does not evoke the intense feelings of terror that the phobia does.

C. Agoraphobia

This involves the intense fear of entering fear-evoking situations that may provoke a panic attack or otherwise cause the individual to lose control in public. Although most cases of agoraphobia accompany panic disorder, occasionally there are cases in which panic disorder is not a feature.

5. Obsessive-Compulsive Disorder (p.252)

This disorder is characterized by intrusive thoughts (obsessions) that are extremely disturbing and which people cannot get out of their mind, and behaviors that people feel compelled to perform over and over again (compulsions). In most cases, the compulsive behavior develops to ward off the obsessional thoughts. For example, repeated and excessive hand washing may develop to ward off fear of contamination.

6. Posttraumatic Stress Disorder (p.256)

In PTSD, the individual has experienced something traumatic, either directly (e.g., being threatened with death) or indirectly (e.g., witnessing someone being threatened with death). There are three primary and essential characteristics of PTSD: hyperarousal, avoidance, and reexperience. PTSD differs from other trauma-related disorders in its seriousness, duration, and poorer prognosis.

A. Vulnerability Factors

Preexisting emotional and behavioral difficulties, particularly depression or alcohol abuse, predispose persons to acquiring PTSD after a traumatic event.

B. Epidemiological Evidence

Studies show that a majority of persons who develop PTSD after a trauma had pre-trauma histories of psychological disorders.

C. The Posttraumatic Experience

Persons tend to reexperience the event, often in the form of flashbacks. Persons also show excessive autonomic arousal, hypervigilance, difficulty concentrating, and sleep disturbances.

7. Interpreting and Treating Anxiety Disorders (P.259)

Because of the overlap between many of the anxiety disorders, differentiating between them in order to make a correct diagnosis presents a complex challenge for the clinician.

A. The Psychodynamic Perspective

This perspective posits that anxiety serves as both an alarm indicating intrapsychic disturbance, and a defense mechanism in which the individual avoids thinking about other troubling issues.

B. The Behavioral Perspective

Behaviorists focus on the individual's learning history as the cause of anxiety. Anxiety, in other words, is the result of environmental contingencies occurring in the person's life. Treatment approaches include eliminating or extinguishing the learned anxious responses.

C. The Cognitive Perspective

The cognitive perspective of anxiety focuses on the meanings that individuals attach to events, objects, and situations they encounter in their lives. These meanings involve unrealistic appraisals of situations, catastrophic thinking about events or situations, overestimations of dangers. Cognitive therapy works to alter the thought patterns of anxious individuals to more realistic interpretations of their environment.

D. The Biological Perspective

There is no doubt that anxiety involves particular biological responses in the person. The biological perspective focuses on genetics, the role of certain brain structures such as the amygdala and hippocampus, as well as the way the brain processes some neurotransmitters as causative factors of anxiety disorders.

TIPS FOR TESTING YOURSELF

Write each of the following key words and concepts on one side of an index card. Then, for each, look up the correct definition in your textbook. Write the definition on the opposite side of the corresponding index card. Now, you have flash cards to study. Keep the cards with you and whenever you have a few minutes, pull them out and test yourself. When you are studying with a study partner, you can test each other. You can also share the duties of looking up the definitions and writing them on the cards. Study them a little each day.

KEY TERMS AND CONCEPTS

anxiety (p.238)
anxiety disorders (p.240)
generalized anxiety disorder (p.240)
panic attack (p.241)
panic disorder (p.241)
phobia (p.245)
phobic disorder (p.245)
specific phobia (p.246)
social phobia (p.247)
agoraphobia (p.251)
obsessive behavior (p.252)
compulsive behavior (p.252)
obsessive-compulsive disorder (p.252)
posttraumatic stress disorder (p.256)
isolation (p.261)
undoing (p.261)
reaction formation (p.261)
implosive therapy (p.261)
flooding (p.261)
cognitive restructuring (p.264)
thought stopping (p.264)
cognitive rehearsal (p.264)
amygdala (p.266)
hippocampus (p.266)
benzodiazepines (p.266)
alprazolam (p.266)

TIPS FOR TESTING YOURSELF

In developing answers for the following questions, turn to the section of your chapter that covers the pertinent material. Read the section thoroughly and spend some time thinking about the information before attempting to frame your answer. Write out each answer without referring to the book, and when you have completed all of them, check their accuracy by returning to the corresponding section in the book. For each question you missed, write out the correct answer. Then test yourself again. Repeat the process until you can answer all the questions correctly.

SHORT ANSWER ESSAY QUESTIONS

1.   How can anxiety facilitate adaptation? In what way are fear and anxiety different?

2.   How do anxiety disorders differ from the simple experience of anxiety?

3.   What are the major symptoms most likely to be manifested in a generalized anxiety disorder?

4.   What are the differences between generalized anxiety disorders and panic disorders?

5.   Define the term "phobia." List its primary characteristics.

6.   Give examples of phobia-creating situations in social and performance settings.

7.   Define obsessions and compulsions. What are the most common features of obsessive-compulsive disorders? What drives compulsive behaviors in the person with obsessive-compulsive disorder?

8.   Define Posttraumatic Stress Disorder, and provide the six diagnostic criteria.

9.   Discuss the epidemiological evidence for the development of PTSD.

10.   How does the psychodynamic perspective explain anxiety disorders? Discuss how this differs from the behavioral perspective.

11.   Describe the techniques used in behavior therapy to treat anxiety disorders.

12.   How does the cognitive model attempt to explain anxiety disorders? List and explain techniques used by cognitive therapists.

13.   How might a person's biological make-up contribute to an anxiety disorder? What treatments are used by this perspective?

14.   Do you think it is possible for a person to develop a phobia of the color red? If yes, why? If no, why not? Support your position either way.

TIPS FOR TESTING YOURSELF

The following sections of self-test questions will test your understanding of the material presented in the chapter. On a separate piece of paper, write the correct answer for each item in the section, then compare your answers with those at the end of the chapter. After you have graded yourself, turn to the chapter and look up the questions you missed. Write out the correct answers. Then test yourself again. Continue doing so until you can answer all the questions correctly.

MULTIPLE CHOICE

1. A diffuse, vague, very unpleasant feeling of fear and dread is characteristic of
   a. a phobia.
   b. anxiety.
   c. motor tension.
   d. hypervigilance.

2. Which of the statements below is not characteristic of a self-description of anxiety?
   a. "My heart thumps often."
   b. "I'm under constant strain."
   c. "I tend to make quick decisions."
   d. "I always seem to be dreading something."

3. Which of the following is not a symptom of generalized anxiety disorder?
   a. motor tension
   b. autonomic reactivity
   c. hypervigilance
   d. sensations of floating

4. The term _____ refers to an abrupt surge of intense anxiety that is cued by a particular stimulus or without obvious cues.
   a. panic attack
   b. obsession
   c. compulsion
   d. hypervigilance

5. A study by Eaton and others (1994) found that _____ of 8,098 people surveyed reported a panic attack during the course of their lives.
   a. 3 percent
   b. 10 percent
   c. 15 percent
   d. 27 percent

6. All of the following statements are true of panic disorders except:
   a. They tend to run in families.
   b. They are usually associated with childhood trauma.
   c. The person may also experience other types of maladaptive behavior.
   d. Severe panic reactions may be followed by psychotic disorganization.

7. Marks (1987) believes that panic and anticipatory anxiety
   a. are essentially the same.
   b. should both be treated with antidepressants.
   c. are not valid DSM categories.
   d. have different sources.

8. The majority of patients with panic disorder experience _____ , while most patients with generalized anxiety disorder experience _____.
   a. muscular weakness; sweating
   b. blurred vision; faintness
   c. heart palpitations; heart palpitations
   d. sweating; chest pain

9. Of the following, which is true of panic disorders?
   a. It is the most common form of anxiety disorder.
   b. It affects more men than women.
   c. It is more frequently found in younger people than in older individuals.
   d. It does not run in families.

10. Which of the following is not one of the general types of phobias?
    a. agoraphobia
    b. claustrophobia
    c. specific
    d. social

11. The most common type of phobia is
    a. fear of heights.
    b. fear of water.
    c. fear of open spaces.
    d. fear of closed spaces.

12. Phobics
    a. must be presented with the feared stimulus in order to become anxious.
    b. spend considerable energy avoiding the feared stimulus.
    c. tend to be predominately male.
    d. both a and c

13. Select the following category that is not typical of phobias.
    a. mutilation fears
    b. animal fears
    c. nature fears
    d. intimacy fears

14. _____ is characterized by fear and embarrassment in dealings with other people.
    a. Simple phobia
    b. Social phobia
    c. Xenophobia
    d. Claustrophobia

15. The fears of _____ and _____ are particularly resistant types of social phobias.
    a. blushing; eating
    b. dating; eating
    c. blushing; dating
    d. blushing; public speaking

16. The following are interpersonal self-help techniques for the person with a social phobia:
    a. approach rather than withdrawal
    b. tolerate silences
    c. initiate conversation
    d. all of the above

17. In helping a phobic person
    a. don't assume that because something was accomplished successfully one time that it will be so easy the next time.
    b. assume that you know best, and force your beliefs where applicable.
    c. both a and b
    d. Throw the phobic a curve ball: do something that is different from what was initially agreed upon.

18. A person who is unable to cope with taking a walk, driving to work....usual business, might be suffering from
    a. obsessive-compulsive disorder.
    b. posttraumatic stress disorder.
    c. agoraphobia.
    d. psychogenic pain disorder.

19. An obsessive compulsive person is usually
    a. lacking in sexual, aggressive, or religious thoughts.
    b. driven by recurrent thoughts and compulsion.
    c. adjusting to a stressor outside the range of normal experience.
    d. obsessed with celebrities.

20. The diagnostic criteria for Posttraumatic Stress Disorder include
    a. responses to intensely frightening events, persistent symptoms of increased arousal, and the avoidance of stimuli associated with a specific trauma.
    b. exposure to a traumatic event, symptoms of more than a month's duration.
    c. hypervigilance, irritability, sleep difficulties, trouble concentrating, and an exaggerated startled response, all following a specific trauma.
    d. all of the above.

21. Sleep and dream disturbances are a symptom of
    a. denial.
    b. repression.
    c. a social phobia.
    d. intrusive thinking.

22. Undoing is
    a. illustrated by a mother who compulsively checks her children's rooms dozens of times while they are asleep.
    b. illustrated when emotions and feelings are separated from thoughts, acts, and consequences.
    c. illustrated by an individual who thinks obsessively "My sister will die" whenever she turns on the water faucet.
    d. illustrated by feelings of generalized pain, with no discernible source.

23. Three types of therapy based on the exposure principle are
    a. undoing, isolation, and reaction formation.
    b. public speaking, public eating, public urinating.
    c. systematic sensitization, implosive exposure, and in vivo therapy.
    d. systematic de-sensitization, implosive therapy, and in vivo exposure.

24. While exposure therapies emphasize the removal of an overwhelming emotional response that may inhibit people who have an anxiety disorder, modeling is another behavioral approach, this one emphasizing
    a. the presence of compulsion-evoking stimuli.
    b. the acquisition of behavioral skills and a feeling of competence.
    c. the tendency of an individual to devalue his or her problem-solving ability.
    d. thought stopping.

25. Cognitive therapy includes all of the following, except
    a. drug therapies.
    b. thought stopping.
    c. rehearsal.
    d. restructuring.

26. Librium and Valium are examples of
    a. anti-depressants
    b. benzodiazepines
    c. co-morbidity
    d. both a and b

NEXT, TRY YOUR HAND AT TRUE/FALSE QUESTIONS.

TRUE AND FALSE QUESTIONS

Indicate whether each statement is true or false. Check your answers at the end of this chapter.

T   F   1. Essentially, fear and anxiety are identical.

T   F   2. Some common anxiety symptoms are trembling, worry, sleeplessness, heart palpitations, and frequency of urination.

T   F   3. "I always have a sharp and intense pain emanating from my stomach" is a self-description indicative of high anxiety.

T   F   4. The clinical features of Generalized Anxiety Disorder include the inability to control worry, restlessness, irritability, sleep disturbances, and muscle tension.

T   F   5. Over fifty percent of patients with panic attacks have attempted suicide.

T   F   6. Persons who experience panic attacks tend to be frequent users of emergency rooms.

T   F   7. Phobic persons seldom develop ways of reducing their fears.

T   F   8. Stimuli that initiate phobias tend to be random.

T   F   9. Xenophobia is a fear of flying.

T   F 10. Fifty percent of people who have panic disorders develop agoraphobia.

T   F 11. Compulsive rituals may become very elaborate.

T   F 12. The exact prevalence of obsessive-compulsive disorder is well known.

T   F 13. Implosive therapy places an individual in direct contact with a feared stimulus.

T   F 14. Thought stopping is essentially a self-control technique.

KEEP GOING.....MATCHING IS NEXT.

MATCHING
Match the following terms with information provided below. The answers are at the end of this chapter.
    a. implosive therapy   g. cormobidity
    b. reaction formation   h. specific phobia
    c. obsession   i. compulsion
    d. in vivo exposure   j. "sense of strangeness"
    e. social phobia   k. social gatherings
    f. hypervigilance   l. Posttraumatic Stress Disorder (PSTD)

_____ 1. overlap of symptoms among patients with different disorders

_____ 2. feature of a panic attack

_____ 3. repetitive thoughts

_____ 4. a phobia arousing situation

_____ 5. presentation of actual feared stimulus

_____ 6. fear and embarrassment in dealing with others

_____ 7. symptom of generalized anxiety disorder

_____ 8. includes fear of animals

_____ 9. repetitive actions

_____ 10. behaving in a manner opposite underlying feelings

_____ 11. imagined recreation of fear-arousing situation

_____ 12. a situation in which the stressor is outside the range of normal experience

CHAPTER 8 ANSWER KEY

Multiple Choice

1.	b	14.	b
2.	c	15.	a
3.	d	16.	d
4.	a	17.	a
5.	a	18.	c
6.	b	19.	b
7.	d	20.	d
8.	c	21.	d
9.	c	22.	c
10.	b	23.	d
11.	a	24.	b
12.	b	25.	a
13.	d		
26.	b		

True/False

1.	F	8.	F
2.	T	9.	F
3.	F	10.	T
4.	T	11.	T
5.	F	12.	F
6.	T	13.	F
7.	F	14.	T

Matching

1.	g	7.	f
2.	j	8.	h
3.	c	9.	i
4.	k	10.	b
5.	d	11.	a
6.	e	12.	l

Chapter 9
SEXUAL VARIANTS AND DISORDERS

CHAPTER OVERVIEW
This chapter considers two types of sexual behaviors: those that are often personally problematic (sexual dysfunctions) and those that differ from the norms of society (paraphilias). Historical perspectives on sexuality are traced, and theories as well as research findings and treatment modalities are discussed. Contemporary views on homosexuality and bisexuality, which are no longer considered to be psychological disorders, are reviewed. Finally, the types and rates of sexual victimization, and the approaches to their treatments are explored.

LEARNING OBJECTIVES
After studying this chapter, you should be able to answer these questions:
1. How do views concerning sexuality change over time?
2. How do views concerning sexuality vary across cultures?
3. Where does most information about sexual practices come from?
4. Why are frequent sex surveys needed?
5. What is the difference between homosexual behavior and being a homosexual?
6. What is the term "gay" used to refer to and why is it used?
7. What determines a person's sexual orientation?
8. What is bisexual behavior?
9. What is a sexual dysfunction?
10. What are the main types of sexual dysfunctions and what are their defining characteristics and features?
11. What is the nature of sex therapy?
12. How effective is sex therapy?
13. What is gender identity disorder of childhood and where does it come from?
14. What is the nature of transsexualism?
15. What is nontranssexual gender identity disorder?
16. What is a paraphilia?
17. What are the defining features and characteristics of the paraphilias?
18. What are the various psychological perspectives on the paraphilias and what do they contribute to the treatment of these disorders?
19. What are some types of sex offenders?
20. What are some of the psychological problems with sexual victimizers and what treatments are promising?

CHAPTER OUTLINE
1. Changing Views of Sexual Behavior (p.271)
Views of sexual behavior have been particularly influenced over the centuries by changing sociocultural factors and religious beliefs. These changes have evolved from the early Greeks, who

believed sexual expression to be a pleasurable and desirable part of human existence, to the later Western European beliefs that sex was a sin and sexual expression should be repressed.

A. Homosexuality: An Example of Changing Views of Sexual Behavior

The views of homosexuality have changed as the result of changing attitudes of society toward sexuality in general. Homosexual orientation refers to affectional and sexual attraction to members of one's own sex. Homosexual behavior refers to sexual behavior with one's own sex. Homosexual orientation is dependent on the self-identification of the individual as being homosexual; one does not have to have had sexual experience to identify as homosexual. At the same time, many persons who identify as heterosexual have had sexual experiences with members of their own sex.

B. Bisexuality: An understudied sexual variant

This includes the capacity for arousal by members of both sexes, sexual activity or desire for sexual contact with both men and women, and self-identification as bisexual. The origins of bisexual orientation remain to be delineated.

C. Origins of Sexual Orientation

Research thus far has indicated that sexual orientation is the result of a complex interplay of multiple psychological and biological factors and suggests multiple pathways to the different orientations.

2. Sexual Dysfunction (p.277)

A sexual dysfunction is defined as persistent impairment of sexual desire, interest, or response that causes significant distress or difficulty in relationships.

A. Types of Sexual Dysfunction

There are three broad categories of sexual dysfunction disorders: disorders of desire, disorders of arousal, and organismic disorders. Psychological factors often contributing to sexual dysfunctions include: a restricted ability to express positive emotions, fear of rejection, inhibitions about nakedness, concerns with being dominated, and low self-esteem.

3. Treatment of Sexual Dysfunction (p.281)

Treatments often consist of integration of psychodynamic, family systems, and cognitive-behavioral techniques. Three general goals for treatment of couples include fostering good communication, reducing the fear of failure, and shifting the couple's attention to the experience of sensory pleasure.

4. Gender Identity Disorder (p.285)

There are two essential parts of the diagnosis of Gender Identity Disorder. These are persistent cross-gender identification, and evidence of discomfort about one's anatomical sex that causes significant distress.

A. Gender Identity Problems in Children

Children who have not yet reached puberty who show considerable distress at being male or female and who express an intense desire to be the opposite sex may have Gender Identity Disorder of Childhood.

B. Gender Identity Disorder in Adults

Transsexuals experience an intense desire to change their sexual status, including their anatomical structure. Nontranssexual gender identity disorder involves a discomfort about the individual's anatomical sex which they deal with by cross-dressing, but does not include preoccupation with changing their anatomy.

C. Possible Causes of Gender Identity Disorder

The causes of GID are not known, but evidence exists to suggest a genetic component. Psychosocial theories emphasize the role of the parents in the development of the child's gender identity, whether as responses to a child's atypical gender role behaviors, or as a causative factor.

5. The Paraphilias (p.289)

Involving nonnormative sexual interests and practices, paraphilias are divided into three general classes: preference for a nonhuman object to induce sexual arousal, repetitive sexual activity that involves real or simulated suffering or humiliation, or repetitive sexual activity with nonconsenting partners.

A. Fetishism

A nonliving object, or fetish, serves as a primary source of sexual arousal and gratification. Fetishists are almost always male, fetishism often begins in adolescence, and rubber fetishes are very popular.

B. Transvestic Fetishism

Most transvestic fetishists are heterosexual males who cross-dress in women's clothing for sexual gratification.

C. Sexual Sadism and Masochism

Sadism and masochism involve pain and indignity. The sadist achieves orgasm by inflicting pain or humiliation on others; the masochist depends on suffering and humiliation at the hands of others.

D. Voyeurism

This involves spying on others, usually strangers, and particularly while the others are having sex.

E. Frotteurism

This refers to rubbing up against or otherwise touching unsuspecting women in a sexual manner while in a crowd.

F. Exhibitionism

Exhibitionists are always male who repeatedly expose their genitals to unsuspecting strangers in public places.

G. Pedophilia

The pedophile experiences repeated and intense urges and sexually arousing fantasies involving a child who has not reached the age of puberty, and has either acted on these urges or is very distressed by them.

H. Perspectives on the Paraphilias

Human sexual behavior has biological underpinnings and is also strongly influenced by the social environment. Deviant sexual behaviors are harder to research and understand because they are relatively rare and are usually concealed by the participants.

6. Sexual Victimization (p.298)

These sexual deviations involve victims who are either unwilling, uninformed, vulnerable, or too young to give consent. The clearest examples are rape and child sexual abuse.

A. Sexual victimizers

Almost all sex offenders are male, and many have other mental illnesses.

B. Sexual harassment

Unwanted sexual attention, including verbal and nonverbal behavior constitutes sexual harassment. A frequent site of sexual harassment is the workplace. Few victims file formal complaints.

TIPS FOR TESTING YOURSELF

Write each of the following key words and concepts on one side of an index card. Then, for each, look up the correct definition in your textbook. Write the definition on the opposite side of the corresponding index card. Now, you have flash cards to study. Keep the cards with you and whenever you have a few minutes, pull them out and test yourself. When you are studying with a study partner, you can test each other. You can also share the duties of looking up the definitions and writing them on the cards. Study them a little each day.

KEY TERMS AND CONCEPTS

sex surveys (p.272)
homosexuality (p.275)
bisexual behavior (p.276)
sexual desire (p.277)
sexual arousal (p.277)
orgasm (p.278)
sexual dysfunction (p.277)
erectile dysfunction (p.278)
inhibited sexual arousal (p.278)
hypoactive sexual desire disorder (p.278)
nocturnal penile tumescence (p.279)
premature ejaculation (p.279)
female orgasmic disorder (p.281)
dyspareunia (p.281)
vaginismus (p.281)
sex therapy (p.281)
Masters and Johnson approach to sex therapy (p.282)
cognitive-behavior approach to sex therapy (p.283)
psychodynamic approach therapy (p.284)
gender identity disorder (p.285)
transsexualism (p.287)
paraphilias (p.289)
fetishism (p.289)
transvestic fetishism (p.292)
covert sensitization (p.293)
sadism (p.294)
masochism (p.294)
voyeurism (p.295)
exhibitionism (p.295)
pedophilia (p.296)
sexual victimization (p.298)

```
┌─────────────────────────────────────────────────────────────────────────┐
│ TIPS FOR TESTING YOURSELF                                                 │
│                                                                           │
│ In developing answers for the following questions, turn to the section of │
│ your chapter that covers the pertinent material. Read the section         │
│ thoroughly and spend some time thinking about the information before      │
│ attempting to frame your answer. Write out each answer without referring  │
│ to the book, and when you have completed all of them, check their         │
│ accuracy by returning to the corresponding section in the book. For each  │
│ question you missed, write out the correct answer. Then test yourself     │
│ again. Repeat the process until you can answer all the questions          │
│ correctly.                                                                │
└─────────────────────────────────────────────────────────────────────────┘
```

SHORT ANSWER ESSAY QUESTIONS

1. What do recent surveys reveal regarding the changing views of sexual behavior in the U.S.?

2. How have our attitudes toward homosexuality changed? What is bisexuality?

3. What is a sexual dysfunction? List the types presented in your text and briefly explain them.

4. How are sexual dysfunctions treated? Describe the Masters and Johnson approach.

5. Explain the behavioral and cognitive approaches to treating sexual dysfunction.

6. Overall, how effective is sex therapy?

7. Discuss the nature of gender identity disorders.

8. Provide a definition for paraphilias. List and discuss the types presented in your text.

9. How do the various theories attempt to explain paraphilia?

10. Review the research on sexual victimization. What is the long-term effect of being a victim of sexual assault?

11. What interventions are promising for sexual victimizers?

TIPS FOR TESTING YOURSELF

The following sections of self-test questions will test your understanding of the material presented in the chapter. On a separate piece of paper, write the correct answer for each item in the section, then compare your answers with those at the end of the chapter. After you have graded yourself, turn to the chapter and look up the questions you missed. Write out the correct answers. Then test yourself again. Continue doing so until you can answer all the questions correctly.

MULTIPLE CHOICE

1. Select the following statement that is not true of Kinsey's research.
    a. It was the first major study of sexual practices in the U.S.
    b. There was a volunteer bias in his sample.
    c. In-depth interviews were used to collect data.
    d. He found that sexual dysfunction could not be treated successfully.

2. Laumann and others' (1994) study through the National Opinion Research Center found
    a. the median number of sexual partners for a man is 10.
    b. monogamous couples have the most sex and are the happiest.
    c. 10 percent of men reported having a sexual encounter with a male in adulthood.
    d. both a and b.

3. It appears that teenagers have sex for the first time because of
    a. affection.
    b. affection and peer pressure.
    c. peer pressure.
    d. none of the above.

4. Which of the following is not a change in social customs found in a recent survey?
    a. There has been an increase in cohabitation before marriage.
    b. There is an increase in rates of divorce and remarriage.
    c. Nontraditional types of sexual relationships are accepted more.
    d. Oral sex is still perceived to be perverted.

5. What percentage of men find group sex very appealing?
    a. 52
    b. 14
    c. 3
    d. 20

6. Choose the statement below that is true of homosexuals.
    a. A person's belief about homosexuality is dependent upon actual behavior.
    b. The term "homosexual" is preferred over the term "gay."
    c. Someone with no sexual experience usually thinks of himself/herself as heterosexual.
    d. Many homosexuals have heterosexual fantasies.

7. According to a recent public opinion poll, _____ percent of American respondents said they believe homosexual relationships are morally wrong.
    a. 10
    b. 57
    c. 44
    d. none of the above

8. Both the American Psychological Association and the American Psychiatric Association
    a. have retained homosexuality as a psychiatric disorder.
    b. have found that homosexuals differ in their psychological adjustment from heterosexuals.
    c. do not consider homosexuality to be a mental illness.
    d. consider bisexuality to be a psychiatric disorder.

9. LeVay (1991) found
    a. no difference in the anatomical structure of the hypothalamus between gay and heterosexual men.
    b. a difference in the form of the hypothalamus between gay men and heterosexual men.
    c. a difference in the level of psychological adjustment between homosexual and heterosexual men.
    d. both a and c

10. A potential confounding factor in the above study was
    a. the age of the subjects.
    b. coronary heart disease.
    c. AIDS.
    d. the sexual orientation of the subjects.

11. The rate of bisexuality in the U.S.
    a. is difficult to estimate.
    b. has decreased over the last several years.
    c. is increasing as a function of changing attitudes.
    d. is estimated to be 29 percent.

12. A sexual dysfunction
    a. refers to an impairment of an organic nature.
    b. refers to an impairment in sexual response.
    c. refers to an impairment of sexual interest.
    d. both b and c

13. Which of the following factors has not been identified as a cause of sexual dysfunction?
    a. infidelity
    b. number of children
    c. alcohol
    d. fatigue

14. Choose the following statement that has not been identified as a psychological correlate of sexual dysfunction.
    a. fear of rejection
    b. inhibitions about nakedness
    c. difficulty expressing tender emotions
    d. need for achievement

15. The DSM includes the following as sexual dysfunctions:
    a. Hypoactive Sexual Desire Disorder
    b. Sexual Aversion Disorder
    c. Orgasmic Disorders
    d. all of the above

16. Erectile dysfunction occurs during the _____ stage of the sexual-response cycle.
    a. excitement
    b. appetitive
    c. resolution
    d. orgasm

17. Identify the statement below that is true of the relationship between sexual dysfunction and the marital relationship.
    a. Sexual problems are only found in the context of a dysfunctional relationship.
    b. Most of the time, sexual problems indicate a problem in the relationship.
    c. Sexual problems can occur in a well-functioning marriage.
    d. none of the above.

18. _____ is a disorder of the orgasm phase in females.
    a. Vaginismus
    b. Inorgasmia
    c. Dyspareunia
    d. Anorgasmia

19. _____ refers to genital pain before, during, or after intercourse.
    a. Vaginismus
    b. Anorgasmia
    c. Dyspareunia
    d. Retarded dysparia

20. LoPiccolo (1994) states that modern sex therapy is a combination of family systems therapy, cognitive and behavioral techniques, and
    a. psychodynamic approaches.
    b. rational emotive approaches.
    c. operant conditioning approaches.
    d. systematic desensitization.

21. Which of the following is not a general goal for couples in sex therapy?
    a. mutual communication
    b. decreasing the fears of failure
    c. shifting attention to the experience of pleasure
    d. increase the rate of orgasms of both partners

22. A couple experiencing a sexual dysfunction is in the early stages of learning Masters and Johnson's sensate focusing techniques. They have most likely been told to
    a. attempt to have sexual intercourse several times a day.
    b. pretend that each person is making love to a "fantasy partner" such as a movie star.
    c. caress and explore the partner's body without attempting sexual intercourse.
    d. analyze the roots of the sexual problem that occurred during early childhood experiences.

23. The case of the twenty-four-year-old lawyer who had an inability to retain an erection is illustrative of
    a. the psychoanalytic approach to treating sexual disorders.
    b. the use of a cognitive behavioral approach to treating sexual dysfunction.
    c. the use of biofeedback in treating sexual dysfunction.
    d. the failure of the Kaplan approach.

24. Which is not a goal of sex therapy for couples?
    a. improve communication
    b. teach new sex techniques
    c. decrease fear of failure
    d. shift focus from fear of failure to enjoying the experience

25. Gender identity refers to a person's
    a. sexual preference.
    b. genetic composition.
    c. feeling of being male or female.
    d. male or female genital organs.

26. Sexual preference is synonymous with
    a. sexual orientation.
    b. one's preference for type of sexual activity.
    c. a preference for certain characteristics with a given sex.
    d. both a and c

27. A young girl refuses to wear dresses and states, "I'm a boy. Boys wear pants." This child would probably be described as exhibiting
    a. childhood homosexuality.
    b. transgender identity conflict.
    c. a gender identity disorder of childhood.
    d. a nontranssexual gender identity disorder of childhood.

28. People who have a very intense desire to change their sexual status, including their   anatomical structures, are called
    a. homosexuals.
    b. transvestites.
    c. paraphilias.
    d. transsexuals.

29. According to Lindemalm and others (1986), what fraction of cases of male-to-female transsexuals experience fair to good sexual adjustment?
    a. 1/2
    b. 1/8
    c. 2/3
    d. 1/3

30. Which of the following is not a paraphilia?
    a. fetishism
    b. transvestism
    c. sadism
    d. homosexuality

31. In a _____, a nonliving object serves as the primary source of sexual arousal and consummation.
    a. parataxia
    b. dysparneuia
    c. fetish
    d. parafetish

32. Select the statement below that is true.
    a. Fetishism usually begins in early adulthood.
    b. Most fetishists are female.
    c. In some cases, crimes are committed to obtain the desired object.
    d. Fetishists prefer to experience arousal in the presence of others.

33. Bill becomes sexually aroused by dressing in women's lingerie. His behavior is characteristic of
    a. transsexualism.
    b. transvestism.
    c. a gender identity disorder.
    d. masochism.

34. Covert sensitization involves
    a. replacing aversive imagery.
    b. pleasurable imagery with aversive imagery.
    c. avoiding anxiety-producing imagery.
    d. both a and c

35. The five features most commonly found in cases of sadomasochism include agreement on dominant and submissive roles, awareness of role playing, a sexual context, a shared understanding of sadomasochism, and
    a. a history of early childhood abuse.
    b. a desire to become the opposite sex.
    c. the consent of both partners.
    d. inhibited sexual desire.

36. Which of the following is not true about individuals who engage in voyeurism or exhibitionism?
    a. It is a compulsive behavior.
    b. They are almost always male.
    c. They are usually harmless.
    d. Most individuals are married.

37. The psychodynamic perspective views paraphilic behavior to be a function of
    a. learning.
    b. modeling the same-sex parent.
    c. unresolved conflicts.
    d. a fixation of the superego.

38. Which of the following is not a consequence for rape survivors?
    a. loss of self-esteem
    b. anxiety
    c. social phobia
    d. posttraumatic stress disorder

NEXT, TRY YOUR HAND AT TRUE/FALSE QUESTIONS.

TRUE/FALSE QUESTIONS
Indicate whether each statement is true or false. Check your answers at the end of this chapter.

T F 1. The early Greeks regarded sex with partners of either sex as normal.

T F 2. Many homosexuals have heterosexual fantasies.

T F 3. Geography plays a role in the formation of homosexual communities.

T F 4. Homosexuality between women is called lesbianism.

T F 5. Denmark allows homosexuals to marry.

T F 6. Homosexuals differ in psychological adjustment from heterosexuals.

T F 7. It appears that sexual orientation is due to a multitude of factors.

T F 8. If a sexual problem is due entirely to organic factors, it is termed a sexual dysfunction.

T F 9. Performance anxiety is not a contributing factor to impotence.

T F 10. In treating sexual dysfunctions, Masters and Johnson emphasize communication between partners.

T F 11. Sexual fantasies are considered maladaptive.

T F 12. Transsexual surgery remains controversial.

T F 13. Fetishism is one of the most puzzling forms of sexual behavior.

T F 14. Covert sensitization is very useful in treating transvestism and other paraphilias.

T F 15. Only women are considered to be transvestites.

T F 16. Sadomasochists may be heterosexual, bisexual, or homosexual.

T F 17. No one type of treatment is superior in treating paraphilias.

T F 18. Cognitive-behavioral techniques have shown some promise for treatment of sex offenders.

KEEP GOING.....MATCHING IS NEXT.

MATCHING

Match the following terms with information provided below. The answers are at the end of the chapter.

a. gender identity
b. nocturnal penile tumescence
c. fetishism
d. sensate focus
e. masochist

f. erectile dysfunction
g. pedophilia
h. paraphilia
i. transvestism
j. voyeurism

_E_ 1. sexual satisfaction is based on pain/humiliation

_____ 2. inability to attain or hold an erection

_H_ 3. means "attraction to the deviant"

_____ 4. changes in penis during sleep

_____ 5. sexual-retraining technique

_A_ 6. refers to person's feeling of being male or female

_C_ 7. use of nonliving object as source of sexual arousal and consummation

_I_ 8. cross-dressing

_G_ 9. victim is a child

_J_ 10. sexual gratification from watching others

GOOD, NOW CHECK YOUR ANSWERS. WHEN YOU'RE DONE GRADING YOURSELF, COVER YOUR ANSWERS, AND START ALL OVER AGAIN. KEEP TESTING YOURSELF UNTIL YOU CAN ANSWER THEM ALL CORRECTLY.

CHAPTER 9 ANSWER KEY
Multiple Choice

1.	b		20.	a
2.	b		21.	d
3.	b		22.	c
4.	d		23.	b
5.	b		24.	b
6.	d		25.	c
7.	d		26.	a
8.	c		27.	c
9.	b		28.	d
10.	c		29.	d
11.	a		30.	d
12.	d		31.	c
13.	b		32.	c
14.	d		33.	b
15.	d		34.	b
16.	a		35.	c
17.	c		36.	d
18.	d		37.	c
19.	c		38.	c

True/False

1.	T		10.	T
2.	T		11.	F
3.	T		12.	T
4.	T		13.	T
5.	T		14.	T
6.	F		15.	F
7.	T		16.	T
8.	F		17.	T
9.	F		18.	T

Matching

1. e
2. f
3. h
4. b
5. d
6. a
7. c
8. i
9. g
10. j

Chapter 10
PERSONALITY DISORDERS

CHAPTER OVERVIEW

Personality disorders are considered to be long-standing, maladaptive patterns of behavior. A primary characteristic of this type of disorder is "inflexibility." In this section, the major types of personality disorders are presented in three broad categories: odd/eccentric, dramatic/emotional/erratic, and anxious/fearful. The chapter also discusses associated diagnostic criteria, relevant theory, and obstacles to classification.

LEARNING OBJECTIVES

After studying this chapter, you should be able to answer these questions:

1. What are personality disorders?
2. On which DSM-IV axis are personality disorders diagnosed?
3. What are the three categories of personality disorders and what personality disorders are in each category?
4. What are the defining characteristics of paranoid personality disorder?
5. How does schizoid personality disorder differ from schizotypal personality disorder? How is it different from avoidant personality disorder?
6. How would someone with histrionic personality disorder be described?
7. What factors are important in the diagnosis of narcissistic personality disorder?
8. What are the main characteristics of borderline personality disorder?
9. What is antisocial personality disorder and how is it related to criminal behavior?
10. What are the main features of avoidant personality disorder?
11. What is the defining characteristic of someone with dependent personality disorder?
12. How might a person with obsessive-compulsive personality disorder be described?
13. Why has research into treatment of personality disorder been limited?
14. Why is it necessary to be attuned to cultural factors when diagnosing and treating personality disorders?
15. What is the outlook for future classification of personality disorders?

CHAPTER OUTLINE

1. Classifying Personality Disorders (p.304)

Personality disorders are long-standing, maladaptive, inflexible patterns of behavior that seriously impair social or occupational functioning. Personality disorders are grouped according to their predominant, common features. The differences between normal personality and personality disorders are not always apparent, and people rarely seek treatment for personality disorders.

2. Odd or Eccentric Behaviors (p.307)

Persons with these disorders are often characterized as withdrawn, cold, and irrational.

A. Paranoid Personality Disorder

The defining feature of this disorder is marked suspicion as evidenced by the tendency to read hidden meanings in benign events or comments, unwarranted suspiciousness and mistrust of others, and the expectation that one will be exploited or otherwise taken advantage of.

B. Schizoid Personality Disorder

Persons who are schizoid are withdrawn, reserved, and secluded. They prefer solitude and not only lack the capacity for close relationships, but they seem to have no desire for them. They do not appear bizarre or eccentric, but do often lack social skills.

C. Schizotypal Personality Disorder

Persons with this personality disorder are characterized by oddities of thinking, perceiving, communicating, and behaving. They are not as extreme as full-blown schizophrenia. They are also withdrawn, isolated, and lack social skills.

3. Dramatic, Emotional, or Erratic Behaviors (p.311)

These are persons who seek attention and are very unpredictable.

A. Histrionic Personality Disorder

The hallmark of this disorder is the tendency to be grossly overdramatic. Being the center of attention is the person's priority. They tend to speak in gushing and dramatic manner, exaggerating every emotion.

B. Narcissistic Personality Disorder

Narcissistic personality disorder is characterized by an extreme sense of self importance, a need for constant attention, a fragile self-esteem, and the inability to experience empathy or warmth for others.

C. Borderline Personality Disorder

The predominant features of this disorder include unstable personal relationships, self-destructive and impulsive behaviors, extreme fears of abandonment, intense dependency and manipulation of others. They show identity disturbances and report chronic feelings of emptiness and an intolerance of being alone.

D. Antisocial Personality Disorder

The person with Antisocial Personality Disorder is one who consistently violates norms and the rights of others, sometimes leading to criminal acts. They seldom show anxiety and rarely experience feelings of guilt. When in tough spots because of their behaviors, they see themselves as faultless, blaming their difficulties on others.

4. Anxious or Fearful Behaviors (p.322)

Each of these disorders has a prominent feature of anxiety or fear.

A. Avoidant Personality Disorder

This is characterized by low self-esteem, fear of negative evaluation, and pervasive avoidance of social situations. Whereas the schizoid personality doesn't desire social contact, the avoidant personality fears social contact out of fear of rejection or fear of criticism.

B. Dependent Personality Disorder

People with dependent personality disorder passively allow other people to make all the important decisions in their lives, and consistently subordinate their own needs to those of others so as to maintain their dependence on those others.

C. Obsessive-Compulsive Personality Disorder

Persons with obsessive-compulsive personality disorder are rigid and restricted in their behavior, but lack the obsessive thinking that is characteristic of obsessive-compulsive anxiety disorder. Extreme perfectionism is a predominant feature, and the individual is inflexible, formal, unusually serious.

5. Treatment of Personality Disorders (p.326)

People with personality disorders rarely seek treatment, rather, they believe their difficulties to be the fault of others.

6. The Outlook for Personality Disorder Classification (p.326)

There is much disagreement among clinicians about this diagnostic category—whether the entire category is appropriate, or whether the individual diagnoses are appropriate. Further research is warranted to explore the vulnerability-resilience interaction in personality disorders.

```
TIPS FOR TESTING YOURSELF

Write each of the following key words and concepts on one side of an index card.  Then, for each,
look up the correct definition in your textbook.  Write the definition on the opposite side of the
corresponding index card.  Now, you have flash cards to study.  Keep the cards with you and
whenever you have a few minutes, pull them out and test yourself.  When you are studying with a
study partner, you can test each other.  You can also share the duties of looking up the definitions
and writing them on the cards.  Study them a little each day.
```

KEY TERMS AND CONCEPTS

personality (p.304)
personality disorder (p.304)
symptom disorder (p.305)
prototypal approach (p.307)
paranoid personality disorder (p.307)
schizoid personality disorder (p.308)
schizotypal personality disorder (p.309)
histrionic personality disorder (p.311)
narcissistic personality disorder (p.312)
borderline personality disorder (p.312)
splitting (p.316)
antisocial personality disorder (p.317)
avoidant personality disorder (p.322)
dependent personality disorder (p.323)
obsessive-compulsive personality disorder (p.324)
dimensional model (p.327)

TIPS FOR TESTING YOURSELF

In developing answers for the following questions, turn to the section of your chapter that covers the pertinent material. Read the section thoroughly and spend some time thinking about the information before attempting to frame your answer. Write out each answer without referring to the book, and when you have completed all of them, check their accuracy by returning to the corresponding section in the book. For each question you missed, write out the correct answer. Then test yourself again. Repeat the process until you can answer all the questions correctly.

SHORT ANSWER ESSAY QUESTIONS

In developing answers for the following questions, turn to the section of your chapter that covers the pertinent material. Read the section thoroughly before attempting to frame your answer.

1. What are the characteristic behaviors of personality disorders?

2. Why do the personality disorders present problems in classification?

3. What is the prototypal approach of DSM-IV?

4. Describe the characteristics associated with paranoid personality disorders.

5. What symptoms might be expected of a schizoid personality disorder?

6. List characteristics associated with the schizotypal personality disorder.

7. Histrionic personality disorders display what symptoms?

8. Describe the symptoms associated with narcissistic personality disorder.

9. What kind of behaviors might one expect of a borderline personality disorder? Recent research suggests three distinctive features of this disorder. What are they?

10. What are the research findings about the brains and cognitive style of people with antisocial personality disorder?

11. List the traits of an avoidant personality disorder.

12. Explain the prominent features in dependent personality disorder.

13. An individual who is diagnosed as having an obsessive-personality disorder presents what behaviors?

14. What are the additional proposed categories of personality disorders and why are they controversial?

15. Why is the treatment of the personality disorders difficult and seldom successful?

152

TIPS FOR TESTING YOURSELF

The following sections of self-test questions will test your understanding of the material presented in the chapter. On a separate piece of paper, write the correct answer for each item in the section, then compare your answers with those at the end of the chapter. After you have graded yourself, turn to the chapter and look up the questions you missed. Write out the correct answers. Then test yourself again. Continue doing so until you can answer all the questions correctly.

MULTIPLE CHOICE

1. Which of the following statements is false regarding personality disorders?
   a. They are long-standing, maladaptive ways of dealing with the environment.
   b. They are usually noticed in childhood or in early adolescence.
   c. They allow for only a rigid and narrow range of responses to situations.
   d. They are estimated to occur in 49 percent of the population.

2. Select the statement below that is correct.
   a. Little is known about the origins and development of a personality disorder.
   b. Personality disorders are severely incapacitating.
   c. Much research exists on the nature of personality disorders.
   d. They are diagnosed on Axis I.

3. The major personality disorders may be divided into three groups: odd/eccentric, dramatic/emotional, and
   a. sadistic/avoidant.
   b. aggressive/fearful.
   c. anxious/fearful.
   d. seductive/sexual.

4. Jim exhibits feelings of suspiciousness, hypersensitivity, and mistrust of his coworkers. He is perceived as "cold" by them. Typically, these types of traits are seen in
   a. paranoid personality disorders.
   b. schizoid personality disorders.
   c. schizophrenia.
   d. prototypal personality disorders.

5. Margo works as a night receptionist in a high rise apartment building. She is viewed by tenants as "weird and aloof" because she never acknowledges them unless spoken to first. She is unmarried and lives alone in the apartment building and does not appear to socialize or date. Margo appears to exhibit characteristics of a(n) _____ disorder.
   a. schizotypal
   b. schizoid
   c. atypical personality
   d. antisocial

6. A schizotypal personality disorder is characterized by
   a. a break from reality.
   b. attention-seeking.
   c. intense emotional attachments.
   d. oddities of speech.

7. Jean is an overly dramatic person. She is seen by others as being vain and immature. Because of her self-centered attitude and manipulative behaviors, relationships with others tend to be stormy. She first came to the attention of a therapist because of a superficial and dramatic attempt to commit suicide by taking an almost toxic dose of vitamins. The therapist would likely diagnose Jean as a
   a. paranoid personality disorder.
   b. schizotypal personality disorder.
   c. narcissistic personality disorder.
   d. histrionic personality disorder.

8. Mary is engaged to marry Joe but has concerns about some things. For example, Joe is very intolerant of others and often seems to require excessive admiration and attention. Given this information, select a tentative diagnosis for Joe.
   a. narcissistic personality disorder
   b. histrionic personality disorder
   c. schizotypal personality disorder
   d. none of the above

9. A therapist who is treating a client who is diagnosed as a borderline personality disorder should expect which of the following to occur?
   a. The client is likely to ask for special favors, and will try to impress the therapist with his brilliance.
   b. Self-destructive behaviors designed to call forth a "saving" response from the therapist have a high probability of occurring.
   c. The thinking of the client is likely to deteriorate under stress and the client might express some delusional thoughts.
   d. A pattern of irresponsible behaviors, lack of conscience, and lying will probably characterize this client's behavior.

10. According to Kernberg, the borderline personality disorder characterized by a failure to integrate the positive and negative experiences that occur between the individual and other people is a phenomenon known as
    a. autism.
    b. egocentric behavior.
    c. egotistical behavior.
    d. splitting.

11. Which of the following is not a problem in cases of borderline personality disorder?
    a. affective disturbances
    b. impulse disturbances
    c. reality disturbances
    d. identity disturbances

12. Choose the following statement that is not true of Linehan's (1993) dialectical behavior therapy for borderline personality disorder.
    a. It combines cognitive, behavioral, and psychodynamic concepts.
    b. It is aimed particularly at suicidal threats and gestures.
    c. It uses individual and group therapy.
    d. It emphasizes that patients become independent of others.

13. The case of Gary Gilmore illustrates many symptoms of
    a. a conduct disorder.
    b. an antisocial personality disorder.
    c. a borderline personality disorder.
    d. a narcissistic personality disorder.

14. According to Gottesman and Goldsmith (1994),
    a. learning theory presents the best explanation of how antisocial personality develops.
    b. heredity may play a role in criminality and antisocial behavior.
    c. brain wave patterns have failed to show significance in the study of antisocial personality disorder.
    d. none of the above.

15. From a cognitive perspective, the study of antisocial behavior focuses on
    a. moral development.
    b. patterns of brain wave activity.
    c. differing levels of neurotransmitters.
    d. left-handedness and right-brain dominance.

16. Select the following statement that is true.
    a. Abused children are at greater risk for being diagnosed as antisocial personality disorder in adulthood.
    b. There is no relationship between abuse in childhood and antisocial personality disorder in adulthood.
    c. People diagnosed as having antisocial personality disorder do not report being abused in childhood.
    d. both b and c

17. A person with an avoidant personality disorder experiences conflict over
    a. desires to be good and impulses toward hostile and violent behavior.
    b. wanting affection and doubting their acceptance by others.
    c. fears of looking foolish and wanting to be the center of attention.
    d. obsessions about germs or dirt and inability to maintain a totally clean environment.

18. _____ personality disorders tend to be "clinging" according to Bornstein (1992).
    a. Avoidant
    b. Narcissistic
    c. Antisocial
    d. Dependent

19. An individual with a dependent personality disorder believes that
    a. he/she deserves the best.
    b. he/she is more important than others.
    c. others are dependent on him/her.
    d. he/she must act meek and obedient to keep another's attention.

20. Morgan describes his friend Dylan as somewhat "stiff and formal." Dylan's rigid perfectionism and morality often drives Morgan over the edge. However, since Dylan has been eccentric since he was a young boy, Morgan tries to overlook Dylan's quirks. Which of the following would most likely apply to Dylan?
    a. obsessive-compulsive personality disorder
    b. obsessive-compulsive anxiety disorder
    c. dependent personality disorder
    d. none of the above

21. Read the following statement and match it with its appropriate diagnosis. "I must save money. That's why I tend to save things and people call me a packrat."
    a. paranoid personality disorder
    b. obsessive-compulsive personality disorder
    c. dependent personality disorder
    d. schizoid personality disorder

22. Which of the following is not a problem related to a lack of knowledge regarding personality disorders?
    a. People with personality disorders are satisfied with their behavior.
    b. Professionals tend to see a restricted sample of people with these disorders.
    c. They view the environment as the source of their problems.
    d. DSM-IV lacks specific criteria for diagnosis.

23. _____ therapy has been used effectively with personality disorders in which anxious or fearful behavior plays a prominent role.
    a. Behavior
    b. Psychodynamic
    c. Drug
    d. Relaxation

24. _____ therapy may be a useful part of the treatment of many individuals with personality disorders.
    a. Group
    b. Family
    c. Reality
    d. both a and b

25. Some clinicians argue that _____ should be included as a category in DSM-IV personality disorders.
    a. a sadistic pattern
    b. a manic pattern
    c. an ego-maniacal pattern
    d. an argumentative pattern

26. Axis II of DSM-IV uses a(n) _____ model for classification.
    a. categorical
    b. dimensional
    c. nosological
    d. ICD

NEXT, TRY YOUR HAND AT TRUE/FALSE QUESTIONS.

TRUE/FALSE QUESTIONS

Indicate whether each statement is true or false. Check your answers at the end of this chapter.

T   F   1. Personality disorders are classified on Axis I of the DSM.

T   F   2. Little is known about the origins of personality disorders.

T   F   3. Personality disorders are often called symptom disorders.

T   F   4. Personality disorders produce the most reliable diagnoses of any DSM disorder.

T   F   5. A person may have a diagnosis on Axis I and Axis II.

T   F   6. Schizoid individuals have a poor prognosis for treatment.

T   F   7. "All the world is a stage" best describes the schizotypal personality disorder.

T   F   8. Devaluing the importance of others is characteristic of the borderline personality disorder.

T   F   9. "Splitting" refers to the failure to integrate positive and negative aspects of experience.

T   F   10. Men are more likely than women to be diagnosed as having histrionic personality disorder.

T   F   11. Borderline personality disorders occur in 10 percent of the general population.

T   F   12. Recently, bulimia has become a destructive tactic for borderlines.

T   F   13. Individuals with obsessive-compulsive personality disorder are quite good at seeing the "big picture."

T   F   14. People with personality disorders frequently seek professional help.

T   F   15. Research demonstrates that drug therapy is the best method of treatment for personality disorders.

KEEP GOING.....MATCHING IS NEXT.

MATCHING

Match the following terms with information provided below. The answers are at the end of the chapter.

a. narcissistic personality disorder
b. borderline personality disorder
c. schizoid personality disorder
d. impulse disturbance
e. personality

f. categorical model
g. prototypal approach
h. dimensional model
i. splitting
j. symptom disorders

I _____ 1. shifting between contradictory images

E _____ 2. characteristic ways of behaving

_____ 3. classification system used in DSM-IV

C _____ 4. few, if any, activities provide pleasure

A _____ 5. may fantasize about unlimited success

B _____ 6. suggests marginal level of functioning

_____ 7. characterized by self-damaging acts

_____ 8. Axis I disorders

_____ 9. approaches classification through a threshold model

_____ 10. focuses on patterns of personality characteristics

CHAPTER 10 ANSWER KEY

Multiple Choice

1.	d	14.	b
2.	a	15.	a
3.	c	16.	a
4.	a	17.	b
5.	b	18.	d
6.	d	19.	d
7.	d	20.	a
8.	a	21.	b
9.	b	22.	d
10.	d	23.	b
11.	c	24.	d
12.	d	25.	a
13.	b	26.	a

True/False

1.	F	9.	T
2.	T	10.	F
3.	F	11.	F
4.	F	12.	T
5.	T	13.	F
6.	T	14.	F
7.	F	15.	F
8.	T		

Matching

1.	i	6.	b
2.	e	7.	d
3.	g	8.	j
4.	c	9.	f
5.	a	10.	h

Chapter 11
MOOD DISORDERS

CHAPTER OVERVIEW

Mood disorders, characterized by a disturbance in mood or emotion are the topic of interest in this section. Mood disorders fall into two broad categories, depression and mania, and include constellations of such symptoms as sadness, feeling blue, elation, or excessive energy expenditure. The chapter explains depression as a mood state and as a disorder, and presents risk factors identified through research. It also discusses disorders in which periods of depressed mood are alternated with mania. Topics covered include dysthymic disorder, major depressive disorder, cyclothymic disorder, and bipolar I and II disorders. The chapter gives an extensive overview to treatments of these disorders and information on factors related to suicide and parasuicide.

LEARNING OBJECTIVES

After studying this chapter, you should be able to answer these questions:
1. What are the three main types of mood disorders?
2. How common is depressive disorder?
3. How do cultural factors affect the rates of depressive and bipolar disorders?
4. How does having the "blues" differ from clinical depression?
5. What are the individual and socioeconomic risk factors for depression?
6. How do dysthymic disorders differ from major depressive disorder?
7. What are current theories about the causes of depression?
8. What are the most effective treatments for depression?
9. What are the four bipolar disorders and what are their distinguishing characteristics?
10. What genetic and psychosocial factors contribute to bipolar disorder?
11. What is the most effective treatment for bipolar disorder?
12. What is the relationship between mental illness and suicide attempts?
13. Which mood disorders have the highest and lowest correlation with suicide rate?
14. What is parasuicide?
15. What are the individual, racial, ethnic, and socioeconomic risk factors for suicide?
16. What life events may precipitate suicide?
17. What is suicide contagion?
18. How can suicide be prevented?

CHAPTER OUTLINE

1. Depressed Mood (p.331)

Feeling depressed is not the same as having a depressive disorder. Various types of life experiences can lead to temporary feelings of depression, and usually these feelings fade quickly when the situation changes.

2. Mood Disorders (p.332)

These are disturbances in mood or emotional reactions that are not due to other mental or physical disorders.

3. Depression (p.333)

Ranging from a relatively mild menalcholy to an extremely negative mood that affects the ability to function, depression can be a temporary or a long-lasting mood state.

A. Vulnerability Factors for Depression

Family and twin studies clearly support a genetic component for both major depression and bipolar disorder. Age and gender are both risk factors for depression. Other risk factors include life events and lack of social supports.

4. Depressive Disorders (p.337)

A. Dysthymic Disorder

This is characterized by a mild and chronic depressed mood that can last for years. For the person with dysthymia, depressive symptoms seems normal, like a way of life. Because of its chronicity, the person with dysthymia feels helpless to make any changes.

B. Major Depressive Disorder

A person with a major depressive disorder has experienced one or more major depressive episodes without ever having had a manic or hypomanic episode. A major depressive episode is marked by depressed mood as well as at least four other symptoms that last at least two weeks and represent a change from the person's usual functioning. At least 50 percent of people who experience a major depressive episode will experience a recurrence. The more episodes they have, the more likely they will continue to have episodes. Major depression can also be accompanied by psychotic symptoms, primarily delusions.

5. Causes and Treatment of Depression (p.341)

The causes are not well understood, but by considering the combination of biological, social, and psychological factors, progress is made in understanding and treating depression.

A. Biological Factors in Depression

Research has shown that depression is related to biochemical factors, specifically with regard to the lack of insufficiency of particular neurotransmitters.

B. Biologically Based Treatment

Two major biologically based treatments for depression are antidepression medications and electroconvulsive therapy.

C. Psychologically Based Treatment

There is considerable evidence to support the effectiveness of psychotherapy in the treatment of depression, but the link between specific treatments and clinical improvement has not been clearly established. There is significant evidence that psychotherapy yields lower relapse rates than courses of medication. The psychodynamic perspective is rarely used in the treatment of depression, but other treatment approaches are used with some success.

D. The Humanistic-Existentialist Perspective

Existential theories focus on the loss of self-esteem, while humanists focus on the discrepancies between a person's view of the ideal and the view of her or his actual self.

E. The Behavioral Perspective

The behaviorists conceptualize depression as a consequence of inadequate skills in getting social reinforcement and poor coping skills.

F. Behavioral Treatment for Depression

Social skills training using role playing to practice the new skills is a primary technique used by behavior therapists.

G. The Cognitive Perspective

The cognitive perspective posits that depression is caused by negative meanings that persons attach to events in their lives. They hold negative beliefs about self, the world, and the future.

H. Cognitive-Behavioral Therapy

CBT challenges and disputes the negative beliefs, replacing them with more functional, rational beliefs. Clients are taught to identify their dysfunctional thoughts and challenge them through the use of homework assignments.

I. The Vulnerability-Resilience Perspective

Both biological and psychological factors contribute to vulnerability and resilience, and together they can determine the outcome when people are experiencing negative environmental stressors.

J. Combined Treatment of Depression

A combination of psychotherapy and medication reduces the likelihood of relapse for the less severe cases of depression.

6. The Bipolar Disorders (p.356)

Formerly called manic-depressive illness, bipolar disorder involves episodes of both depression and mania. People often experience swings in mood from euphoria, grandiosity, irritability, and hostility to episodes of sadness and hopelessness with periods of normalcy in between.

A. Bipolar I Disorder

A person with Bipolar I disorder experiences manic episodes and major depressive episodes as well. People are diagnosed on the basis of the manic episodes, the assumption being that they will eventually experience a depressive episode.

B. Bipolar II Disorder

In Bipolar II disorder, the manic episodes are somewhat less extreme than in Bipolar I disorder. These episodes, called hypomania, lack the florid drama of the full-blown mania of Bipolar I.

C. Cyclothymic Disorder

This disorder is best characterized as periods of hypomania along with periods of dysthymia that are most noticeable as changes in energy, do not meet the criteria for either mania or major depressive disorder, and are more chronic in course. Episodes of cyclothymia often have a seasonal component and are more common in spring or fall.

7. Causes and Treatment of Bipolar Disorder (p.361)

A. Genetic Factors
The evidence for a genetic predisposition to bipolar disorder is very strong, meaning that the vulnerability is inherited, not necessarily the disorder itself.

B. Biologically Based Treatment of Bipolar Disorder
The most common treatment is lithium. It is primarily an anti-manic drug, but it does reduce depressive symptoms in some persons. However, lithium has serious side effects and is not effective for about half of bipolar patients. Adherence is a problem, too, because people may be unwilling to give up the sensations associated with the elevated mood.

C. Psychosocial Factors and Bipolar Episodes
Psychosocial factors play a role in both triggering new episodes as well as in preventing them. Both environmental stressors and family stressors can play a part.

D. Psychological Approaches for Bipolar Patients and Their Families
Family psychoeducational interventions can be helpful in preventing relapse, nonadherence to the medication regimen, and to educate the family in ways of interacting with the bipolar patient.

8. Suicide (p.364)
Suicide is one of the top ten causes of death in the U.S. U.S. suicide rates averaged 12.5 per 100,000 in the 20th century.

A. Mental Illness and Suicide
Mental illness greatly increases the probability of a suicide attempt. Parasuicide refers to suicidal behavior that does not result in death. Parasuicidal behavior predicts completed suicide within a year following a parasuicidal behavior.

B. Risk Factors for Suicide
Adolescents and young adults, and people over 70 are at greater risk for suicide. Women make more attempts than men, but men are more likely to complete the suicide. Native American and Alaskan native men are at particular risk for suicide.

C. Life Events and Suicide
Life events involving loss are precipitating factors for suicide for some people.

D. Suicidal Contagion
Sometimes referred to as the 'copycat effect,' this refers to the phenomenon of increased suicide attempts in a community after the suicide of a well-known person makes headline news.

E. Prevention of Suicide
Increasing awareness of possible suicidal thinking, providing crisis intervention services, and changing cultural expectations about how to deal with problems all contribute to the prevention of suicide.

TIPS FOR TESTING YOURSELF

Write each of the following key words and concepts on one side of an index card. Then, for each, look up the correct definition in your textbook. Write the definition on the opposite side of the corresponding index card. Now, you have flash cards to study. Keep the cards with you and whenever you have a few minutes, pull them out and test yourself. When you are studying with a study partner, you can test each other. You can also share the duties of looking up the definitions and writing them on the cards. Study them a little each day.

KEY TERMS AND CONCEPTS
mood disorder (p.332)
depression (p.333)
unipolar disorder (p.334)
major depressive disorder (p.333)
dysthymic disorder (p.337)
dysthymia (p.337)
major depressive episode (p.339)
catecholomines (p.341)
dopamine (p.341)
gamma aminobutyric acid (p.342)
acetylcholine (p.342)
seasonal affective disorder (p.343)
monoamine oxidase (MAO) (p.342)
monoamine oxidase inhibitors (p.342)
reversible inhibitors of monoamine oxidase (RIMAs) (p.342)
tricyclic antidepressants (p.342)
selective serotonin reuptake inhibitors (SSRIs) (p.342)
seasonal affective disorder (SAD) (pp.343, 344)
electroconvulsive therapy (ECT) (p.346)
interpersonal psychotherapy (p.350)
humanistic-existentialist psychotherapy (p.350)
social skills training (p.351)
schemata (p.352)
cognitive triad (p.352)
learned helplessness (p.352)
automatic thoughts (p.353)
cognitive-behavior therapy (p.353)
cyclothymic disorder (pp.357, 361)
bipolar disorder (p.356)
rapid cycling (p.357)
bipolar I disorder (p.357)
mania (pp.357, 358)
bipolar II disorder (p.359)
hypomania (p.359)
hypomanic episode (p.359)

suicide (p.364)
parasuicide (p.364)
postvention (p.367)

```
TIPS FOR TESTING YOURSELF

In developing answers for the following questions, turn to the section of your chapter that covers the
pertinent material. Read the section thoroughly and spend some time thinking about the information
before attempting to frame your answer. Write out each answer without referring to the book, and when
you have completed all of them, check their accuracy by returning to the corresponding section in the
book. For each question you missed, write out the correct answer. Then test yourself again. Repeat the
process until you can answer all the questions correctly.
```

SHORT ANSWER ESSAY QUESTIONS

In developing answers for the following questions, turn to the section of your chapter that covers the
pertinent material. Read the section thoroughly before attempting to frame your answer.

1. What are the different categories of mood disorders?

2. How can you differentiate between clinical depression and sadness? The term depression
    can refer to a symptom and to a disorder. Explain this.

3. What are the risk factors for depression?

4. Discuss the contribution of stressful life events to mood disorders.

5. What is a dysthymic disorder? Describe its symptoms.

6. What are the characteristics of a major depression?

7. How do the biological theories explain the origin of a mood disorder? Discuss the
    research presented throughout the chapter that strongly points to a biological basis for
    mood disorders. What types of research designs are typically used to assess the biological
    contributions to mood disorders?

8. What is the dexamethasone suppression test (DST), and what is its effectiveness?

9. Describe the biological treatments used in treating depression. How effective are these
    interventions?

10. Present the psychodynamic views of depression.

11. How do the behaviorists conceptualize depression?

12. Explain how the cognitive model views and treats depressive disorders. Describe Beck's
    cognitive-distortion model.

13. Explain the existential-humanistic position on depression.

14. What are the characteristics and causes of a bipolar disorder? Describe the two types discussed in your text. What is mania? What is a cyclothymic disorder?

15. What treatments are available for individuals with bipolar disorders?

16. What are the risk factors of suicide for persons with mood disorders? Discuss the causes of suicide.

17. Explain how parasuicidal behavior differs from suicidal behavior.

18. Discuss some useful methods of suicide prevention, and then discuss the impact of suicide on others when it does occur.

19. How is postvention useful in helping survivors of suicide handle their grief?

TIPS FOR TESTING YOURSELF

The following sections of self-test questions will test your understanding of the material presented in the chapter. On a separate piece of paper, write the correct answer for each item in the section, then compare your answers with those at the end of the chapter. After you have graded yourself, turn to the chapter and look up the questions you missed. Write out the correct answers. Then test yourself again. Continue doing so until you can answer all the questions correctly.

MULTIPLE CHOICE

1. The essential feature of a mood disorder is
   a. a delusion.
   b. a disturbance in mood or emotional reaction not due to any other physical or mental disorder.
   c. a manic episode.
   d. parasuicidal behavior.

2. About _____ percent of the adults in the United States have experienced some type of mood disorder.
   a. 20
   b. 10
   c. 5.5
   d. 24

3. After a death, survivors often experience
   a. grief.
   b. the blues.
   c. cyclothymia.
   d. none of the above

4. Depressed mood is an important symptom in a(n):
   a. dysthymic disorder
   b. unipolar disorder
   c. adjustment disorder without depressed mood
   d. adjustment disorder with depressed mood

5. Major depressive disorder is the _____ greatest cause of disability affecting quality of life and productivity worldwide.
   a. second
   b. fifth
   c. first
   d. tenth

6. Which of the following is a risk factor for depression?
   a. heredity
   b. age
   c. gender
   d. all of the above

7. Depression appears to be related to up to _____ of all suicides.
   a. one-half
   b. one-fourth
   c. one-third
   d. one-fifth

8. Which of the following is true regarding the changing rate of major depression?
   a. A person's birth cohort is not a significant predictor of major depression.
   b. There has been an increase in the rate of major depression over time in all countries.
   c. While the birth cohort has changed, there is no associated change in rates for major depression.
   d. both a and c

9. Henderson (1992) found which of the findings below in relationship to unsupportive behaviors and depression?
   a. Unsupportive behaviors can render social support ineffective.
   b. Social support is more important than unsupportive behaviors in buffering the effects of depression.
   c. Unsupportive behavior is not a risk for depression.
   d. Social support and unsupportive behaviors are not directly related to depression.

10. Select the symptom below which is not characteristic of a depressive disorder.
    a. feelings of guilt
    b. loss of interest
    c. difficulty concentrating
    d. impulsive decisions

11. The term "unipolar" describes
    a. persons who experience mania and depression.
    b. persons who experience depression only.
    c. persons whose grieving is extended.
    d. persons who experience delusions.

12. The term "dysthymia" means
    a. distorted body image.
    b. different moods.
    c. defective or diseased mood.
    d. chronic mood.

13. Epidemiological studies show an added risk of depression for people who
    a. lack social support.
    b. have overbearing social support.
    c. feel isolated and alone.
    d. both a and c

14. Which of the following is not a diagnostic criterion for dysthymic disorder?
    a. depressed mood most of the day, more days than not, for at least two years
    b. the disturbance is not part of a chronic psychotic disorder
    c. the disturbance is the result of some chemical substance or general medical condition
    d. poor appetite, overeating, insomnia, low energy, poor concentration, all coupled with depression

15. Tim reports feeling tired, sad, and experiencing difficulty eating. He also states that he derives no enjoyment out of life and that his problems began approximately 4 years ago. Tim would most probably be diagnosed as having
    a. cyclothymia.
    b. dysthymia.
    c. parasuicidal behavior.
    d. low libido.

16. The term "double depression" refers to
    a. the presence of dysthymic disorder and major depression, concurrently.
    b. the belief that postpartum depression is twice as high a risk for suicide as dysthymia.
    c. the presence of dysthymia in twins.
    d. bipolar II disorders.

17. In some major depressive episodes, the patient experiences depression and psychotic features. An example of this would be
    a. a man who thinks he is the devil.
    b. a woman who thinks she's a sinner.
    c. a woman who thinks she is a goddess.
    d. both a and c

18. Among the diagnostic criteria for major depressive disorder are
    a. no history of manic or hypomanic episodes.
    b. presence of major depressive episode with or without history of same.
    c. hallucinations and delusions.
    d. all of the above

19. The most widely held view regarding depression is that
    a. it results from an interaction of personal and situational factors.
    b. it is primarily genetic.
    c. it is a learned phenomenon.
    d. situational characteristics are less important than once thought.

20. Which of the following is not a neurotransmitter that has been associated with depression?
    a. GABA
    b. dopamine
    c. acetylcholine
    d. inderamine

21. Antidepressants work
    a. by increasing the flow of GABA.
    b. by destroying receptor sites.
    c. primarily through producing increased serotonin.
    d. by blocking the ability of MAO to change serotonin into another form.

22. Dysphoric mood and an inability to experience pleasure appear to be related to
    a. changes in blood flow in the cerebrum.
    b. different metabolic rates within the medulla.
    c. differences in metabolism in the frontal-temporal areas of the cortex.
    d. both a and c

23. Jacobs (1994) found that during REM sleep
    a. the serotonin neurons increase in transmission.
    b. the circadian rhythms in the brain cease.
    c. the limbic system suspends functioning.
    d. none of the above.

24. Which of the following is not a major sleep disturbance found in depression?
    a. shallow sleep
    b. fragmented sleep
    c. short sleep
    d. dream sleep

25. Freud believed that the depressed patient
    a. lacked adequate superego functioning.
    b. had a punishing superego.
    c. had a rigid ego.
    d. had an insatiable id.

26. _____ has been successfully treated with light therapy.
    a. Hormonal depression
    b. Bipolar depression
    c. Postpartum depression
    d. Seasonal affective disorder

27. A major assumption of interpersonal psychotherapy is
    a. that depression is caused by interpersonal conflict.
    b. that depression is best understood in an interpersonal context.
    c. that drugs are not necessary.
    d. none of the above.

28. Beck's concept of cognitive triad refers to thoughts of
    a. oneself, one's family, and the future.
    b. oneself, the situation, and the future.
    c. sadness, helplessness, and suicide.
    d. sadness, the situation, and the future.

29. A person who assumes, "I am the center of everyone's attention, especially of bad performances or personal attributes," is making which of the following cognitive errors according to Beck?
    a. overgeneralizing
    b. selective abstraction
    c. self-references
    d. dichotomous thinking

30. According to Beck's cognitive-distortion model
    a. depression is primarily a distortion of mood.
    b. depression is primarily a distortion of thinking.
    c. depression is primarily a distortion of mood and thought.
    d. none of the above

31. "Cognitive product variables" would include
    a. pessimistic expectations for the future.
    b. self-critical thoughts.
    c. negative self-attributions.
    d. all of the above.

32. Martin Seligman coined the term
    a. hopelessness depression.
    b. learned helplessness.
    c. suicidal depressive episode.
    d. schemata.

33. The loss of _____ is the focus of humanistic-existential therapists.
    a. self-esteem
    b. the real self
    c. a loved one
    d. hope

34. A woman in her 40s maintains multiple roles such as wife, mother, and employee. If this woman were to become depressed, Carl Rogers would assume
    a. she had a genetic predisposition for the disorder.
    b. there was a discrepancy between the ideal and real selves.
    c. she was fixated at the latency stage.
    d. she has depressive schemata.

35. Which of the following is not a side effect of tricyclics?
    a. rigidity
    b. constipation
    c. dry mouth
    d. ringing in the ears

36. Select the drug below which is thought to alleviate depression and have an effect on personality disorders.
    a. Elavil
    b. Tofranil
    c. Nardil
    d. none of the above

37. MAO inhibitors have potentially dangerous side effects because
    a. when combined with certain foods they form a toxic substance.
    b. they cause lethargy and have been implicated in auto accidents.
    c. they increase suicidal ideation.
    d. they can lead to psychotic delusions.

38. Select the statement below that is true of ECT.
    a. It is effective for mild to severe depressions.
    b. It results in permanent changes in brain structure.
    c. ECT is rarely used.
    d. ECT treatments prevent recurrence of depression.

39. Choose the option below that accurately identifies the process of cognitive-behavior therapy for depression.
    a. review, agenda, discussion, homework
    b. agenda, discussion, summary, homework
    c. homework, discussion, review, summary
    d. discussion, agenda development, summary, homework

40. The occurrence of _____ is a prerequisite for a diagnosis of bipolar disorder.
    a. delusions of persecution
    b. mania
    c. depression
    d. a sleep disorder

41. A cyclothymic disorder presents as a milder version of
    a. a bipolar I disorder.
    b. a dysthymic disorder.
    c. a bipolar II disorder.
    d. none of the above.

42. The poet Robert Lowell was affected by
    a. depression with psychotic features.
    b. hypomania.
    c. depression.
    d. bipolar disorder.

43. Linda is described as being elated, talkative and hyperactive on the weekends. Her sister recalled that Linda went on a shopping binge and purchased ten purses in the same color. The sister also noted that in a recent conversation, Linda had difficulty staying on a topic. Linda was most probably experiencing a
   a. depressive-anxiety disorder.
   b. hypomanic episode.
   c. depressive episode.
   d. sleep deprivation.

44. Research suggests that there is a linkage between chromosome(s) _____ and bipolar disorder.
   a. 16
   b. 12
   c. X
   d. all of the above

45. Bipolar is _____.
   a. an acute, curable disorder.
   b. a chronic, life-long disorder.
   c. a chronic, curable disorder.
   d. none of the above

46. The most common treatment of bipolar disorders is
   a. ECT.
   b. lithium.
   c. psychotherapy.
   d. none of the above

47. Suicide is
   a. the second leading cause of death on college campuses.
   b. not a significant factor in deaths of college students.
   c. on the decrease among high school students.
   d. both b and c

48. Of the following, which is not a factor associated with suicide in people with mood disorders?
   a. previous suicide attempts
   b. death of a loved one
   c. hopelessness
   d. anxiety

NEXT, TRY YOUR HAND AT TRUE/FALSE QUESTIONS.

TRUE/FALSE QUESTIONS

Indicate whether each statement is true or false. Check your answers at the end of this chapter.

T F 1. Almost one out of four hospitalized medical patients has depressive symptoms.

T F 2. Men are twice as likely as women to experience depression.

T F 3. The "pile-up" of stressful life events affects a person's long-term vulnerability to depression.

T F 4. Dysthymic disorder shows little variability with age.

T F 5. Fifty percent of people diagnosed with a major depressive episode will have at least one more episode in their lifetime.

T F 6. Depression is probably the result of a lack of certain chemical neurotransmitters at particular sites in the brain.

T F 7. Beck believes that the tendency to have negative cognitions may have a basis in childhood experiences.

T F 8. Depressed patients are not very realistic about their own social skills.

T F 9. It is believed that President Lincoln experienced bouts of major depression.

T F 10. Antidepressants are the drugs most commonly involved in prescription overdose.

T F 11. ECT is not very effective in treating severe depression.

T F 12. Recent research suggests that psychodynamic interpersonal therapy may be as effective as the cognitive approach.

T F 13. Genetic studies of families suggest that mood disorders have a genetic basis.

T F 14. Under 10 percent of successful suicides also involve another psychiatric condition.

T F 15. According to research by Young and others (1994), subjects who were low on Beck's Hopelessness Scale were at highest risk for suicide.

T F 16. A history of suicide among family members, previous suicide attempts, and a high level of anxiety are not factors related to an increased risk of suicide in those with mood disorders.

T F 17. The tendency to set unrealistically high standards for oneself is called perfectionism, and it is often an important factor in suicide.

T F 18. Parasuicide is a term used to describe suicidal behavior resulting immediately in death.

T   F   19. In the Western world, suicide is considered noble and honorable, while in the far east, such as Japan, suicide is considered a dishonorable act.

T   F   20. Postvention prevents survivors from experiencing the grief and feelings of guilt surrounding the suicide of a friend.

KEEP GOING.....MATCHING IS NEXT.

MATCHING

Match the following terms and names with definitions presented below. The answers are at the end of the chapter.

a. postvention
b. seasonal affective disorder
c. electroconvulsive shock therapy
d. cognitive triad
e. unipolar disorder
f. schemata

g. Bowlby
h. social skills training
i. lithium
j. dysthymia
k. parasuicide
l. hopelessness

_____ 1. an important theme for those who bear suicidal preoccupations

_____ 2. believed depression was a complex reaction to loss

_____ 3. group discussion and intervention following a suicide

_____ 4. includes individuals who have either had one or more episodes of depression but no manic episodes

_____ 5. tend to involve less lethal means than suicides

_____ 6. drug used to treat bipolar disorder I

_____ 7. has been treated using light therapy

_____ 8. focuses on appropriate behavior

_____ 9. involves passing electrical current through patient's head

_____ 10. negative thoughts about self, situation, and future

_____ 11. Beck identified these as thought patterns

_____ 12. "defective or diseased mood"

GOOD, NOW CHECK YOUR ANSWERS. WHEN YOU'RE DONE GRADING YOURSELF, COVER YOUR ANSWERS, AND START ALL OVER AGAIN. KEEP TESTING YOURSELF UNTIL YOU CAN ANSWER THEM ALL CORRECTLY.

CHAPTER 11 ANSWER KEY
Multiple Choice

1.	b		25.	b
2.	b		26.	d
3.	a		27.	b
4.	d		28.	b
5.	a		29.	c
6.	d		30.	b
7.	c		31.	d
8.	b		32.	b
9.	a		33.	a
10.	d		34.	b
11.	b		35.	a
12.	c		36.	d
13.	d		37.	a
14.	c		38.	c
15.	b		39.	b
16.	a		40.	b
17.	d		41.	a
18.	d		42.	d
19.	a		43.	b
20.	d		44.	d
21.	d		45.	b
22.	d		46.	b
23.	d		47.	a
24.	d		48.	b

True/False

1.	T	11.	F
2.	F	12.	T
3.	F	13.	T
4.	T	14.	F
5.	T	15.	T
6.	T	16.	F
7.	T	17.	T
8.	F	18.	F
9.	T	19.	F
10.	T	20.	T

Matching

1. l
2. g
3. a
4. e
5. k
6. i
7. b
8. h
9. c
10. d
11. f
12. j

Chapter 12
SCHIZOPHRENIA AND OTHER PSYCHOTIC DISORDERS

CHAPTER OVERVIEW

The concept of schizophrenia is highlighted in the present chapter. Definition and characteristic symptoms are presented along with incidence rates, theoretical positions, and historical perspectives. The subtypes of disorganized, catatonic, undifferentiated, and paranoid schizophrenia are explained and prognostic factors evaluated. Therapeutic approaches such as antipsychotic drugs, skills training, family interventions, and community support are highlighted, and their effectiveness summarized. The results of long-term outcome studies of schizophrenic prognosis are also evaluated.

LEARNING OBJECTIVES

After studying this chapter, you should be able to answer these questions:
1. What are the features of a psychotic order?
2. What are the DSM-IV-TR categories of psychotic disorders?
3. What are the four subtypes of schizophrenia and what are the distinguishing characteristics of each?
4. What is the difference between positive and negative symptoms of schizophrenia?
5. What causes schizophrenia?
6. What do family, twin, and adoption studies tell us about vulnerability to schizophrenia?
7. What do community factors and stress contibute to the development of schizophrenia?
8. What problems of attention and cognition are markers for schizophrenia?
9. What are some adverse side effects from taking antipsychotic medications?
10. Why are skills training, family programs, and community support important for people with schizophrenia and their families?
11. What is the long-term prognosis for people with schizophrenia?
12. What are the characteristics of schizoaffective disorder?
13. What is the difference between delusions in schizophrenia and in a delusional disorder?
14. What is a shared psychotic disorder?

CHAPTER OUTLINE

1. Psychotic Disorders (p.373)

Psychotic disorders are typically characterized by bizarre thinking and/or behavior. There is a marked departure from reality in persons with psychotic disorders.

2. Schizophrenia (p.374)

Schizophrenia is not a single disorder. Instead, it is a cluster of disorders that are grouped together because they frequently appear together and because there is not yet enough understanding of the critical factors that differentiate them.

A. DSM-IV-TR Subtypes of Schizophrenia

Classification of schizophrenia by subtype is only moderately stable, as subtypes tend to fluctuate as the individual's symptoms fluctuate and the schizophrenia progresses. Currently, the subtype categories are Paranoid, marked by delusions and sustained extreme suspiciousness, Catatonic, marked by psychomotor disturbances ranging from immobility to extreme agitation, and Disorganized, marked by incoherence, extreme disorganization in thought and behavior, and flat or wildly inappropriate and labile affect.

B. Positive and Negative Symptoms

The more valid grouping of symptoms of schizophrenia are into two broad categories; positive symptoms and negative symptoms. Positive symptoms reflect a distortion or excess of normal function and tend to be most frequent in the early episodes. Negative symptoms reflect behavioral deficits or the loss or decrease of normal function. To put it quite simply, positive symptoms are things that are present which should not be, and negative symptoms represent things that should be present but are not.

3. Schizophrenic Spectrum Disorders (p.383)

These are disorders that resemble schizophrenia but do not meet the diagnostic criteria for schizophrenia. Such disorders include some personality disorders, particularly Schizotypal Personality Disorder. Other personality disorders from the odd and eccentric cluster, schizoid and paranoid personality disorders are found with more frequency in family members of persons with schizophrenia.

4. The Development of Schizophrenia (p.383)

The causes are not known, but there is evidence to suggest that schizophrenia is produced by the interaction of vulnerability factors and environmental stress.

A. Genetic Factors

There is a wealth of evidence supporting the role of heredity in the development of schizophrenia, although specific modes of genetic transmission have not been identified. Whether or not a person with particular genetic makeup experiences a disorder in the schizophrenic spectrum depends on the influence of physical and psychosocial factors in the environment.

B. Prenatal Factors

Vulnerability to schizophrenia has been linked by maternal exposure to viruses and other stressors during certain periods of prenatal development, specifically during the second trimester of fetal development. The neural development model of schizophrenia suggests that persons who develop schizophrenia may, because of disruptions in fetal development during the second trimester, may have inadequately developed brains. This inadequacy may involve a disruption of synaptic pruning, or an inadequate number of dendritic branches.

5. Studying Vulnerability to Schizophrenia (p.392)

In addition to the biological factors discussed thus far, researchers have also looked to the environment as a contributing factor in the development of schizophrenia.

A. Family Studies

Studies of families in which both parents have schizophrenia indicate a significantly higher risk for development of schizophrenia in the children. Equally interesting, however, is the finding that about 25 percent of those children showed no type of disordered behavior, startling because of the degree of stress involved in living in a household with schizophrenic parents.

B. Twin Studies

Twin studies have indicated that although the concordance rate for monozygotic twins is significant, it is still less than 50 percent, meaning that heredity alone is not responsible for schizophrenia.

C. Adoption Studies

There are two primary types of adoption studies: those that compare adopted children whose biological parents were diagnosed with schizophrenia with adopted children whose parents did not have this disorder, and those studies examining the incidence of schizophrenia in biological and adoptive families of adopted children who develop schizophrenia.

D. Vulnerability and Adoptive Family Characteristics

Study results indicate that healthy family environments protect children who are at risk for developing schizophrenia. The incidence of psychotic disorders is greatly reduced when vulnerable children are reared in psychologically healthy families.

E. High-Risk Studies and the Search for Markers

Knowledge of the markers that predict vulnerability or risk can help to develop primary prevention, or interventions that can help keep the disorder from developing.

6. Therapeutic Approaches (p.398)

Biological, behavioral, and family-centered approaches appear to show the most promise in helping to deal with the symptoms of schizophrenia.

A. Antipsychotic Drugs

These are the mainstay of treatment for schizophrenia, although they have unpleasant side effects and can cause permanent damage to some organs such as the liver after long-term use.

B. Psychosocial approaches

Formal psychotherapy is not effective; however, some interventions such as problem solving, reality testing, psychoeducation, and some behavioral techniques can be helpful in improving adherence to medications, improving social functioning, and preventing relapse.

C. Family Programs

These interventions include education about schizophrenia, information about treatments, identification of probable causes, problem solving, and crisis management skills for family members.

D. Community Support

Halfway houses or group homes, daycare facilities, and mental health clinics can be sources of both treatment and practical help.

E. Combined Treatment Approaches

Preferred treatment includes both medication and psychosocial interventions, although in reality it is rare that this happens.

F. Long-Term Outcome Studies

Most studies focus on a lessening of symptoms and psychosocial adjustment between relapses. Studies have also shown that changes based on medication last a year or less after hospitalization, while changes based on intense psychosocial intervention were still apparent after several years.

7. Other Psychotic Disorders (p.407)

A. Schizoaffective Disorder

This refers to the collection of symptoms of some individuals that do not quite fit into either the category of mood disorder or the category of schizophrenia. The individual experiences major mood disturbance during periods of schizophrenia-like symptoms as well as when such symptoms are absent.

B. Delusional Disorder

The prominent feature of delusional disorder is delusional thinking, however, the delusions are not as bizarre as those in schizophrenia.

C. Shared Psychotic Disorder

Quite rare, this disorder involves the transfer of delusions from one person to another. The two people usually are from the same family and live together in social isolation. The more dominant of the two is the one who holds the beliefs and the secondary person then takes on the beliefs of the first.

TIPS FOR TESTING YOURSELF

Write each of the following key words and concepts on one side of an index card. Then, for each, look up the correct definition in your textbook. Write the definition on the opposite side of the corresponding index card. Now, you have flash cards to study. Keep the cards with you and whenever you have a few minutes, pull them out and test yourself. When you are studying with a study partner, you can test each other. You can also share the duties of looking up the definitions and writing them on the cards. Study them a little each day.

KEY TERMS AND CONCEPTS

psychotic disorder (p.373)

schizophrenia (p.374)

positive symptoms (p.378)

negative symptoms (p.378)

delusion (p.378)

hallucination (p.380)

perseverative speech (p.381)

monogenic model (p.385)

polygenic model (p.385)

multifactorial polygenic model (p.385)

dominant gene (p.385)

recessive gene (p.385)

index case (p.384)

schizophrenic spectrum disorders (p.383)

synaptic pruning (p.389)

neurodevelopmental model of schizophrenia (p.389)

physical anomalies (p.390)

dopamine hypothesis (p.391)

cerebral ventricles (p.390)

assortative mating (p.392)

dyzygotic twins (p.393)

vulnerability(pp.392, 394)

markers (p.395)

high risk study (p.395)

Continuous Performance Test (p.397)

smooth pursuit eye movements (p.397)

prodromal symptoms (p.398)

tardive dyskenesia (p.400)

expressed emotion (p.405)

schizoaffective disorder (p.407)

delusional disorder (p.408)

shared psychotic disorder (folie a deux) (p.408)

SHORT ANSWER ESSAY QUESTIONS
In developing answers for the following questions, turn to the section of your chapter that covers the pertinent material. Read each section thoroughly before attempting to frame your answer.

1. What is a psychosis? List the types of disorders included in this category.

2. Discuss the epidemiological research findings on schizophrenia and the economic impact of the disorder.

3. List and briefly describe the major characteristics of a schizophrenic disorder. Differentiate positive from negative symptoms.

4. What specific subtypes of schizophrenic disorder does DSM-IV recognize? List the unique characteristics of each subtype.

5. What were Kraepelin's and Bleuler's definitions of schizophrenia? How were their perspectives different? What are first and second rank symptoms?

6. Define the concepts "positive" and "negative" symptoms. How are these used in research?

7. What are schizophrenic spectrum disorders?

8. Present the genetic and biological perspectives on schizophrenic disorders.

9. What methods are used to study genetic and environmental factors in schizophrenia?

10. How do vulnerability, resilience, and stress figure into the complexity of schizophrenia? What information do studies of high-risk factors contribute on the topic?

11. What role does heredity play in schizophrenic tendencies? Explain the Mendelian pattern of heredity, and differentiate between the monogenic model and the polygenic model.

12. How are schizotypal personality disorders, paranoid personality disorders, and schizoaffective disorders similar? What factors differentiates them from one another?

13. What role might brain structure play in the development of a schizophrenic disorder?

14. How are family studies important to the diagnosis of paranoid schizophrenia? Twin studies? Adoption studies?

15. What are the disadvantages present in traditional antipsychotic drugs, and how do clozapine and risperidone solve these problems?

16. In treating schizophrenic patients to cope, name five skills and goals for medication management and four skills and goals for symptom management.

17. List and explain some remedial strategies for coping with the cognitive deficits of schizophrenia.

18. Catalog and explain the scales of expressed emotion (EE).

19. What do long-term outcome studies of those people diagnosed with schizophrenia tell us about the ability to recover from or adapt to it?

TIPS FOR TESTING YOURSELF

The following sections of self-test questions will test your understanding of the material presented in the chapter. On a separate piece of paper, write the correct answer for each item in the section, then compare your answers with those at the end of the chapter. After you have graded yourself, turn to the chapter and look up the questions you missed. Write out the correct answers. Then test yourself again. Continue doing so until you can answer all the questions correctly.

MULTIPLE CHOICE
1. Schizophrenic disorders are a type of
   a. mood disorder.
   b. insanity.
   c. organic brain syndrome.
   d. psychosis.

2. About _____ percent of the population will be diagnosed as having a schizophrenic disorder in any given year.
   a. 1
   b. 5
   c. 10
   d. 15

3. Individuals diagnosed with a schizophrenic disorder
   a. consume 2 ½ percent of total annual health care expenditures in the U.S.
   b. constitute 10 percent of the permanently and totally disabled population.
   c. make-up 14 percent of the homeless population in large cities.
   d. all of the above

4. Which of the characteristics below is not a symptom of schizophrenia?
   a. changes in perception of the environment
   b. difficulty in differentiating oneself from the environment
   c. a change in motivation
   d. pathological lying

5. Often, a family member may notice behavioral changes in a person before the active phase of the schizophrenic episode begins. These symptoms may include impairment in functioning, odd beliefs, lack of interest, and
   a. loss of memory.
   b. a decreased concern for personal hygiene.
   c. bulimic behavior.
   d. waxy flexibility.

6. Select the disorder below that is not a principal psychotic disorder.
   a. delusional disorder
   b. substance-induced psychotic disorder
   c. schizophreniform disorder
   d. paranoid personality disorder

7. Which of the following represents a positive symptom for schizophrenia?
   a. flattened affect
   b. apathy
   c. bizarre behavior
   d. poverty of speech

8. A delusion is
   a. a faulty interpretation of reality.
   b. not found in a psychotic disorder.
   c. never found in schizophrenia.
   d. none of the above.

9. Joe attends a rock concert and is struck by the fact that the singer is referring to him in a number of songs. Joe's belief would be considered a
   a. tangential delusion.
   b. command delusion.
   c. referential delusion.
   d. residual delusion.

10. C. T. Harrison, author of an article in *Military Review*, was found
    a. to have been misdiagnosed.
    b. to be diagnosed as a paranoid schizophrenic.
    c. to be competent to stand trial.
    d. both a and c

11. Unlike hallucinations experienced in delirium in other disorders, schizophrenics
    a. experience them in a clear, conscious state.
    b. rarely experience auditory hallucinations.
    c. primarily experience tactile hallucinations.
    d. hallucinations are not somatic.

12. The theory that intelligence may play a critical role in hallucinations is proposed by
    a. the psychodynamic position.
    b. the cognitive advocates.
    c. the dopamine hypothesis.
    d. rational-emotive proponents.

13. The therapist greets his client by stating, "Good morning, did you sleep well last night?" The client responds, "Yes, but night is when the moon is blue, and sadness brings with it tears of rage, like a lion who stalks the forest to kill." The client's response to this therapist's greeting is most likely due to
    a. hallucinations.
    b. loosening of associations.
    c. delusions.
    d. poverty of content.

14. When we discuss disorganized behavior as it pertains to schizophrenic disorder, we are referring to
    a. problems carrying out activities of daily living.
    b. impaired social functioning.
    c. changes in goal-directed behavior.
    d. all of the above.

15. _____ denotes the lack of movement of a person diagnosed with schizophrenic disorder.
    a. Catatonic rigidity
    b. Catatonic static
    c. Catatonic inexcitement
    d. Catatonic posture

16. Which of the following is not characteristic of a schizophrenic's impaired social functioning?
    a. emotional detachment
    b. violations of personal space
    c. inappropriate sexual behaviors
    d. none of the above

17. According to Baron and others (1992), negative symptoms appear to be associated with
    a. a high rate of schizophrenic concordance in other family members.
    b. nongenetic causes for schizophrenia.
    c. a genetic basis for schizophrenia.
    d. an early onset of schizophrenia.

18. Select the term below that is not a DSM-IV subtype of schizophrenic disorder.
    a. paranoid
    b. undifferentiated
    c. hebephrenic
    d. disorganized

19. Marty believes that the FBI has planted a radio transmitter in her brain. She claims they are transmitting her thoughts to their local field office. Marty would most probably be diagnosed as a(n)
    a. catatonic schizophrenic.
    b. undifferentiated schizophrenic.
    c. paranoid schizophrenic.
    d. disorganized schizophrenic.

20. Schneider emphasized
    a. the importance of developing a reliable classification system.
    b. the importance of adequate treatment for the mentally ill.
    c. the nature of early childhood experiences in the development of first rank symptoms.
    d. the transitional nature of first and second rank symptoms.

21. _____ schizophrenics behave in a childish manner and their behavior appears to be aimless.
    a. Paranoid
    b. Undifferentiated
    c. Simple
    d. Disorganized

22. The risk rate for identical twins to develop schizophrenia is
    a. exactly 100 percent.
    b. no more than 22 percent.
    c. slightly below 50 percent.
    d. not presently known.

23. The Genain sibling case is illustrative of
    a. early childhood sexual abuse and its subsequent consequences.
    b. a genetic basis for schizophrenia.
    c. the role of NIMH in treating schizophrenia.
    d. the relationship between substance abuse and schizophrenia.

24. The study of schizophrenic disorders by genetic theorists has led them to favor a _____ model.
    a. monogenic
    b. multifactorial polygenic
    c. polygenic
    d. penetrant

25. The results of using scanning techniques to study the brains of schizophrenics have led to the observation that schizophrenics
    a. have significantly larger cerebral ventricles than normals.
    b. have more head trauma than normals.
    c. have brains smaller in actual size than normals.
    d. have less cerebrospinal fluid than normals.

26. The dopamine hypothesis posits that
    a. an excess of dopamine at certain synapses is associated with schizophrenia.
    b. the schizophrenic's brain lacks dopamine at certain synapses.
    c. the development of schizophrenia is related to a deficiency in the number of receptor sites in the brain.
    d. none of the above

27. The studies on D3 as a marker for schizophrenia have
    a. been encouraging to geneticists.
    b. been confounding in their designs that render them uninterpretable.
    c. not supported it as a marker for schizophrenia.
    d. provided support for its association with schizophrenia.

28. In an NIMH study of identical twins and schizophrenia (Torrey et al., 1994), differences in behavior between twins was noted as early as age
    a. two.
    b. five.
    c. eight.
    d. thirteen.

29. The studies of adoption in Denmark tend to suggest a(n)_____ view of schizophrenic disorders.
    a. environmental
    b. genetic
    c. transpersonal
    d. discordant

30. The diathesis-stress model of schizophrenia hypothesizes
    a. that stress alone is enough to produce a schizophrenic disorder.
    b. that genetics alone will result in schizophrenia.
    c. that schizophrenia is the result of an interaction between genetics and environmental stressors.
    d. none of the above.

31. A Swedish study (Lewis et al., 1992) lends support to
    a. the increased-stress theory.
    b. the social-selection theory.
    c. the foster-parent theory.
    d. the immunological theory.

32. The search for early markers for schizophrenia suggests that all of the following are indicators except
    a. impaired attention.
    b. attention dysfunction.
    c. attentional dysfunction associated with adjustment problems in adolescence and adulthood.
    d. overinvolvement in fantasy.

33. Communication deviance is defined as
    a. the inability to maintain a shared focus of attention during interactions.
    b. the inability to actively express hostile feelings.
    c. the inability to think logically.
    d. the inability to actively participate in an ongoing conversation.

NEXT, TRY YOUR HAND AT TRUE/FALSE QUESTIONS.

TRUE/FALSE QUESTIONS

Indicate whether each statement is true or false. Check your answers at the end of this chapter.

T   F   1. In someone experiencing a schizophrenic disorder, a good predictor of outcome is the person's level of adjustment prior to the onset of symptoms.

T   F   2. The annual total treatment cost for schizophrenia in the U.S. is $3 million.

T   F   3. A schizophrenic may experience foul odors coming from their bodies.

T   F   4. According to the psychodynamic perspective, hallucinations represent the freeing of unconscious information.

T   F   5. Schizophrenic behavior is often difficult to predict.

T   F   6. Paranoid thinking does not tend to fall along a continuum.

T   F   7. The cause of schizophrenia is not known.

T   F   8. There is evidence to suggest that if a pregnant mother has influenza, the offspring has an increased risk of schizophrenia.

T   F   9. Low doses of amphetamines can worsen the symptoms of schizophrenic disorders.

T   F   10. Assortative mating refers to marrying someone with dissimilar characteristics.

KEEP GOING.....MATCHING IS NEXT.

MATCHING
Match the following terms with information provided below. The answers may be found at the end of the chapter.

a. Kraepelin
b. D1, D2, D3, D4
c. negative symptoms
d. residual type
e. waxy flexibility
f. cross-fostering study
g. social-selection theory
h. disordered speech
i. schizophrenic spectrum disorders
j. assortative mating
k. expressed emotion (EE)

l. the dopamine hypothesis
m. diathesis
n. increased-stress theory
o. CPT
p. problem-solving skills
q. polygenic model
r. risperidone
s. emotional overinvolvement
t. smooth-pursuit eye movement
u. tardive dyskinesia
v. second-rank symptoms

_____ 1. occurs when a person tracks a slow-moving object

_____ 2. focuses on the amount of stress experienced by people in different socio-economic classes

_____ 3. alternative solutions to a crisis or difficulty

_L_ 4. states that an excess of dopamine at certain brain synapses relates to schizophrenic disorder

_____ 5. measure of attitudes expressed by family members when talking about a person whose behavior is disturbed

_____ 6. symptoms sometimes found in other psychotic disorders

_____ 7. loss or decrease in normal functions

_____ 8. loosening of associations

_____ 9. dementia praecox

_____ 10. has negative (or some mild) but not positive symptoms

_____ 11. arm remains in position it is placed

_____ 12. mating with similar partner

_____ 13. includes schizotypal and paranoid personality disorder

_____ 14. dopamine receptor sites in brain

_____ 15. study involving foster children of adoptive, schizophrenic parents

_____ 16. poor coping skills lead to a socioeconomic decline

_____ 17. skin color and weight can be predicted from it

_____ 18. simply put, a predisposition

_____ 19. one of the new generation of antipsychotic drugs

____ 20. a test measuring sustained attention of up to 20 minutes

____ 21. involuntary motion of the lips, tongue, legs, or body

____22. an exaggerated emotional response to an illness

GOOD, NOW CHECK YOUR ANSWERS. WHEN YOU'RE DONE GRADING YOURSELF,
COVER YOUR ANSWERS, AND START ALL OVER AGAIN. KEEP TESTING YOURSELF
UNTIL YOU CAN ANSWER THEM ALL CORRECTLY.

CHAPTER 12 ANSWER KEY

Multiple Choice

1.	d		18.	c
2.	a		19.	c
3.	d		20.	a
4.	d		21.	d
5.	b		22.	c
6.	d		23.	b
7.	c		24.	b
8.	a		25.	a
9.	c		26.	a
10.	b		27.	c
11.	a		28.	b
12.	b		29.	b
13.	b		30.	c
14.	d		31.	a
15.	a		32.	d
16.	d		33.	a
17.	b			

True/False

1.	T
2.	F
3.	T
4.	T
5.	T
6.	F
7.	T
8.	T
9.	T
10.	F

Matching

1. t
2. n
3. p
4. l
5. k
6. v
7. c
8. h
9. a
10. d
11. e
12. j
13. I
14. b
15. f
16. g
17. q
18. m
19. r
20. o
21. u
22. s

Chapter 13
COGNITIVE IMPAIRMENT DISORDERS

CHAPTER OVERVIEW
Disorders of the brain leading to cognitive, affective, and behavioral problems are discussed in this portion of the text. This is one of the few clusters of disorders for which there are specific behavioral symptoms and known causative factors. Memory impairment, disorientation, and confusion are prominent features of all of the disorders discussed. In addition to assessing vulnerability for brain disorders, techniques for determining cognitive dysfunction will be explored. The characteristics of major brain syndromes are reviewed as well as actual/potential causes discussed. Lastly, the contributions of psychological treatment interventions for brain-disordered patients are explored.

LEARNING OBJECTIVES
After studying this chapter, you should be able to answer these questions:
1. What areas of brain research are especially important in understanding normal and abnormal behavior?
2. What factors influence vulnerability to brain disorders?
3. How is brain damage assessed?
4. What is the mental status examination?
5. What is neuropsychology?
6. What are the distinguishing characteristics of delirium and dementia?
7. What are the characteristics, causes, and effects of Alzheimer's disease?
8. What is Pick's disease and how is it diagnosed?
9. What is Huntington's disease and where does it come from?
10. What are the symptoms and course of Parkinson's disease?
11. What are the cognitive and behavioral consequences of brain traumas like injuries, tumors, and infections?
12. What are the three classifications of brain injuries?
13. What are the defining features of amnestic disorders?
14. What are the causes and effects of cerebrovascular accidents (CVAs) or strokes?
15. What causes Korsakoff's syndrome?
16. What are the main types of epilepsy and how are they treated?
17. Why is it important to approach brain disorders from an integrative perspective?

CHAPTER OUTLINE
1. The Brain: An Interactional Perspective (p.414)
    Brain function, whether normal or abnormal, is the result of the total interaction between the structural and neurochemical makeup of the brain and the social, environmental, and behavioral experiences of the individual.

    A. Vulnerability to Brain Disorders
    Factors that determine the degree of vulnerability to brain disorders include age, social support, stress, personality factors, and physical condition.

B. Assessing Brain Damage

The task of identifying behavior changes associated with brain damage is important, but made complicated by the fact that damage to particular areas of the brain can have diverse effects. Procedures used to assess the effects of brain damage include mental status examination, neuropsychological testing, as well as a variety of brain imaging techniques that help pinpoint the areas of damage.

2. Delirium (p.418)

The symptoms of delirium develop over a short period of time and include cognitive impairment, disorientation, and confusion, along with altered consciousness. Delirium can be caused by disease, systemic infection, intoxication, or withdrawal from an addictive substance.

A. Delirium Tremens

An extreme example of delirium, delirium tremens result from prolonged addiction to alcohol and usually occur after the person has stopped drinking. The mechanism underlying DTs is poorly understood, but appears to be the result of interference of alcohol with brain metabolism.

3. Dementia (p.419)

The predominant feature of dementia is a gradual loss of intellectual abilities that interferes with social or occupational functioning. Memory impairment, loss of judgment, language and motor problems, changes in personality, confusion, and behavior changes all are symptoms. Onset is insidious and the course is gradual and progressive.

A. Alzheimer's Disease

Marked by memory lapses and confusion, dementia of the Alzheimer's type severely impairs short-term memory, leaving long term memory relatively intact at first. This is a progressive and eventually fatal deterioration that occurs as more and more of the brain becomes involved.

B. Pick's Disease

The symptoms of Pick's disease are so similar to those of Alzheimer's that it takes an autopsy to tell the two apart. Pick's is most likely to develop between the ages of 60 and 70, after which the risk decreases.

C. Huntington's Disease

This is a rare heredity disease transmitted by a single gene and characterized by progressive degeneration of the brain tissue. The disease involves four types of symptoms including dementia, irritability and apathy, depression and anxiety, and hallucinations and delusions.

D. Parkinson's Disease

Parkinson's disease may develop by the age of 50 and is characterized by tremor, rigidity, loss of vocal power, social withdrawal, reduced intellectual abilities, and difficulty coping with problems. Parkinson's has been associated with reduced levels of the neurotransmitter dopamine. Treatment has traditionally consisted of the drug L-dopa; however, gene therapy is now being evaluated as a viable treatment.

E. Brain Trauma: Injuries, Tumors, and Infections

Injury to the brain is a common cause of mental disorders. Severe brain injury can cause profound cognitive and behavioral problems, but even mild to moderate injuries can produce lasting disabilities as well. Brain injuries are grouped into concussions, contusions, or lacerations. Diagnosing the extent of brain injury can be difficult and although some head injuries lead to specific losses in functioning, other causes of brain damage such as tumors or infections result in more diffuse or generalized loss of function.

4. Amnestic Disorders (p.433)

Amnestic disorders are disturbances of memory due to either the effects of a medical condition or a substance.

5. The Diversity of Cognitive Impairment Disorders (p.433)

There is a wide diversity of impairments resulting from a wide variety of insults to the brain such as cerebral vascular accidents, vascular dementia, Korsakoff's syndrome, and epilepsy.

A. Cerebrovascular Disorders

These include cerebrovascular accidents, or strokes, vascular dementia characterized by series of smaller strokes having a cumulative effect on the brain.

B. Korsakoff's Syndrome

Korsakoff's syndrome results from a combination of a deficiency of vitamin B1 and alcoholic drinking. It is irreversible and is characterized by the loss of both recent and past memories as well as perceptual deficits and confabulation.

C. Epilepsy

Epilepsy is a disturbance of brain function which is the result of transient electrical activity of the brain and culminates in a seizure. Approximately 30 to 50 percent of persons with epilepsy experience psychological difficulties.

6. An Integrative Approach to Brain Disorders (p.435)

The effects of brain injury on behavior are influenced by the person's history and personality, environmental and social factors, as well as the person's physical makeup. In addition, the person's responses to the injury and its consequences can have a further impact on both the degree of impairment and the degree of recovery.

TIPS FOR TESTING YOURSELF

Write each of the following key words and concepts on one side of an index card. Then, for each, look up the correct definition in your textbook. Write the definition on the opposite side of the corresponding index card. Now, you have flash cards to study. Keep the cards with you and whenever you have a few minutes, pull them out and test yourself. When you are studying with a study partner, you can test each other. You can also share the duties of looking up the definitions and writing them on the cards. Study them a little each day.

KEY TERMS AND CONCEPTS
mental-status examination (p.416)
neuropsychology (p.417)
neuropsychological testing (p.417)
brain imaging (p.417)
delirium (p.418)
delirium tremens (p.419)
dementia (p.420)
confabulation (p.420)
Alzheimer's disease (p.422)
Pick's disease (p.428)
Huntington's disease (p.428)
autosomal dominant disorder (p.428)
GABA (gamma-aminobutyric acid) (p.429)
Parkinson's disease (p.430)
brain tumor (p.430)
HIV-associated cognitive impairment (p.431)
general paresis (p.432)
amnestic disorders (p.433)
cerebrovascular accident (p.434)
stroke (p.434)
vascular dementia (p.434)
Korsakoff's syndrome (p.434)
epilepsy (p.434)
grand mal seizure (p.434)
petit mal seizure (p.435)
psychomotor epilepsy (p.435)

SHORT ANSWER ESSAY QUESTIONS

In developing answers for the following questions, turn to the section of your chapter that covers the pertinent material. Read each section thoroughly before attempting to frame your answer.

1. What are the factors that influence vulnerability to brain damage and brain disorders? Is an interactional perspective important when considering brain disorders?

2. What are the major procedures used to assess brain damage? What factors are assessed in a mental status examination?

3. List the deficits associated with delirium. What are the four organic causes of delirium?

4. Describe the symptoms of dementia. Differentiate between senile dementia and pre-senile dementia.

5. What is Alzheimer's disease? Explain its potential physiological causes. Is this disease a major health threat for the U.S.? Describe the impact Alzheimer's disease has on family members and treatment interventions for the patient.

6. Differentiate the following disorders: Pick's disease, Huntington's disease, and Parkinson's disease.

7. What is HIV-associated cognitive impairment? General paresis is the result of what untreated medical condition?

8. Describe the dimensions of amnestic disorders. Discuss both vascular dementia and Korsakoff's syndrome.

9. Describe the differences among the following disorders: grand mal seizures, petit mal epilepsy, and psychomotor epilepsy. How is epilepsy treated?

10. How have the psychodynamic, behavioral, cognitive, and community perspectives contributed to treatment of brain disorders?

TIPS FOR TESTING YOURSELF

The following sections of self-test questions will test your understanding of the material presented in the chapter. On a separate piece of paper, write the correct answer for each item in the section, then compare your answers with those at the end of the chapter. After you have graded yourself, turn to the chapter and look up the questions you missed. Write out the correct answers. Then test yourself again. Continue doing so until you can answer all the questions correctly.

MULTIPLE CHOICE

1. Select the factor below that does not influence vulnerability to brain damage and brain disorders.
   a. personal variables
   b. intelligence
   c. social support
   d. age

2. _____ can often ease adjustment to a brain condition.
   a. A supportive physician
   b. Aphasia
   c. Social support
   d. Social isolation and total bed rest

3. In order to assess damage or deterioration of the brain, which of the options below may be used?
   a. general physical evaluation
   b. mental-status examination
   c. PET scan
   d. all of the above

4. Which of the following is not generally a part of a mental status exam?
   a. language
   b. sleep habits
   c. mood
   d. general appearance

5. Which of the following is able to image the brain in all planes?
   a. a PET scan
   b. a CT scan
   c. an MRI
   d. an x-ray

6. The most common syndromes involving disorders of the brain and cognitive impairment include disturbances of memory, imagination, thought processing, problem-solving skills, judgment, and
   a. identity.
   b. perception.
   c. gait.
   d. fine motor coordination.

7. A person going through severe withdrawal from alcohol is likely to experience
   a. amnesia.
   b. Pick's disease.
   c. delirium.
   d. primary degeneration dementia.

8. Which of the following is not one of the general organic causes of delirium?
   a. brain disease
   b. confabulation
   c. intoxication
   d. substance withdrawal

9. Delirium tremens are characterized by
   a. tremors.
   b. prolonged sleep patterns.
   c. visual hallucinations.
   d. both a and c

10. Which of the following is true about dementia?
    a. Personality changes are rare
    b. Dementia may be reversible
    c. Delirium seems to prevent dementia
    d. Dementia often involves rapid deterioration

11. Senile dementia occurs in people
    a. under the age of 70.
    b. under the age of 65.
    c. over the age of 65.
    d. over the age of 70.

12. In dementia syndromes, confabulations refers to _____ when the person's memory has lapsed.
    a. being unable to recall the names of common objects
    b. filling in memory gaps with inaccurate details
    c. reliving earlier memories
    d. none of the above

13. Martha is an eighty-two-year-old grandmother who was found wandering down the highway by the local police. She did not know where she lived or the date or time when asked. When the police asked her to come to the local hospital, Martha began screaming hostile insults. Upon arriving at the hospital, Martha was most probably diagnosed as having
    a. Pick's disease.
    b. Alzheimer's disease.
    c. multi-infarct dementia.
    d. HIV-associated cognitive impairment.

14. Alzheimer's victims constitute over _____ of all people in nursing homes.
    a. 50 percent
    b. 70 percent
    c. 20 percent
    d. 10 percent

15. The development of plaques and clumps in the brain is associated with
    a. Alzheimer's disease.
    b. multi-infarct dementia.
    c. organic hallucinosis.
    d. Huntington's chorea.

16. The only way to be absolutely certain that a person has Alzheimer's disease is to
    a. carefully conduct an in-depth mental status examination.
    b. perform a PT scan.
    c. perform a PT scan and confirm the diagnosis with a follow-up MRI evaluation.
    d. examine the brain after death.

17. _____ is associated with a particular form of brain atrophy and its symptoms are very similar to those of Alzheimer's disease.
    a. Epilepsy
    b. General paresis
    c. Huntington's disease
    d. none of the above

18. The folk singer and composer Woody Guthrie who died at age fifty-five in 1967 after being misdiagnosed an alcoholic was really suffering from
    a. epilepsy.
    b. Korsakoff's syndrome.
    c. pellagra.
    d. Huntington's chorea.

19. By studying the blood of Iris del Valle Soto and other members of her family, researchers
    a. have identified the location on chromosome pair 4 where the Huntington gene is located.
    b. have developed a diagnostic genetic test to screen for Huntington's disease.
    c. have shown that Huntington's disease is not genetically transmitted.
    d. both a and b

20. In patients with _____, the most prominent symptoms are dementia, irritability, depression, hallucinations, delusions, and choreiform movements.
    a. Huntington's disease
    b. Pick's disease
    c. HIV-associated cognitive impairment
    d. Alzheimer's disease

21. Research on Parkinson's disease
    a. suggests that brain cell implantation may be an effective treatment.
    b. raises ethical issues by considering "sham surgery."
    c. focuses on increased production of dopamine.
    d. all of the above.

22. Traumatic neurosis refers to
    a. reactions that come after a startling event.
    b. a neurotic who has a psychogenic head injury.
    c. the damaging of neurons due to head injury.
    d. PTSD when it occurs because of head injury.

23. Major tears or ruptures in the brain tissue are called:
    a. lacerations.
    b. concussions.
    c. contusions.
    d. intracranial adhesions.

24. Which of the following is true regarding HIV-associated cognitive impairment?
    a. It closely resembles psychological depression.
    b. It is reversible.
    c. It is seen only in the last stages of life.
    d. A positive test for HIV means that individuals also have HIV-associated cognitive impairment

25. One of the results of untreated syphilis in its late stage is:
    a. seizures.
    b. general paresis.
    c. pellagra.
    d. choreiform movements.

26. Amnestic disorders may be defined as disturbances of memory due to the effects of a medical condition or
    a. chronic tumor.
    b. the persistent effects of a chemical substance.
    c. cerebrovascular stroke.
    d. none of the above

27. Multi-infarct dementia is another name for
    a. epilepsy.
    b. pellagra.
    c. hypertensive dementia.
    d. vascular dementia.

28. Korsakoff's syndrome is characterized by the loss of recent and past memories and an inability to form new memories. Which of the following is the most likely to be diagnosed as having this disorder?
    a. a schizophrenic
    b. an anorectic
    c. a chronic alcoholic
    d. an epileptic

29. Which of the following is caused by a dietary deficiency?
    a. Parkinson's disease
    b. general paresis
    c. dementia paralytica
    d. pellagra

30. The most severe form of epilepsy is
    a. grand mal.
    b. petit mal.
    c. psychomotor.
    d. posttraumatic.

31. Which of the following is not one of the major ways to treat epilepsy?
    a. phenobarbitol
    b. antipsychotic medication
    c. psychological management
    d. surgery

32. The majority of epileptics
    a. have the same intellectual abilities as the general population.
    b. suffer mild disturbances in psychological functioning in between seizures.
    c. seldom have a warning that a seizure is about to occur.
    d. often suffer from hallucinations and periods of unpredictable behavior.

33. When treating the organic brain disorders, behavioral psychologists
    a. focus on such factors as personality and early experiences as an indicator of how much a person might recover.
    b. focus on people's ability to adapt and learn new responses.
    c. teach the patient memory-aid techniques and help relieve depression associated with dementia.
    d. leave the treatment methods to the neurologists in this case.

NEXT, TRY YOUR HAND AT TRUE/FALSE QUESTIONS.

TRUE/FALSE QUESTIONS

Indicate whether each statement is true or false. Check your answers at the end of this chapter.

T   F   1. A person's adaptation to brain disorders is highly idiosyncratic.

T   F   2. Behavioral deficits caused by brain injury in childhood may not be noticed until later on in life.

T   F   3. Stress, sensory and sleep deprivation, and severe fatigue contribute to the onset of delirium.

T   F   4. Delirium tremens is not life threatening.

T   F   5. Depressive features are not typically seen in dementia.

T   F   6. The leading cause of mental deterioration among the elderly is Alzheimer's disease.

T   F   7. Alzheimer's and Pick's disease appear to have a genetic basis.

T   F   8. Traumatic brain injury is a common cause of mental disorder.

T   F   9. A person may expect to recover from a concussion in about four or five weeks.

T   F   10. Because HIV-associated cognitive impairment occurs in younger people, the disorder may be misdiagnosed.

T   F   11. An epileptic seizure appears to be the result of an "electrical storm" in the brain.

T   F   12. Petit mal seizures are obvious and therefore easy to identify.

T   F   13. Cases of brain damage are highly concentrated in the segment of the population with low socioeconomic status.

T   F   14. Vascular dementia is the result of a series of major strokes occurring over an instant of time.

KEEP GOING.....MATCHING IS NEXT.

MATCHING

Match the following terms with the information provided below. The answers are at the end of the chapter.

a. grand mal seizure
b. Pick's disease
c. contusions
d. amnestic syndrome
e. Korsakoff's syndrome

f. confabulation
g. delirium
h. mental status examination
i. syphilitic infection
j. neuropsychologist

_____ 1. rupturing of tiny blood vessels

_____ 2. has symptoms very similar to Alzheimer's disease

_____ 3. loss of consciousness and extreme spasms

_____ 4. may lead to irreversible brain disorders

_____ 5. detailed but inaccurate memories

_____ 6. caused by a deficiency of the vitamin thiamine

_____ 7. an interview

_____ 8. specialist in assessment of cognitive dysfunction in brain disorders

_____ 9. symptoms include disorientation, confusion, and cognitive impairment

_____ 10. memory difficulty involving inability to learn new material or recall information acquired in the past

CHAPTER 13 ANSWER KEY

Multiple Choice

1.	b	18.	d
2.	c	19.	d
3.	d	20.	a
4.	b	21.	d
5.	b	22.	a
6.	b	23.	a
7.	c	24.	a
8.	b	25.	b
9.	d	26.	b
10.	b	27.	d
11.	c	28.	c
12.	b	29.	d
13.	b	30.	a
14.	a	31.	b
15.	a	32.	a
16.	d	33.	b
17.	d		

True/False

1.	T	8.	T
2.	T	9.	F
3.	T	10.	T
4.	F	11.	T
5.	F	12.	F
6.	T	13.	T
7.	T	14.	F

Matching

1.	c	6.	e
2.	b	7.	h
3.	a	8.	j
4.	i	9.	g
5.	f	10.	d

Chapter 14
SUBSTANCE-RELATED DISORDERS

CHAPTER OVERVIEW

This chapter introduces you to the topic of substance-related disorders. Alcohol abuse and dependence issues are reviewed; treatment strategies and prevention programs are delineated. Other drugs including barbiturates, opioids, cocaine, amphetamines, hallucinogens, cannabis, nicotine, and caffeine are also discussed in terms of addictive properties, physiological impact, and therapeutic interventions. Questions about a common neurotransmitter pathway, particularly involving dopamine, the role of society and governmental units in shaping policies regarding the availability and use of illicit substances, and whether there are behavioral addictions are also addressed.

LEARNING OBJECTIVES

After studying this chapter, you should be able to answer these questions:
1. What are the effects of substance-related disorders on human functioning?
2. What are two categories of substance-related disorders?
3. What are the two subgroups of substance-use disorders?
4. What are the characteristics of substance dependence?
5. What is tolerance?
6. What causes withdrawal?
7. What behaviors are associated with compulsive substance use?
8. How does substance abuse differ from substance dependence?
9. What are the main types of substance-induced disorders and the common features that each share?
10. What happens when someone is in a state of substance intoxication?
11. How does alcohol affect the brain and body?
12. What are the major theories concerning the origins of alcohol related disorders?
13. What programs treating alcohol-related disorders are most effective?
14. What are some promising prevention programs for alcohol-related disorders?
15. What are the effects of barbiturates and tranquilizers?
16. What are the natural opioids and what effect do they have on the brain and body?
17. What are the two main opioids in use today, and how do they affect the brain and body?
18. Where does cocaine come from?
19. What is the difference between crack and powder cocaine?
20. How do amphetamines affect the brain and body?
21. What is the difference between methamphetamine and amphetamine?
22. What are the effects of hallucinogens?
23. What are the dangers of phencyclidine use?
24. What substances are inhaled and how do they affect an individual?
25. What are the forms of cannabis in use today?
26. What is the major active ingredient in cannabis and what are the ramifications of long-term use?
27. How does nicotine affect the brain?
28. What are the symptoms of caffeine intoxication?
29. What might be the common pathway that substance-related disorders take in the brain?

30. What role does society and government play in the availability and use of substances?
31. What behavioral addictions are being studied today?
32. What are the most promising programs for substance-related treatment and prevention?

CHAPTER OUTLINE

1. Substance-Use Disorders (p.442)

These disorders include problems associated with the way people use and abuse drugs that alter the way that people think, feel, and behave. There are two groups of disorders: those dealing with substance abuse, and those dealing with substance dependence.

A. Substance Dependence

Substance dependence is a maladaptive pattern of substance use that seriously impairs social or occupational functioning. Dependence is defined by the development of tolerance, which is the need to take more and more of a drug to get the same effect. Dependence is also defined by the onset of withdrawal symptoms upon cessation of the drug use.

B. Substance Abuse

Substance abuse refers to the continuation of substance use despite a pattern of adverse consequences resulting from the drug use such as legal, social, and interpersonal problems.

2. Substance Induced Disorders (p.443)

Substance induced disorders refer to a variety of symptoms such as delirium and psychosis that result from substance use.

3. Alcohol-Related Disorders (p.444)

When alcohol is consumed, it first affects the frontal lobes, then the cerebellum, and finally the medulla and spinal cord. Overuse of alcohol is linked to physical, psychological, and behavioral impairment. Studies of the effects of alcoholic drinking on the brain have found the presence of brain dysfunction in over half of detoxified alcoholics.

A. Excessive Alcohol Use

About 70 percent of persons drink alcohol on occasion; and an estimated 12 percent are heavy drinkers. Overuse of alcohol is influenced by age and sociocultural factors.

B. Theories and Treatment

There is much evidence that individual differences in sensitivity to alcohol influences people's ability to metabolize alcohol, and that some of these differences are gender related. Some of the differences in sensitivity also may be related to ethnicity. Other differences between alcoholic and nonalcoholic drinkers may include levels of sensitivity of nerve cells and variations in neurochemicals in the brain. Differing etiologies of alcohol dependence require different treatment approaches. One major argument in the treatment of alcoholism is the abstinence versus controlled drinking approach. However, some research does support a controlled drinking approach with some alcoholics; for others, abstinence is the appropriate approach.

C. Preventing Alcohol-Related Disorders

One way of approaching this task is to identify risk factors for overuse and then develop interventions to address those risks. Such risks include socioeconomic, interpersonal, familial factors, among others.

4. Other Drugs (p.457)

It is very common for alcoholism to occur together with dependence on other drugs; substance abuse has significant co-morbidity with a variety of other conditions.

A. Barbiturates and Tranquilizers

These are central nervous system depressants. Both reduce anxiety and insomnia and tolerance for both quickly develops. Death can result from sudden abstinence, and the margin between an intoxicating dose and a fatal dose can become extremely small.

B. The Opioids

The term opioid refers to a substance that acts on the nervous system in a manner similar to the opium poppy. Opiate refers to opioid drugs derived from or similar to the juice of the opium poppy. Opioids produce both sedative and analgesic effects, including mood changes, sleepiness, mental clouding, constipation, and slowing of the brain's respiratory center. Overdoses may cause death due to cessation of breathing, and withdrawal can be severe and life-threatening.

C. Cocaine

Cocaine is the main active substance in the leaves of the coca bush. It is the only drug known to be both a local anesthetic and a central nervous system stimulant. Cocaine increases heart rate, blood pressure, and body temperature while decreasing appetite. Researchers have posited that cocaine causes the release of large amounts of dopamine in the brain.

D. Amphetamines

Amphetamines are powerful central nervous stimulants. They are believed to act by influencing norepinephrine and dopamine receptors in the brain. Amphetamines are used medically in the treatment of certain conditions, but are very much drugs of abuse as well. Tolerance develops rapidly.

E. Hallucinogens

These drugs act on the central nervous system to produce alterations of consciousness. There is sensory displacement and a variety of hallucinations as well with use. They also sometimes produce extreme panic attacks and some serious effects including psychosis, severe depression, and flashbacks.

F. Phencyclidine (PCP)

Originally developed as a surgical anesthetic, PCP was found to induce hallucinations and delirium and so its legal use was discontinued. It continues to be manufactured illegally and has become a street drug available in a number of forms such as tablets, powder, or a capsule. It is classified as a dissociative anesthetic and in small doses, it produces insensitivity to pain; in large doses it produces a coma-like state.

G. Inhalants
The surface area of the lungs with the extensive capillary network makes inhalation a prime method for ingesting many substances. The effects of inhalation can be more intense than intravenous injection. Tolerance and withdrawal have been reported by users.

H. Cannabis
Pharmacologically, marijuana is not a narcotic, although legally, it is classified as one. It can be ingested by either smoking or eating parts of the plant. When it is ingested, the major active ingredient, tetrahydrocannabinol, is quickly absorbed. The effects produced are grandiosity, lethargy, impaired short-term memory, impaired motor performance, distortions in time perception.

I. Nicotine
Nicotine acts by influencing receptors sensitive to acetylcholine which results in effects on the central and peripheral nervous systems and the heart. It seems to work by releasing dopamine and speeding neural message transmission. It is also causes measurable declines in cognitive functioning.

J. Caffeine
Caffeine exhibits effects similar to other psychoactive drugs and caffeine drinkers develop both tolerance and withdrawal.

5. Is There a Final Common Pathway? (p.472)
Researchers believe that no matter what the psychoactive substance is, they all appear to activate a pleasure circuit in the brain. Another question to be answered by research is whether an inability to absorb enough dopamine creates drug-seeking behavior in people.

6. Substance Dependence and Social Policy (p.472)
Some treatment approaches show promise in dealing with the use of illicit and addictive drugs. Social policy, however, continues to make substance users criminals rather than patients.

7. Are There Behavioral Addictions? The Dilemma of Pathological Gambling (p.472)
Pathological gambling involves craving, compulsion, loss of control, and continuing the behavior in spite of negative consequences. It does not involve ingesting a substance. There are few professionals trained in treating pathological gambling and few studies investigating effective treatments.

```
TIPS FOR TESTING YOURSELF

Write each of the following key words and concepts on one side of an index card.  Then, for each, look
up the correct definition in your textbook.  Write the definition on the opposite side of the corresponding
index card.  Now, you have flash cards to study.  Keep the cards with you and whenever you have a few
minutes, pull them out and test yourself.  When you are studying with a study partner, you can test each
other.  You can also share the duties of looking up the definitions and writing them on the cards.  Study
them a little each day.
```

KEY TERMS AND CONCEPTS

substance-use disorder (p.442)
substance dependence (p.442)
withdrawal (p.442)
compulsive substance use (p.442)
substance abuse (p.443)
intoxication (p.445)
physiological dependence on alcohol (p.445)
alcohol abuse (p.445)
detoxification (p.447)
sensitivity to alcohol (p.449)
naltrexone (p.449)
balance placebo design (p.451)
aversive conditioning (p.451)
controlled drinking (p.451)
relapse prevention (p.453)
abstinence violation affect (p.453)
Alcoholics Anonymous (p.454)
barbiturates (p.459)
tranquilizing drugs (p.459)
opioids (p.459)
endorphins (p.459)
enkephalins (p.459)
dymorphins (p.459)
naloxone (p.459)
opiates (p.460)
morphine (p.460)
heroin (p.460)
methadone (p.462)
methadone maintenance (p.462)
cocaine (p.463)
amphetamine (p.465)
methamphetamine (p.465)
hallucinogen (p.465)
lysergic acid dimethylamide (LSD) (p.465)
post-hallucinogen perceptual disorder (p.466)

```
TIPS FOR TESTING YOURSELF

In developing answers for the following questions, turn to the section of your chapter that covers the
pertinent material. Read the section thoroughly and spend some time thinking about the information
before attempting to frame your answer.  Write out each answer without referring to the book, and when
you have completed all of them, check their accuracy by returning to the corresponding section in the
book.  For each question you missed, write out the correct answer.  Then test yourself again.  Repeat the
process until you can answer all the questions correctly.
```

SHORT ANSWER ESSAY QUESTIONS

1. Differentiate substance dependence disorders from substance abuse disorders. Define intoxication, addiction, withdrawal, and flashbacks.

2. Define addictive behavior and tolerance.

3. What is alcohol abuse? List some facts about the problems of alcohol. Explain the concepts of problem drinking and alcoholism.

4. What effects does alcohol have on the body and mental health? Enunciate the diagnostic criteria for alcohol intoxication.

5. Present the biological, psychodynamic, and learning perspectives on alcoholism.

6. What cognitive factors have been related to problem drinking?

7. How may social conditions and community factors contribute to excessive use of alcohol? Present the "addictive cycle" of the interactional model.

8. What is detoxification? List the symptoms of withdrawal.

9. Contrast the biological and community approaches to the treatment of alcoholism.

10. Discuss the learning and cognitive models of alcoholism.

11. Discuss alcohol abuse and relapse prevention.

12. Briefly describe opioids as a psychoactive drug and discuss their addictive potential. What treatment strategies are available for this addiction?

13. Delineate the effects and treatment of cocaine addiction.

14. Describe the characteristics associated with the use of amphetamines, LSD, PCP, and marijuana.

15. What are the withdrawal symptoms of nicotine? Describe the treatments available for smoking addiction. Why is the transdermal nicotine patch considered a promising development?

16. How addictive is caffeine?

MULTIPLE CHOICE

1. Psychoactive substances
   a. are used by only a small minority of the population.
   b. have very different effects than the medications typically prescribed by a physician.
   c. cause psychotic-like symptoms.
   d. affect thoughts, emotions, and behaviors.

2. A 1991 study showed that _____ percent of the U.S population aged 18 and older meet the criteria for drug abuse or dependence on a substance other than alcohol or tobacco.
   a. 13.8
   b. 6.2
   c. 7.7
   d. 2.9

3. Physiological dependence on a substance can be shown in two ways:
   a. tolerance or withdrawal.
   b. tolerance or repeated intoxications.
   c. frequent and continued use of the substance.
   d. a "high" feeling and withdrawal symptoms.

4. Compulsive substance abuse involves
   a. drug-seeking behavior.
   b. ingestion or use of substances.
   c. hiding alcohol and other drugs.
   d. both a and b

5. DSM-IV
   a. does not consider physiological dependence in its cataloguing of disorders.
   b. distinguishes between substance abuse and dependence.
   c. reports that there is no difference between substance abuse and substance dependence.
   d. none of the above

6. Which of the following is not an indication of substance intoxication?
   a. mania
   b. perceptual problems
   c. wakefulness
   d. judgment problems

7. Which of the following in the only type of alcohol safe for human consumption?
    a. isopropyl
    b. ethyl alcohol
    c. wood alcohol
    d. methyl alcohol

8. Betty drank until she reached a blood/alcohol level of .50. You would expect her to
    a. show uninhibited and silly behaviors.
    b. have problems with reasoning powers, memory and judgment.
    c. have poor motor coordination and stagger when walking.
    d. possibly die.

9. A 220-pound man has four alcoholic drinks at happy hour. Is he intoxicated?
    a. no
    b. maybe
    c. probably
    d. yes

10. Children with fetal alcohol syndrome
    a. usually become alcoholics like their parents.
    b. are often mentally retarded.
    c. have a high incidence of childhood leukemia
    d. are often born with alcohol in their bloodstreams.

11. The greatest and most immediate effects of alcohol are on the
    a. central nervous system.
    b. liver.
    c. stomach.
    d. sense organs.

12. There is evidence of a high prevalence of sensitivity to alcohol among people of _____ derivation.
    a. Eastern European
    b. Latin American
    c. Asian
    d. Swedish

13. According to the psychodynamic view, which would not be a characteristic of the oral-dependent personality?
    a. self-doubt
    b. passivity
    c. depression
    d. dependence

14. Most researchers agree that alcohol is
    a. an unconditioned response.
    b. a punishing stimulus.
    c. a reinforcer.
    d. a negative reinforcer.

15. Which of the following is not one of the cultural conditions that minimize alcohol problems?
    a. Alcohol is not used at all in the family.
    b. Children are exposed to alcohol at an early age in family settings.
    c. Alcohol is considered a food and usually served with meals.
    d. Abstinence is socially acceptable but intoxication is not.

16. When a person is intoxicated
    a. black coffee can be an effective way to "sober him/her up."
    b. a very cold shower can be an effective sobering agent.
    c. making the person walk around in fresh air can be an effective sobering agent.
    d. There is no effective sobering agent.

17. During therapy, Jim, who is a problem drinker, is told to visualize that he is about to drink some alcohol. Then he imagines he is feeling nauseous and feels like vomiting. This type of technique is called
    a. aversive conditioning.
    b. covert sensitization.
    c. systematic desensitization.
    d. disulfiram therapy.

18. Relapse-prevention programs and concern about the abstinence-violation effect is most likely to be part of
    a. the psychodynamic approach to treatment of alcohol problems.
    b. the Alcoholics Anonymous approach to treatment of alcoholism.
    c. the cognitive approach to treating problem drinking behavior.
    d. detoxification.

19. Which of the following is not a way your text suggests that students can help themselves before they drink?
    a. select a designated driver
    b. pace drinks to three per hour
    c. focus an event on something other than drinking
    d. have nonalcoholic drinks available

20. A natural opioid produced by the brain is (are)
    a. hallucinogens.
    b. barbiturates.
    c. endorphins.
    d. methadone.

21. Heroin is a derivative of
    a. morphine.
    b. marijuana.
    c. endorphins.
    d. none of the above.

22. The opiates cause mood changes, sleepiness, metal dulling, and
    a. hyperventilation.
    b. appetite loss.
    c. depression of the brain's respiratory center.
    d. both a and c

23. The ability of American service personnel in Vietnam to so easily leave heavy drug use behind when they returned to the U.S. is best explained by
    a. the exposure orientation.
    b. the interactional orientation.
    c. the methadone maintenance approach to drug addiction.
    d. successful detoxification techniques.

24. Which of the following is not one of the effects of cocaine?
    a. euphoria
    b. feelings of separation from one's body
    c. increased heart rate
    d. increased energy

25. Estimates of the number of "crack babies" born each year ranges from ____ to ____.
    a. 20,000; 50,000
    b. 50,000; 120,000
    c. 200,000; 500,000
    d. 50,000; 200,000

26. The effects of _____ are produced with as little as fifty micrograms of the substance.
    a. cocaine
    b. amphetamines
    c. LSD
    d. PCP

27. A predominant feature of post-hallucinogen perceptual disorder is
    a. loss of time.
    b. loss of depth perception.
    c. rapid eye movements.
    d. flashbacks.

28. _____ is (are) classified as a dissociative anesthetic.
    a. Cocaine
    b. Amphetamines
    c. LSD
    d. PCP

29. Which of the following is not true of marijuana?
    a. It suppresses male hormones.
    b. It can cause harm to an unborn child.
    c. It can damage chromosomes.
    d. It can be secreted in breast milk.

30. Select the term below that is not a stage of change in smoking cessation.
    a. action
    b. maintenance
    c. contemplation and commitment
    d. continuation

NEXT, TRY YOUR HAND AT TRUE/FALSE QUESTIONS.

TRUE/FALSE QUESTIONS
Indicate whether each statement is true or false. Check your answers at the end of this chapter.

T   F   1. Teen use of alcohol and marijuana appear to be on the increase.

T   F   2. The term "addiction" is not used in the DSM-IV.

T   F   3. People differ in their vulnerabilities to the negative side effects of particular substances.

T   F   4. Seventy percent of all traffic fatalities are alcohol related.

T   F   5. Moderate use of alcohol may lessen the chance of heart attack.

T   F   6. There does not appear to be a genetic basis for alcoholism.

T   F   7. The effects of barbituates and alcohol are addictive.

T   F   8. Endorphins are natural opiates.

T   F   9. Methadone maintenance's popularity as a form of treatment has decreased in recent years.

T   F   10. Naltrexone blocks opioid receptors.

T   F   11. The use of inhalants to "get high" includes gasoline and lighter fluid.

T   F   12. Caffeine is the world's most widely used mind-altering drug.

KEEP GOING.....MATCHING IS NEXT.

MATCHING

Match the following terms with the information provided below. The answers are at the chapter.

a. morphine
b. exposure orientation
c. barbiturates
d. interactional orientation
e. abstinence-violation effect
f. cocaine
g. naltrexone

h. PCP
i. inhalants
j. detoxification
k. nystagmus
l. distilled spirits
m. transdermal nicotine patch
n. balanced placebo design

_____ 1. a person's belief about alcohol content can be tested by this study

_____ 2. involuntary spasmodic motion of eyeballs

_____ 3. drug used by Freud

_____ 4. important factor in relapse

_____ 5. hard liquor

_____ 6. prescribed for anxiety relief or to prevent convulsions

_____ 7. drug used to treat opioid addiction

_____ 8. a dissociative anesthetic

_____ 9. most important active ingredient of opium

_____ 10. considers both the person and situation in development of addiction

_____ 11. "drying out"

_____ 12. addiction is a function of mere exposure to opioids

_____ 13. examples include gasoline and aerosol sprays

_____ 14. multilayered pad containing nicotine, applied to the skin with a pressure-sensitive adhesive

---

GOOD, NOW CHECK YOUR ANSWERS. WHEN YOU'RE DONE GRADING YOURSELF, COVER YOUR ANSWERS, AND START ALL OVER AGAIN. KEEP TESTING YOURSELF UNTIL YOU CAN ANSWER THEM ALL CORRECTLY.

CHAPTER 14 ANSWER KEY

Multiple Choice

1.	d		16.	d
2.	b		17.	a
3.	a		18.	c
4.	d		19.	b
5.	b		20.	c
6.	a		21.	a
7.	b		22.	c
8.	d		23.	b
9.	b		24.	b
10.	b		25.	d
11.	a		26.	c
12.	c		27.	d
13.	c		28.	d
14.	c		29.	c
15.	a		30.	d

True/False

1.	T		7.	T
2.	T		8.	T
3.	T		9.	F
4.	F		10.	T
5.	T		11.	T
6.	F		12.	T

Matching

1.	n		8.	h
2.	k		9.	a
3.	f		10.	d
4.	e		11.	j
5.	l		12.	b
6.	c		13.	i
7.	g		14.	m

Chapter 15
DISORDERS OF CHILDHOOD AND ADOLESCENCE

CHAPTER OVERVIEW
Childhood development presents a unique set of vulnerabilities to a variety of problems. A selection of disorders of childhood and adolescence is presented in this chapter. Among those discussed are the externalizing disorders of attention-deficit/hyperactivity disorder, tic disorders, Tourette's disorder, oppositional defiant disorder, and conduct disorder, and the internalizing disorders of separation anxiety disorder, social phobia, generalized anxiety disorder, and obsessive-compulsive disorder. The chapter examines depression in children. Various types of treatment for children and adolescents are also examined.

LEARNING OBJECTIVES
After studying this chapter, you should be able to answer these questions:
1. What are the characteristics of externalizing behaviors?
2. What are the main externalizing disorders?
3. What are the features of attention-deficit/hyperactivity disorder (ADHD)?
4. What are some examples of motor and vocal tics?
5. What are the causes and symptoms of Tourette's disorder?
6. What are the causes and characteristics of oppositional defiant disorder (ODD)?
7. What is conduct disorder and where does it come from?
8. What are internalizing behaviors?
9. What are the main DSM-IV internalizing disorders?
10. What causes separation anxiety disorder?
11. What are the effects of social phobia in children?
12. How do the symptoms of generalized anxiety disorder differ in children and adults?
13. What are the causes and symptoms of obsessive-compulsive disorder in children?
14. What are the most effective treatments for anxiety disorders in children?
15. What are the differences in adult and childhood depression?
16. What is the prognosis for children who suffer from depression?
17. What are some of the main differences in therapy for children and adults?
18. What is the goal of play therapy?
19. What behavioral and cognitive-behavioral techniques have been effective with children?
20. What is the focus of family therapy?
21. What do we know about the overall effectiveness of therapy with children?

CHAPTER OUTLINE
1. Externalizing Disorders (p.481)
Children with externalizing disorders are undercontrolled, and exhibit behaviors that annoy or otherwise create problems for other people. Such behaviors include temper tantrums, fights, or disobedient or destructive behaviors.

A. Attention-Deficit/Hyperactivity Disorder

ADHD is characterized by symptoms of inattention, hyperactivity, and impulsivity, and also frequently occurs together with learning disabilities, depression, anxiety, conduct disorder or oppositional defiant disorder.

B. Oppositional Defiant Disorder

This disorder involves negativistic, defiant, disobedient, and hostile behavior directed at authority figures that is more frequent than what would be expected for children of comparable ages and developmental levels.

C. Conduct Disorder

Conduct disorder is characterized by aggressive behavior that causes or threatens harm to people or animals, property damage, deceitfulness, theft, and serious rule violations.

2. Internalizing Disorders (p.495)

In internalizing disorders, children see themselves as inadequate or undeserving. These are more likely to be disturbances of mood or emotion, and because they do not involve readily apparent behaviors, are often overlooked.

A. Separation Anxiety Disorder

Children with separation anxiety show excessive anxiety when not with major attachment figures or in familiar environments. They may be unable to stay in rooms by themselves, go to school, or even visit friends. All children experience some separation anxiety, but this is transient and part of normal development. For the child with separation anxiety disorder, the symptoms last for a significantly longer period of time and cause significant distress or impairment in functioning,

B. Other Anxiety Disorders Found in Children

Other anxiety disorders found in adults can also be found in children. These include social phobia, generalized anxiety disorder, posttraumatic stress disorder, and obsessive-compulsive disorder.

C. Treatment of Anxiety Disorders in Children

Medication is appropriate for treating OCD, and cognitive-behavioral therapy has also been successful in the treatment of phobias and simple fears. Since anxious children likely have parents with anxiety problems, family therapy can also be helpful.

D. Depression

DSM-IV-TR criteria for diagnosing depression in children is not very different for that of adult depression; only minor modifications are made. There are differences in the frequency of depression as well as gender-based patterns of depression. Feelings of sadness are quite common in children, but when the depression is more severe, a diagnosis of depressive disorder is made.

3. Therapy for Children and Adolescents (p.506)

Small children are difficult to treat because they can't verbalize their feelings or describe their thoughts. The therapist must ask specific questions to help the child describe her or his sad feelings. Medications are used, but more research is needed to investigate the efficacy of medication use for childhood depression as well as to determining the long-term effects. Some psychological treatment approaches that have been successful with adults are also useful for treating depression in adolescents.

For example, behavioral therapy and cognitive-behavioral therapy have shown promise in use with both children and adolescents. And, because mood disorders also tend to run in families, family therapy is a useful treatment approach as well.

TIPS FOR TESTING YOURSELF

Write each of the following key words and concepts on one side of an index card. Then, for each, look up the correct definition in your textbook. Write the definition on the opposite side of the corresponding index card. Now, you have flash cards to study. Keep the cards with you and whenever you have a few minutes, pull them out and test yourself. When you are studying with a study partner, you can test each other. You can also share the duties of looking up the definitions and writing them on the cards. Study them a little each day.

KEY TERMS AND CONCEPTS
externalizing disorders (p.481)
attention-deficit/hyperactivity disorder (ADHD) (p.481)
oppositional defiant disorder (ODD) (p.489)
conduct disorder (p.490)
internalizing disorders (p.495)
separation anxiety disorder (p.496)
social phobia (p.497)
generalized anxiety disorder (p.498)
posttraumatic stress disorder (p.500)
obsessive-compulsive disorder (p.500)
depression (p.502)
tics (p.505)
Tourette's disorder (p.505)
coprolalia (p.506)
play therapy (p.508)

TIPS FOR TESTING YOURSELF

In developing answers for the following questions, turn to the section of your chapter that covers the pertinent material. Read the section thoroughly and spend some time thinking about the information before attempting to frame your answer. Write out each answer without referring to the book, and when you have completed all of them, check their accuracy by returning to the corresponding section in the book. For each question you missed, write out the correct answer. Then test yourself again. Repeat the process until you can answer all the questions correctly.

SHORT ANSWER ESSAY QUESTIONS
In developing answers for the following questions, turn to the section of your chapter that covers the pertinent material. Read each section thoroughly before attempting to frame your answer.

1. How do behavioral problems impact a child's development?

2. What are the characteristics associated with attention-deficit/hyperactivity disorder?

3. Describe the possible causes of attention-deficit/hyperactivity disorder. What treatments are used?

4. What are the diagnostic criteria for chronic tic disorder? For Tourette's disorder? For oppositional defiant disorder?

5. Name four behavioral features of conduct disorder.

6. Explain the term "conduct disorder," listing clinical features. Contrast this with the term "oppositional defiant disorder." Review characteristics and treatment strategies for these disorders.

7. Explain the nature of internalizing disorders. List the most common internalizing disorders seen in children and their symptoms.

8. Differentiate between social phobia and generalized anxiety disorder. How does obsessive-compulsive disorder differ from both of these disorders?

9. What are the characteristic signs of depression in girls and boys? Discuss the causes of depressive disorders in children and adolescents.

10. What therapeutic approaches are used to treat depressed children and adolescents?

11. Describe the therapies used to treat children and adolescents.

12. What factors are especially crucial for the treatment of children and adolescents from diverse cultural backgrounds?

TIPS FOR TESTING YOURSELF

The following sections of self-test questions will test your understanding of the material presented in the chapter. On a separate piece of paper, write the correct answer for each item in the section, then compare your answers with those at the end of the chapter. After you have graded yourself, turn to the chapter and look up the questions you missed. Write out the correct answers. Then test yourself again. Continue doing so until you can answer all the questions correctly.

MULTIPLE CHOICE

1. Select the statement below that is incorrect.
    a. Behavioral problems may interfere with development by delaying academic and social learning.
    b. Withdrawn children are less likely to be referred to a mental health specialist than an active child.
    c. Parents may feel guilty about a child who exhibits maladaptive behavior.
    d. Reading problems are not associated with underlying pathology.

2. Select the best estimate of children less than eighteen years of age who meet the criteria for one or more mental disorders.
    a. 10–12 percent
    b. 6–8 percent
    c. 17–22 percent
    d. 2–3 percent

3. What ratio of children who need help for maladaptive behavior receive it?
    a. two out of five
    b. one out of two
    c. one out of three
    d. one out of four

4. Which of the following is not a risk factor for childhood disorders?
    a. low socioeconomic status
    b. parental psychopathology
    c. family discord
    d. low birth weight

5. One reason researchers believe that childhood disorders are distinct from disorders of adulthood is that
    a. childhood disorders tend to have brief durations.
    b. sex ratios for these disorders switch from childhood to adulthood.
    c. the symptoms tend to be dramatically different.
    d. disorders of childhood appear to incorporate developmental milestones as themes.

6. Warren is easily distracted, fails to pay close attention to the teacher's instructions, and often leaves his assigned desk in the second grade classroom. Warren's behavior is indicative of
    a. pica.
    b. attention-deficit/hyperactivity disorder.
    c. oppositional deficit disorder.
    d. an internalizing disorder.

7. Which of the following is not one of the categories where ADHD children show inappropriate behaviors of their ages?
   a. destructiveness
   b. impulsiveness
   c. inattention
   d. hyperactivity

8. The three types of ADHD include the inattentive type, the hyperactive-impulsive type, and the
   a. contained type.
   b. constitutional type.
   c. convoluted type.
   d. combined type.

9. Prevalence estimates for ADHD range from _____ percent of school age children and constitute _____ percent of referrals to child clinics.
   a. 3–5; 30–40
   b. 7–12; 10–30
   c. 4–5; 30–40
   d. 2–10; 20–30

10. The study cited in the text that involved ADHD children as "negative social catalysts" found that children
    a. lacked appropriate socialization.
    b. elicited maladaptive behaviors from others around them.
    c. use their social skills in a negative fashion.
    d. regress in social situations.

11. The research study involving simulation of an astronaut and mission control revealed that ADHD boys
    a. lacked enough attention to play the game.
    b. had difficulty learning by observation of models.
    c. were more enthusiastic about the game than controls.
    d. none of the above

12. Select the statement that best summarizes the research on the causes of attention-deficit/hyperactivity disorder.
    a. A genetic cause has been found.
    b. The cause appears to be environmental.
    c. Birth defects cause the disorder.
    d. The causes are unknown.

13. The most common treatment for hyperactive children is
    a. tranquilizers.
    b. stimulant medication.
    c. mainstreaming.
    d. amniocentesis.

14. Research on therapeutic intervention for attention-deficit/hyperactivity disorder has demonstrated that
    a. behavioral therapies work best.
    b. drugs alone are effective.
    c. psychodynamic therapies are the most effective.
    d. drugs and behavioral interventions are most effective.

15. William's mother describes his behavior in the following manner: resentful, defiant, argumentative in interactions, and irritable. These symptoms suggest the presence of a(n)
    a. anxiety disorder of childhood.
    b. oppositional defiant disorder.
    c. disruptive disorder.
    d. obsessive-compulsive disorder.

16. Children who develop conduct disorders before age 10 are more likely to develop _____ in adulthood.
    a. aggressive personality disorder
    b. antisocial personality disorder
    c. paranoid personality disorder
    d. schizotypal personality disorder

17. Select a typical prevention measure for conduct disorder from the list of strategies below.
    a. a project designed to improve an adolescent's social skills
    b. group therapy for parents of children diagnosed as having conduct disorders
    c. a project designed to enhance preschoolers' creativity
    d. none of the above

18. Which of the following is not considered to be an internalizing disorder?
    a. separation anxiety
    b. phobias
    c. ADHD
    d. depression

19. Obsessions involve _____, while compulsions are described as
    a. rituals; thoughts.
    b. thoughts; rituals.
    c. dreams; thoughts.
    d. thoughts; fears.

20. Of the following, which is true of separation anxiety disorder?
    a. Treatment failure is often due to parents' inability to comply with the treatment program.
    b. It has a physiological basis.
    c. It is best treated with drugs.
    d. Children with this disorder usually become agoraphobic.

21. Overanxious disorder of childhood is analogous to _____ in adults.
    a. separation anxiety disorder
    b. dependent personality disorder
    c. dysthymia
    d. none of the above

22. Which of the following is not a common symptom of depression in girls?
    a. eating erratically
    b. feeling ugly
    c. being unhappy about social life
    d. denying being unhappy

23. A questionnaire that is often used to screen children for depression is the
    a. Daily Depression Scale.
    b. Affective Checklist for Kids.
    c. Emotional Factor Inventory.
    d. Children's Depression Inventory.

24. The most frequently used method to treat children with maladaptive behaviors is
    a. behavioral therapy.
    b. family therapy.
    c. play therapy.
    d. peer therapy.

NEXT, TRY YOUR HAND AT TRUE/FALSE QUESTIONS.

TRUE/FALSE QUESTIONS
Indicate whether each statement is true or false. Check your answers at the end of this chapter.

T F 1. In order to diagnose ADHD, symptoms must be observed after age seven.

T F 2. Research has indicated a potential problem in the area of the corpus collosum in children with ADHD.

T F 3. Medicated ADHD children have better prognoses in the future than nonmedicated ADHD children.

T F 4. ADHD criteria have been modified so that they also apply to adults.

T F 5. Conduct disorders are found predominantly in females.

T F 6. If separation anxiety disorder begins in adolescence, it may result in substantial psychopathology.

T F 7. For kids with obsessive-compulsive disorders, Prozac has been used with some success.

T F 8. The peak risk period for depression is mid and late adolescence.

T F 9. The most effective approach to therapy for young children is to work with the parent instead of the child.

KEEP GOING.....MATCHING IS NEXT.

MATCHING

Match the following terms with information provided below. The answers are at the end of the chapter.

a. conduct disorder
b. hyperactivity
c. separation anxiety disorder
d. play therapy
e. ritualistic behaviors
f. internalizing disorder
g. copralalia

h. tics
i. Tourette's disorder
j. destruction of property
k. oppositional defiant disorder
l. social phobia
m. depression

_____ 1. a type of tic disorder that may begin as early as age 2

_____ 2. includes hostile behavior toward authority figures

_____ 3. may involve harming animals

_____ 4. the uttering of obscenities

_____ 5. not a special diagnostic category in the DSM-IV for children

_____ 6. recurrent, rapid vocalizations

_____ 7. child shows excessive anxiety when not with parent

_____ 8. includes jumping around and wiggling when sitting down

_____ 9. used to help children act out their feelings

_____10. conditions characterized by anxiety and depression

_____11. a behavioral feature of a conduct disorder

_____12. children show an excessive shrinking from contact with unfamiliar people

_____13. may be a normal part of childhood

GOOD, NOW CHECK YOUR ANSWERS. WHEN YOU'RE DONE GRADING YOURSELF, COVER YOUR ANSWERS, AND START ALL OVER AGAIN. KEEP TESTING YOURSELF UNTIL YOU CAN ANSWER THEM ALL CORRECTLY.

CHAPTER 15 ANSWER KEY

Multiple Choice

1.	d		13.	b
2.	c		14.	d
3.	c		15.	b
4.	d		16.	b
5.	b		17.	a
6.	b		18.	c
7.	a		19.	b
8.	d		20.	a
9.	a		21.	d
10.	b		22.	d
11.	b		23.	d
12.	d		24.	a

True/False

1.	T		5.	F
2.	T		6.	T
3.	F		7.	T
4.	T		8.	T

Matching

1.	i		8.	b
2.	k		9.	d
3.	a		10.	f
4.	g		11.	j
5.	m		12.	l
6.	h		13.	e
7.	c			

Chapter 16
PERVASIVE DEVELOPMENTAL DISORDERS AND MENTAL RETARDATION

CHAPTER OVERVIEW
This chapter reviews two forms of developmental disorders: autism and mental retardation. These disorders affect or relate to every aspect of an individual's life. Both autism and mental retardation are evident early in life and represent significant impairment in social, behavioral, communicative, and intellectual abilities. The characteristics, etiology and courses of the disorders are presented and research findings and current issues are discussed. The effect of legislation is highlighted as it applies to mental retardation, and the impact of retardation upon the family is reviewed.

LEARNING OBJECTIVES
After studying this chapter, you should be able to answer these questions:
1. How does a pervasive developmental disorder impact a child's development?
2. What are the main pervasive developmental disorders?
3. What are the characteristics, causes, and effects of autistic disorder?
4. How is autistic disorder treated?
5. What is Asperger's disorder and how does it differ from autistic disorder?
6. What is meant by childhood disintegrative disorder and when do its symptoms appear?
7. What is the distinguishing symptom of Rett's disorder and how does it affect a child's development?
8. What is mean by an autistic disorder spectrum?
9. How is mental retardation defined and categorized?
10. How have views about mental retardation changed in the past 130 years?
11. What was the eugenics movement?
12. What are the two main categories of causes of mental retardation?
13. What disorders are most associated with biologically caused mental retardation?
14. What is Down syndrome and what causes it?
15. How might the fetal environment cause mental retardation?
16. What are the features of fetal alcohol syndrome?
17. What birth experiences cause mental retardation?
18. What early childhood experiences may cause mental retardation?
19. What psychosocial factors are related to mental retardation?
20. What specific primary, secondary, and tertiary prevention efforts are directed toward mental retardation?
21. What early intervention programs may provide some protection for children who are at risk for mental retardation?
22. What vocational and social skills training programs are available for mentally retarded individuals?
23. What Axis I psychological disorders are often experienced by people who are mentally retarded?
24. What stresses and crises do the families of mentally retarded individuals face?

CHAPTER OUTLINE
1. Pervasive Developmental Disorders (p.515)
These are conditions that become apparent early in the child's development and affect all of the major abilities and areas of functioning that develop as the child gets older, including social, cognitive, language abilities.

A. Autistic Disorder
Typical of autistic disorder is an unusual pattern of social and cognitive development marked by significant social and communication problems and frequently accompanied by mental retardation. Autism is found in boys nearly five times as frequently as girls.

B. Asperger's Disorder
This disorder is similar to autism in that there are severe impairments in social interaction and restricted and negative patterns of behavior. Unlike autism, this disorder has no significant impairment in language or cognitive development or in adaptive skills.

C. Childhood Disintegrative Disorder
The child with this disorder begins to show symptoms between the ages of three and four.

D. Rett's Disorder
This is a progressive disorder which begins to appear after about five months of age and is characterized by a slowing of the normal growth of the child's head resulting in microcephaly and the loss of abilities and skills that had previously been learned, such as early language development and social interaction. They then lose motor skills and show signs of mental retardation. This disorder typically affects only girls.

E. Is There an Autistic Spectrum?
Arguments for an autistic spectrum point to the common features of the disorders including impairments in social interaction, communication, and imagination as well as a restricted range of interests and behaviors.

2. Mental Retardation (p.532)
The primary defining characteristic of mental retardation is subaverage intellectual functioning that begins before age 18 and is accompanied by impaired adaptive functioning,

A. Causes of Mental Retardation
Mental retardation can be traced to a variety of causes. Genetic abnormalities, including gene mutations, chromosomal damage, specific recessive or dominant genes all have been found to cause deficits in intellectual functioning.

B. Historical Views of Mental Retardation
Attempts to understand and classify mental retardation date back centuries, but it wasn't until John Down sparked an interest in classification of the disorder that scientists began to seriously study it. In France, Binet began developing tests to measure intelligence in order to select mentally retarded students for special education programs. In the 1960s, a task force report on mental retardation began to erase much of the stigma of the disorder.

C. Fragile X Syndrome

Many kinds of retardation are related to genes on the X chromosome. Fragile X syndrome refers to the fact that the X chromosome will show a fragile spot when grown in the laboratory. Affected individuals are likely to have retardation, aggression, language impairments, and other disorders such as learning disorders or ADHD.

D. Down Syndrome

This is caused by a chromosomal abnormality affecting the 21st chromosome pair. Most persons have mild to moderate mental retardation and distinctive physical features. They tend to be shorter than average, obese, and have congenital heart abnormalities.

E. The Fetal Environment and Mental Retardation

Sometimes disorders associated with mental retardation come about as the result of conditions in the prenatal environment. Damage to the developing fetus can occur as the result of maternal infection, blood abnormalities, radiation, malnutrition, chemicals the mother may have ingested, age of the mother, or stress the mother is experiencing,

F. Fetal Alcohol Syndrome

Associated with heavy maternal drinking, this disorder is characterized by mental retardation, and physical features including small eyes, drooping eyelids, a short, upturned nose with a low bridge, flat cheeks, thin upper lip, low-set ears, bulging forehead, and an unusually large space between nose and mouth.

G. Problems During and After Birth

A relatively large number of mentally retarded individuals experienced injury during the birthing process. Factors that increase the likelihood of this happening include prematurity, low birth weight, lack of oxygen, and too-rapid progress through the birth canal. Damage can also occur after birth from infection, blows to the head, oxygen deprivation, or poisons.

H. Psychosocial Disadvantage

A large proportion of persons with mild mental retardation come from low socioeconomic classes with limited education and cultural opportunities. It is likely that heredity combined with environmental disadvantage result in reduced intellectual functioning, and early interventions aimed at aspects of the environment and psychosocial enrichment are appropriate and effective.

I. Types of Prevention and Intervention in Mental Retardation

Primary prevention aims at preventing the disorder from occurring in the first place. Secondary prevention treats the problem to minimize its effects. Tertiary prevention helps the individual make the most of her or his strengths and adapt to limitations.

J. Early Intervention Programs

Early intervention programs are tertiary prevention programs designed to help children at risk for retardation as the result of impoverished environment or parents whose IQ falls in the retarded range. Intervention in infancy and early childhood has been shown to decrease the incidence of lowered intellectual functioning due to environmental factors.

K. Vocational and Social Skills Training Programs

Basic social skills training, along with skills necessary to keep a job, such as hygiene, and awareness that it is important to get to work on time and complete assignments are all taught in such training programs, which rely on behavioral training techniques.

L. Recognition and Treatment of Psychological Problems

Significant percentages of mentally retarded persons have comorbid personality disorders or at least dysfunctional personalities. Most also have a variety of other psychological disorders; in other words, most mentally retarded individuals are dually diagnosed. However, many are not adequately treated. Specialized training in recognizing the association between retardation and other disorders is required in order to provide adequate care.

M. The Families of Mentally Retarded Children

Having a mentally retarded child puts significant stress on the parents and other family members.

KEY TERMS AND CONCEPTS

pervasive developmental disorder (p.515)
autistic disorder (p.516)
theory of mind (p.520)
executive functions (p.520)
joint attention behaviors (p.522)
childhood schizophrenia (p.525)
Asperger's disorder (p.529)
childhood disintegrative disorder (p.530)
Rett's disorder (p.530)
microcephaly (p.530)
autistic disorder spectrum (p.531)
mental retardation (p.532)
eugenics movement (p.533)
phenylketornuria (PKU) (p.534)
fragile X syndrome (p.535)
Down syndrome (p.536)
trisomy 21 (p.537)
translocation (p.537)
mosaicism (p.537)
amniocentesis (p.538)
fetal alcohol syndrome (p.539)
psychosocial disadvantage (p.540)
primary prevention (p.540)
secondary prevention (p.541)
tertiary prevention (p.541)
dyslexia (p.543)

SHORT ANSWER ESSAY QUESTIONS

1. What are pervasive developmental disorders? Name the four types of pervasive developmental disorders.

2. What are the characteristics of autistic disorders? What are the diagnostic criteria for autistic disorders? What are the similarities between autistic disorders and childhood schizophrenia? What are the differences?

3. Describe the research on autism. What types of therapeutic approaches are used to treat autism?

4. List the characteristics and diagnostic criteria for Asperger's disorder, Rett's disorder, and child disintegrative disorder.

5. What is mental retardation and how is it distinguished from autism? What are the four levels of mental retardation, and the characteristics for each (at least three per level).

6. What are the different genetic causes of mental retardation?

7. Define phenylketonuria (PKU) and tuberous sclerosis.

8. What is fragile X syndrome? Describe how it got its name.

9. Describe the features and causes of Down syndrome.

10. What prenatal environmental factors can result in mental retardation?

11. What are the characteristics and causes of fetal alcohol syndrome?

12. What problems at and after birth can increase the probability of mental retardation?

13. What types of social and psychological problems do the retarded experience in daily living?

14. Discuss the impact of mental retardation on the family.

> **TIPS FOR TESTING YOURSELF**
>
> The following sections of self-test questions will test your understanding of the material presented in the chapter. On a separate piece of paper, write the correct answer for each item in the section, then compare your answers with those at the end of the chapter. After you have graded yourself, turn to the chapter and look up the questions you missed. Write out the correct answers. Then test yourself again. Continue doing so until you can answer all the questions correctly

MULTIPLE CHOICE

1. Which of the following is not a clinical feature of autism?
   a. lack of awareness of others
   b. speech abnormalities
   c. insistence on sameness
   d. psychotic features

2. Leo Kanner (1943) first described autism as "extreme autistic aloneness" and
   a. an aversion to language.
   b. clinging dependency.
   c. an obsession for sameness.
   d. profound retardation.

3. The approximate age of onset for Asperger's disorder is ____.
   a. usually between ages 1 and 2
   b. over age 2
   c. before age 3, generally much earlier
   d. school age

4. Research studies have shown that the emotional facial expressions, gestures, and vocalizations of an autistic child are often
   a. normal.
   b. flat.
   c. idiosyncratic.
   d. overly expressive.

5. Osterling and Dawson (1994) used a creative technique to diagnose autism. They
   a. reviewed snapshots of children.
   b. had the children tell a story with puppets.
   c. reviewed videotapes of first birthday parties.
   d. none of the above

6. What percentage of autistic children develop seizures after birth?
   a. 25
   b. 33
   c. 43
   d. 72

7. The genetics of autism suggest that
   a. autism is inherited directly.
   b. autism is not a genetic phenomenon.
   c. it is not inherited directly.
   d. it appears to skip a generation after transmission.

8. Through the use of scanning technology, researchers have discovered that autistic individuals appear to
   a. have a defective Y chromosome.
   b. have deficits in right hemisphere functioning.
   c. show stunted development in a part of the cerebellum.
   d. both b and c.

9. Which of the following is not among the diagnostic criteria for Rett's disorder?
   a. seemingly normal development before and after birth
   b. abnormal head circumference at birth
   c. poorly coordinated movements of the body
   d. severely impaired language development

10. Which of the following is among the diagnostic criteria for childhood disintegrative disorder?
    a. normal social interaction
    b. restricted, stereotyped patterns of behavior
    c. good bowel and bladder control
    d. expressive and receptive language

11. Which of the following is true regarding autism versus mental retardation?
    a. Self-stimulation is equally common among autistic and mentally retarded persons.
    b. Autistic children are motivated to please adults but retarded children are not so motivated.
    c. Retarded children show delays in language but autistic children show severe language deficits.
    d. Self-stimulation is common in retardation but uncommon in autism.

12. Which of the statements below is not one of the diagnostic criteria for mental retardation?
    a. The person has a significantly below-average level of intellectual functioning as measured by an IQ test.
    b. The person has at least two out of eight standard physical characteristics that make a person appear retarded.
    c. Social functioning is impaired.
    d. It is an irreversible condition that begins before the age of 18.

13. The "first person" story of Temple Grandin, an autistic person, illustrates
    a. a successful adjustment in life through development of an interest.
    b. the shortened life span of the disorder.
    c. that autistic individuals can also be psychotic.
    d. the importance of behavior modification as a treatment for autism.

14. The majority of retarded people fall into the category of
    a. mild retardation.
    b. moderate retardation.
    c. severe retardation.
    d. savant retardation.

15. Mary is retarded but does not talk. She tends to respond to very simple commands and spends a great portion of her time rocking back and forth. Mary's retardation is probably in the _____ range.
    a. severe
    b. profound
    c. mild
    d. moderate

16. While it was formerly believed that mild mental retardation was due to a combination of heredity and environmental conditions, a Swedish study has shown that at least 50 percent of the mentally retarded people have
    a. some chromosomal defect.
    b. a specific genetic disease.
    c. a pre, or postnatal disease.
    d. all of the above

17. Disorders caused by predictable parental contributions are referred to as
    a. polygenic.
    b. innate.
    c. constitutional.
    d. recessive.

18. _____ is due to an abnormality of the sex chromosomes.
    a. Down syndrome
    b. Fragile X syndrome
    c. PKU
    d. Tay-Sachs disease

19. Amniocentesis cannot be performed until the _____ month of pregnancy.
    a. third
    b. fifth
    c. fourth
    d. none of the above

20. Which is not a typical characteristic of children with Down syndrome?
    a. tallness
    b. flat face
    c. small nose
    d. congenital heart abnormality

21. Generally speaking, Down children seem especially weak in tactile perception, higher-level abstraction and reasoning, and
    a. socialization.
    b. perceptual-motor skills.
    c. facial discrimination.
    d. auditory perception.

22. Down syndrome children often learn better by
    a. seeing material rather than hearing it.
    b. hearing material rather than seeing it.
    c. using verbal information rather than other methods of learning.
    d. tactile perception rather than abstract reasoning.

23. Select the statement that is true of the average intellect of an adolescent or adult with Down syndrome.
    a. They do not develop mentally beyond childhood.
    b. Their cognitive abilities do not decrease with aging.
    c. They are unemployable.
    d. Stimulating environments may lead to intellectual development well into middle age.

24. Retardation may occur if a pregnant mother
    a. contracts the rubella virus.
    b. has syphilis.
    c. has herpes.
    d. all of the above

25. Children born to mothers who drink heavily may
    a. suffer retarded growth.
    b. be born with physical deformities.
    c. be born with mental retardation.
    d. all of the above

26. Approximately ____ to ____ percent of variability in intelligence test scores is related to environmental influences.
    a. 30, 50
    b. 10, 20
    c. 80, 90
    d. 20, 30

27. The results of studies focusing on psychosocial enrichment
    a. have demonstrated long-term effects.
    b. have not yet demonstrated long-term effects.
    c. are not concerned with long-term effects.
    d. show moderate but not long-term effects.

28. The 1975 Education for All Handicapped Children Act required
    a. parents to have children tested for mental retardation if a developmental delay was present before the age of five.
    b. public schools to provide free appropriate education to all handicapped children.
    c. required students to be "mainstreamed" at least for several hours during the school day.
    d. separate but equal learning facilities available for all handicapped children up to the age of eighteen years.

29. The ____ often leads to a vulnerability for personal, sexual, and financial exploitation.
    a. diminished cognitive abilities of retarded persons
    b. lack of social skills training in retarded persons
    c. use of group homes for the retarded
    d. tendency of retarded people to answer "yes"

30. An important part of a community-living program is
    a. the emphasis on contact with the family physician.
    b. the focus on job training.
    c. support offered by the federal government.
    d. the lack of supervision.

31. At present, theories of psychopathology among retarded persons
    a. lag behind those for the general population.
    b. are being intensively tested.
    c. are identical to those for the general population.
    d. point to commonalities between retarded persons and people from the general population.

NEXT, TRY YOUR HAND AT TRUE/FALSE QUESTIONS.

TRUE/FALSE QUESTIONS

Indicate whether each statement is true or false. Check your answers at the end of this chapter.

T   F   1. Autistic disorder is diagnosed on Axis II in DSM-IV.

T   F   2. Approximately 75 percent of autistic cases involve some degree of mental retardation.

T   F   3. Childhood schizophrenia usually occurs before age seven.

T   F   4. Fifty percent of autistic children show a lack of symbolic play.

T   F   5. According to research, there may be a hereditary factor in autism.

T   F   6. Autistic children have difficulty generalizing learned responses.

T   F   7. The genetics of autism suggest that a general tendency to have language or cognitive abnormalities is what is inherited from parents rather than autism.

T   F   8. Mental retardation can be due to several factors.

T   F   9. Many parents of retarded children retain some optimism about their child's future progress while the child is still young.

T   F   10. The risk of giving birth to a child with Down syndrome increases dramatically with the age at which a woman becomes pregnant.

T   F   11. Infants of adolescents are at high risk for retardation and other problems.

T   F   12. Until the 1870s, mental retardation was regarded as a homogeneous category with no distinctions.

KEEP GOING.....MATCHING IS NEXT.

MATCHING

Match the following terms with the information provided below. The answers are at the end of the chapter.

a. phenylketonuria (PKU)
b. Rett's disorder
c. microcephaly
d. fetal alcohol syndrome
e. childhood disintegrative disorder
f. trisomy 21
g. moderate mental retardation
h. rubella virus
i. fragile X syndrome
j. pervasive developmental disorder
k. object substitution
l. joint attention behaviors
m. eugenics movement
n. John Down
o. theory of mind
p. executive function

_____ 1. the ability to infer the mental states of others and to engage in symbolic thinking

_____ 2. a condition in which an infant's head stops growing, and is much smaller than normal

_____ 3. disorder associated with a deterioration of the central nervous system, for reasons unknown

_____ 4. progressive disorder that develops only after an infant has appeared to be developing normally for the first five months of life

_____ 5. accounts for 10 percent of cases diagnosed as retarded

_____ 6. behaviors involving coordination of a child and another person

_____ 7. disorders resulting in severe and long-lasting impairment in several aspects of childhood development

_____ 8. cognitive operations

_____ 9. author of *The Mongolian Type of Idiocy*

_____ 10. another name for Down syndrome

_____ 11. result of mother's heavy drinking while pregnant

_____ 12. German measles

_____ 13. abnormality of the sex chromosomes

_____ 14. metabolic disorder for which newborns are screened

_____ 15. to "pretend" that one object is playing the role of another

_____ 16. a school of thought focused on the improvement of the population's genetic stock

GOOD, NOW CHECK YOUR ANSWERS. WHEN YOU'RE DONE GRADING YOURSELF, COVER YOUR ANSWERS, AND START ALL OVER AGAIN. KEEP TESTING YOURSELF UNTIL YOU CAN ANSWER THEM ALL CORRECTLY.

CHAPTER 16 ANSWER KEY

Multiple Choice

1.	d		17.	b
2.	c		18.	b
3.	d		19.	c
4.	c		20.	a
5.	c		21.	d
6.	b		22.	a
7.	c		23.	d
8.	c		24.	d
9.	b		25.	d
10.	b		26.	a
11.	c		27.	b
12.	b		28.	b
13.	a		29.	d
14.	a		30.	b
15.	b		31.	a
16.	d			

True/False

1.	F		7.	T
2.	T		8.	T
3.	F		9.	T
4.	T		10.	T
5.	T		11.	T
6.	T		12.	T

Matching

1. o
2. c
3. e
4. b
5. g
6. l
7. j
8. p
9. n
10. f
11. d
12. h
13. i
14. a
15. k
16. m

Chapter 17
SOCIETY'S RESPONSE
TO MALADAPTIVE BEHAVIOR

CHAPTER OVERVIEW

This chapter concentrates on the issue of prevention and the role of the family, school, and community in preventing and treating maladaptive behavior. Specific examples of existing programs for juvenile delinquency and suicide prevention are reviewed and the effectiveness of community programs are evaluated. Legal aspects of treatment and prevention are explored and the use of paraprofessionals and self-help groups are evaluated.

LEARNING OBJECTIVES

After studying this chapter, you should be able to answer these questions:
1. What are the goals of primary, secondary, and tertiary prevention?
2. What is the aim of situation-focused prevention?
3. How does competency-focused prevention help people cope with stressful situations?
4. What types of prevention efforts are aimed at families?
5. What is the focus of school-based prevention?
6. How are community agencies and organizations involved in prevention?
7. How do paraprofessionals and self-help groups aid prevention efforts?
8. What is community psychology and what is its role in prevention?
9. What is the focus of community treatment programs?
10. How can community treatment be improved?
11. What is the purpose of voluntary commitment?
12. When might a person be civilly committed?
13. What is criminal commitment and when is it used?
14. What is the meaning of the term "insanity"?
15. What does it mean to be legally incompetent?
16. What has been the history of the various legal tests of insanity?
17. What is the doctrine of *parens patriae*?
18. What is the right of informed consent?
19. What rules of confidentiality arise in clinical settings?
20. When might a clinician's duty to warn supersede the duty of confidentiality to a patient?
21. What was the holding of the Tarasoff decision?
22. What is the rule of public policy in influencing society's perception of maladaptive behavior?

CHAPTER OUTLINE

1. Types of Prevention (p.551)

    A. Levels of Prevention

        Primary prevention is aimed at preventing new cases of disorders from occurring. Secondary prevention attempts to reduce the impact of an existing maladaptive condition by decreasing the duration or intensity of the condition. Tertiary prevention is aimed at reducing the impairment that has resulted from an already existing disorder.

B. Situation-focused and Competency-focused Prevention

Situation–focused prevention is aimed at eliminating the environmental causes of maladaptive behavior. Competency-focused prevention enhances people's ability to successfully cope with the conditions that result in maladaptive behavior.

2. Sites of Prevention

C. The Family

Parents affect their children's development genetically, prenatally, and in the environment they raise them in. Prevention efforts at the site of the family addresses maladaptive responses and behaviors at all levels.

D. The School

Many problems are not identified or do not emerge until the child is in school. So, prevention efforts involve school personnel such as teachers and staff.

E. The Community

Community agencies can provide positive experiences for children that may help them develop adaptive coping strategies and prevent the development of maladaptive behavior by putting children in contact with positive adult role models.

3. The Diverse Paths to Prevention (p.561)

A. Community Psychology

This is concerned with the role of social systems and the community as a whole in prevention.

B. Paraprofessionals

Paraprofessionals, who do not have formal training but who are culturally similar to the target groups can be trained to bridge the gap between the mental health system and the community.

C. Self-Help Groups

Self-help groups are made up of people who share a common problem and can be helpful to persons experiencing extreme stress or loss.

4. Treatment in the Community (p.564)

A network of community services can help prevent rehospitalization for the chronically mentally ill, as well as serve to monitor and assist those mentally ill persons living in the community.

A. Problems with Community Programs

Some problems include lack of integraged services and continuity of care.

B. Improving Treatment in the Community

Alternatives to full-time hospitalization include transitional settings such as halfway houses and day programs which can provide housing and monitoring as the individual transitions to and adjusts to living in the community.

5. Legal Aspects of Treatment and Prevention (p.568)

A. Institutionalization

Commitment may be either voluntary or involuntary through a legal procedure called civil commitment. Criminal commitment may be imposed if the person's criminal act is deemed to be the result of insanity. Insanity is a legal term, not a psychological term, and refers to a person's state of mind during the commission of a crime. Competency refers to a person's state of mind during a legal proceeding.

B. The Rights of Patients

Patients' rights include informed consent,which means that the patient is given all the information regarding the risks and benefits and nature of the treatment in order to make an informed decision to participate or not. They also have the right to terminate treatment at any time.

C. Confidentiality and the Duty to Warn

There is a broad legal protection of confidentiality in clinical settings,and mental health professionals may not reveal any information about a patient without that patient's express written permission. However, there are exceptions to the confidentiality laws. The duty to warn laws mandate that the therapist must report to potential victims a patient's intent to harm them.

6. A Final Word (p.577)

```
TIPS FOR TESTING YOURSELF

Write each of the following key words and concepts on one side of an index card.  Then, for each, look
up the correct definition in your textbook.  Write the definition on the opposite side of the corresponding
index card.  Now, you have flash cards to study.  Keep the cards with you and whenever you have a few
minutes, pull them out and test yourself.  When you are studying with a study partner, you can test each
other.  You can also share the duties of looking up the definitions and writing them on the cards.  Study
them a little each day.
```

KEY TERMS AND CONCEPTS

primary preventions (p.552)
secondary prevention (p.552)
tertiary prevention (p.552)
juvenile delinquency (p.552)
situation-focused prevention (p.554)
competency-focused prevention (p.554)
paraprofessionals (p.562)
community psychology (p.562)
self-help groups (p.563)
custodial housing (p.564)
alternative housing (p.564)
dormitory-inn (p.567)
partial hospitalization (p.567)
criminal commitment (p.568)
civil commitment (p.568)
insanity defense (p.569)
M'Naughten rule (p.569)
Durham rle (p.569)
American Law Institute guidelines (p.569)
parens patriae (p.571)
outpatient commitment (p.574)
Wyatt v. Stickney (p.575)
O'Connor v. Donaldson (p.575)
informed consent (p.575)
confidentiality (p.576)
duty to warn (p.576)
Tarasoff case (p.576)
public policy (p.577)

```
┌─────────────────────────────────────────────────────────────────────────────┐
│ TIPS FOR TESTING YOURSELF                                                     │
│                                                                               │
│ In developing answers for the following questions, turn to the section of your│
│ chapter that covers the pertinent material. Read the section thoroughly and   │
│ spend some time thinking about the information before attempting to frame your │
│ answer. Write out each answer without referring to the book, and when you have │
│ completed all of them, check their accuracy by returning to the corresponding │
│ section in the book. For each question you missed, write out the correct       │
│ answer. Then test yourself again. Repeat the process until you can answer all  │
│ the questions correctly.                                                       │
└─────────────────────────────────────────────────────────────────────────────┘
```

SHORT ANSWER ESSAY QUESTIONS

In developing answers for the following questions, turn to the section of your chapter that covers the pertinent material. Read each section thoroughly before attempting to frame your answer.

1. What is the difference between situation and competency-focused prevention? Give examples of each.

2. What are the goals of primary, secondary, and tertiary prevention?

3. Define juvenile delinquency and list conditions associated with this phenomenon.

4. Explain the concept of child abuse. What are the characteristics of abusing families? What interventions are used to prevent child abuse?

5. What is spouse abuse? List the different self-statements used to treat victims of this abuse.

6. How does divorce impact children? Describe the role of parents as therapists.

7. What role can the school play in primary prevention of disordered behavior?

8. How can the community assist in prevention efforts?

9. Explain the issues involving treatment in the community.

10. What is the difference between civil and criminal commitment?

11. How are competency and insanity defined?

12. Do mentally ill patients have rights? Explain the concept of "informed consent."

13. How has the use of paraprofessionals and self-help groups contributed to prevention efforts?

TIPS FOR TESTING YOURSELF

The following sections of self-test questions will test your understanding of the material presented in the chapter. On a separate piece of paper, write the correct answer for each item in the section, then compare your answers with those at the end of the chapter. After you have graded yourself, turn to the chapter and look up the questions you missed. Write out the correct answers. Then test yourself again. Continue doing so until you can answer all the questions correctly.

MULTIPLE CHOICE

1. The reduction or elimination of the environmental causes of distressed behavior is an example of
   a. tertiary prevention.
   b. situation-focused prevention.
   c. competency-focused prevention.
   d. community intervention.

2. Which of the following would be an example of primary prevention?
   a. premarital counseling
   b. marital therapy
   c. behavior therapy for a hyperactive child
   d. post-rape supportive group counseling

3. Prenatal classes for parents to be, which focus on the importance of an appropriate diet and provide information about the effects of smoking and drinking during pregnancy, would be a type of
   a. primary prevention.
   b. secondary prevention.
   c. tertiary prevention.
   d. behavioral intervention.

4. Tertiary prevention is aimed at reducing
   a. the number of new cases of a disorder in a given population.
   b. the duration of an existing abnormal condition.
   c. the intensity of an existing disorder.
   d. the impairment that may result from a disorder or event.

5. Which of the following conditions has been associated with an increased risk of delinquency?
   a. parental support for academic achievement
   b. alcoholic parents
   c. birth order
   d. none of the above

6. Which of the following is not one of the typical characteristics of an abusive parent compared to a nonabusive parent?
   a. lower level of intelligence
   b. less self-critical
   c. more aggressive
   d. more tense

7. Parents can be taught to respond therapeutically to their children's behavioral problems mainly through the techniques of
   a. play therapy and sharing feelings.
   b. modeling, behavioral rehearsal, and reinforcement.
   c. unconditional positive regard and listening.
   d. sharing their negative feelings with children and allowing them to know what problems the adult is experiencing.

8. _____ percent of the women murdered in the U.S. were killed by a husband, ex-husband, or suitor.
   a. Fifty-one
   b. Twenty-nine
   c. Three
   d. none of the above

9. Which of the following characteristics is not typical of a wife abuser?
   a. tension
   b. resentment
   c. suspicion
   d. narcissism

10. Select the characteristic that is typical of a boy's reaction to familial conflict.
    a. troubled peer relations
    b. poor school grades
    c. overidentification with the father
    d. rejection of peers

11. If a therapist is trying to advise parents on how to soften the blow of divorce, she might suggest
    a. not telling the children ahead of time.
    b. explaining the reasons for the divorce.
    c. setting strong limits on the child's anger.
    d. reinforcing the notion that things will pretty much continue on as before.

12. After a year of participation in the cognitive and social skills program designed by Sarason and Sarason, participating high school students
    a. were rated as being more popular by peers than a control group.
    b. had better school attendance and less tardiness than the control group.
    c. were more likely to find after-school jobs than the control group.
    d. had higher grade point averages than the control group.

13. The study by Ross and Glaser of male residents in a large city ghetto found that higher success in work situations is related to
    a. approval from peers.
    b. more independence from family.
    c. early diet and nutrition.
    d. encouragement and discipline at home.

14. Paraprofessionals
    a. have not been found to be effective in community mental health centers.
    b. tend to vary in age, education, and cultural background.
    c. are labor-intensive to train.
    d. none of the above

15. Self-help groups benefit their members through
    a. providing models on how to cope effectively with stress.
    b. encouraging catharsis.
    c. providing a social outlet.
    d. allowing the participant to accurately lay blame.

16. Community psychology is
    a. a subdiscipline of clinical psychology.
    b. concerned with the role of social systems in preventing maladaptive behavior.
    c. currently undergoing a dramatic revision.
    d. both a and b

17. In community psychology, alternative housing refers to
    a. halfway houses.
    b. nursing homes.
    c. special-care homes.
    d. custodial housing.

18. The Oxford House concept
    a. has not been effective in reducing rehospitalization.
    b. is fully supported by federal funding.
    c. is synonymous with self-governance.
    d. points to the need for dramatic reform of the half-way house concept.

19. The case of Sylvia Frumkin has led to
    a. a focus on system and legal reforms.
    b. increased use of lithium in the elderly.
    c. a recognition of schizophrenia as a genetic problem.
    d. both b and c

20. Which of the following is required by the chronically mentally ill living in the community?
    a. support for family members
    b. clinical services
    c. adequate, supervised housing
    d. all of the above

21. Civil commitment involves whether the individual
    a. is capable of holding a job.
    b. has had a history of violent behavior in the past.
    c. is sane or insane.
    d. is a risk to himself or herself, or to others.

22. _____ refers to a person's state of mind at the time of a judicial proceeding.
    a. Competency
    b. Schizophrenia
    c. Insanity
    d. Illness

23. The M'Naughten rule is most closely associated with
    a. crimes committed by normal people.
    b. a knowledge of right or wrong.
    c. John Hinckley's plea of sanity.
    d. none of the above.

24. "Irresistible impulse" means
    a. the individual's behavior was not necessarily illegal.
    b. the individual could not discriminate right from wrong.
    c. the individual could not control his behavior.
    d. both b and c

25. *Parens patriae* is a Latin term which means
    a. parenthood to the state.
    b. parents should be parents.
    c. parenting makes patriots.
    d. parenthood is achieved through patience.

26. According to Appelbaum (1991), a mental health practitioner's success rate for predicting near future dangerous behavior is between
    a. eighty to ninety percent.
    b. fifty to seventy percent.
    c. forty to sixty percent.
    d. twenty to forty percent.

27. Informed consent requires
    a. that patients receive adequate information about planned treatment before they agree to submit to it.
    b. that patients tell their therapists relevant background information prior to the onset of treatment.
    c. that both patient and therapist agree through a contract on treatment goals.
    d. that a patient has a "sanity hearing" within 7 days of entering an institution under commitment.

28. In the formula P=KxW, the P, K, and W stand for
    a. prevention, knowledge, and will.
    b. personality, knowledge, and work.
    c. professionals, knowledge, and willingness to help.
    d. personal effectiveness, kindness, and willingness to help.

NEXT, TRY YOUR HAND AT TRUE/FALSE QUESTIONS.

TRUE/FALSE
Indicate whether each statement is true or false. Check your answers at the end of this chapter.

T   F   1. Between 4 and 5 percent of American teens are referred to courts annually.

T   F   2. The adolescent pregnancy rate is approximately 500,000 cases per year.

T   F   3. There appears to be a strong link between being abused as a child and abusing your own children.

T   F   4. Twenty-five to thirty percent of all women with a spouse or living with a partner have been beaten at least once in the relationship.

T   F   5. Divorce and familial conflict appear to affect the development of children.

T   F   6. Unemployment appears to be stressful only to those of lower economic status.

T   F   7. Confidentiality in the context of mental health treatment is absolute.

T   F   8. The insanity defense is rarely used and even more rarely successful.

T   F   9. All states allow the insanity defense.

T   F   10. All states have laws concerning competence to stand trial.

KEEP GOING.....MATCHING IS NEXT.

MATCHING

Match the following terms with the information provided below. The answers are at the end of the chapter.

a. paraprofessional
b. competency
c. P=KxW
d. *Rennie v. Klein*
e. community psychology

f. spouse abuse
g. self-help groups
h. *Jaffe v. Redmond*
i. criminal commitment
j. informed consent

_____ 1. 25 to 30 percent of all women living with a partner have been beaten at least once while in this relationship

_____ 2. applies to patients and experimental subjects

_____ 3. allowed patients to refuse treatment

_____ 4. may fill gap between professionals and lower socioeconomic groups

_____ 5. involves placing someone who has broken the law into a mental hospital

_____ 6. members share common concerns

_____ 7. concerned with role of social systems in preventing human distress

_____ 8. prevention formula

_____ 9. U.S. Supreme Court case establishing confidentiality in the provision of mental health treatment

_____ 10. may refer to adequacy of coping skills; in a legal sense refers to whether a person who is the object of a legal proceeding has the capacity to profit from consultation with a lawyer, and to understand the purpose of the legal proceedings.

GOOD, NOW CHECK YOUR ANSWERS. WHEN YOU'RE DONE GRADING YOURSELF, COVER YOUR ANSWERS, AND START ALL OVER AGAIN. KEEP TESTING YOURSELF UNTIL YOU CAN ANSWER THEM ALL CORRECTLY.

CHAPTER 17 ANSWER KEY

Multiple Choice

1.	b		15.	a
2.	a		16.	b
3.	a		17.	a
4.	d		18.	c
5.	b		19.	a
6.	b		20.	d
7.	b		21.	d
8.	b		22.	a
9.	d		23.	b
10.	a		24.	c
11.	b		25.	a
12.	b		26.	c
13.	d		27.	a
14.	b		28.	a

True/False

1.	T		6.	F
2.	F		7.	T
3.	T		8.	T
4.	T		9.	F
5.	T		10.	T

Matching

1.	f
2.	j
3.	d
4.	a
5.	i
6.	g
7.	e
8.	c
9.	h
10.	b